P9-CFM-777

Betty Crocker

the big book of cupcakes

WILEY

Wiley Publishing, Inc

General Mills

Editorial Director: Jeff Nowak

Publishing Manager: Christine Gray

Editors: Karen Schiemo, Kathy Saatzer and Grace Wells

Food Editor: Catherine Swanson

Recipe Development and Testing: Betty Crocker Kitchens

Photography: General Mills Photography Studios and Image Library

Photographers: Val Bourassa and Kayla Pieper

Food Stylists: Carol Grones, Karen Linden and Jerry Dudycha

Wiley Publishing, Inc.

Publisher: Natalie Chapman

Associate Publisher: Jessica Goodman

Executive Editor: Anne Ficklen

Editor: Adam Kowit

Editorial Program Coordinator: Meaghan McDonnell

Production Editor: Liz Britten

Cover Design: Suzanne Sunwoo

Art Direction and Design: Tai Blanche

Layout: Indy Composition Services

Manufacturing Manager: Kevin Watt

The Betty Crocker Kitchens seal guarantees success in your kitchen. Every recipe has been tested in America's Most Trusted Kitchens™ to meet our high standards of reliability, easy preparation and great taste.

FIND MORE GREAT IDEAS AT
BettyCrocker.com

This book is printed on acid-free paper.

Copyright © 2011 by General Mills, Minneapolis, Minnesota. All rights reserved.

Published by Wiley Publishing, Inc., Hoboken, New Jersey

Published simultaneously in Canada

No part of this publication may be reproduced, stored in a retrieval system, or transmitted in any form or by any means, electronic, mechanical, photocopying, recording, scanning, or otherwise, except as permitted under Section 107 or 108 of the 1976 United States Copyright Act, without either the prior written permission of the Publisher, or authorization through payment of the appropriate per-copy fee to the Copyright Clearance Center, Inc., 222 Rosewood Drive, Danvers, MA 01923, (978) 750-8400, fax (978) 750-4470, or on the web at www.copyright.com. Requests to the Publisher for permission should be addressed to the Permissions Department, John Wiley & Sons, Inc., 111 River Street, Hoboken, NJ 07030, (201) 748-6011, fax (201) 748-6008, or online at http://www.wiley.com/go/permissions.

Trademarks: Wiley and the Wiley Publishing logo are trademarks or registered trademarks of John Wiley & Sons and/or its affiliates. All other trademarks referred to herein are trademarks of General Mills. Wiley Publishing, Inc., is not associated with any product or vendor mentioned in this book.

Limit of Liability/Disclaimer of Warranty: While the publisher and author have used their best efforts in preparing this book, they make no representations or warranties with respect to the accuracy or completeness of the contents of this book and specifically disclaim any implied warranties of merchantability or fitness for a particular purpose. No warranty may be created or extended by sales representatives or written sales materials. The advice and strategies contained herein may not be suitable for your situation. You should consult with a professional where appropriate. Neither the publisher nor author shall be liable for any loss of profit or any other commercial damages, including but not limited to special, incidental, consequential, or other damages.

For general information on our other products and services or for technical support, please contact our Customer Care Department within the United States at (877) 762-2974, outside the United States at (317) 572-3993 or fax (317) 572-4002.

Wiley also publishes its books in a variety of electronic formats. Some content that appears in print may not be available in electronic books. For more information about Wiley products, visit our web site at www.wiley.com.

Library of Congress Cataloging-in-Publication Data

Crocker, Betty.
 Betty Crocker big book of cupcakes.
   p. cm.
  title: Big book of cupcakes
  Includes index.
   ISBN 978-0-470-90672-9 (pbk); ISBN 978-0-470-94684-8 (ebk); ISBN 978-0-470-94683-1 (ebk); ISBN 978-0-470-94685-5 (ebk)
  1. Cupcakes. 2. Cookbooks. I. Title. II. Title: Big book of cupcakes.
 TX771.C6977 2011
 641.8'653--dc22

                                2010040977

Manufactured in the United States of America

10 9 8 7 6 5 4 3 2 1

Cover photos: (clockwise) Lamb Cupcakes (page 208), Fancy Flower Cupcakes (page 282), Somewhere Over the Rainbow Cupcakes (page 122), "From the Heart" Cupcakes (page 196), Peanut Butter High Hats (page 268), Cosmopolitan Cupcakes (page 296)

Dear Friends,

Cupcakes! Everybody loves them—and what's not to love? These tasty treats have it all, they're a teeny bit decadent, a lot of fun to eat, and each one delivers the perfect ratio of cake to frosting. Not to mention, no one expects you to *share* a cupcake—it's yours and yours alone!

Maybe it's the endless variety or maybe it's because cupcakes are the ideal indulgence, but there's no denying that these irresistible temptations continue to be all the rage. Cupcakeries (bakeries that specialize in cupcake perfection) have sprouted up in nearly every town, in malls and shopping centers, and even online!

The best thing about cupcakes may just be this: Each one delivers a little love and caring from you the baker. With the endless flavors and ways to decorate, they're the perfect choice for any occasion—selling at a bake sale, welcoming a new neighbor, hosting a bridal shower—because they tell the recipients how much you care.

Because we love cupcakes as much as you, here in *Betty Crocker The Big Book of Cupcakes* you'll find oodles of taste-temping recipes we've developed in our kitchens, as well as some recipes from cupcake bloggers—fans who have dedicated themselves to creating cupcake magic. Most of the recipes are from scratch but there are some terrific ones using cake mix and many that have cake mix variations, for when you don't have as much time. Also included are loads of decorating ideas, from simple to elegant and cute to clever, along with beautiful photos and helpful tips, so that any baker will have beautiful and tasty success. It's sweet baking bliss!

So let's get baking!

Warmly,
Betty Crocker

contents

all about cupcakes

No one knows for sure when the first cupcake was made, and even the experts argue about when the first cupcake recipe appeared in a cookbook. It was either in the late 1700s or the mid-1800s, depending on the source. There's even some confusion about how cupcakes got their name. Was it because these dainty treats were first baked in cups or because of the measurements used to make them? While there are variations on cupcakes in many cuisines—the British have fairy or Queen cakes, the Dutch are known for their traditional cakejes—what everyone knows for sure is that cupcakes are delicious!

Did you know?
The first commercial cupcake was introduced in 1919.

Cupcakes used to be the baked good of choice for children's birthday parties, but lately the cupcake has gone upscale, appearing at adult dinner parties, on the dessert menus of upscale restaurants, and at center stage at weddings.

Along with the explosion of the cupcake's popularity, there has been what can only be called a creative revolution when it comes to flavors. While the classics endure—yellow cupcakes with chocolate frosting and sprinkles, red velvet topped with cream cheese frosting, and devil's food dripping with fudgy deliciousness—you can now find cupcakes that are clearly made with adults in mind. These combinations are unusual in terms of traditional cupcakes, but they so delight today's sophisticated taste buds! Treat yourself to our new creative cupcakes such as Aztec Chile-Chocolate Cupcakes (page 84), Mango-Jalapeño Cupcake Stacks (page 316) or Sunnyside-Up Bacon Cupcakes (page 314). Yes, we did say bacon!

Baking Bloggers: They Dream of Cupcakes

We've tapped into cupcake bloggers—those who dedicate themselves to fulfilling cupcake wishes. Surely they must think of cupcakes every hour of the day to have this kind of passion! Look for these inspired blogger recipes, a treat for the eye as well as the taste buds, sprinkled throughout the book.

Clockwise from top left:

Deborah Harroun, www.tasteandtellblog.com (Chocolate-Amaretto Cupcakes, p. 94)

Angie Dudley, www.bakerella.com (Fire and Ice Cupcakes, p. 324)

Christy Denney, www.thegirlwhoateeverything.blogspot.com (Strawberry Colada Cupcakes, p. 116 and Somewhere Over the Rainbow Cupcakes, p. 122)

Lindsay Landis, www.loveand oliveoil.com (Peach Bourbon Cupcakes, p. 130)

Bree Hester, www.baked bree.com (Toasted Almond Cupcakes, p. 137 and Peanut Butter High Hats, p. 268)

Anna Ginsberg, www.cookie madness.net (Banana-Coffee Caramel-Filled Cupcakes, p.306)

baking cupcakes

Stock Up

With a few basic items, you can make and decorate a batch of cupcakes in a snap. You can shop at your supermarket, specialty cooking or baking stores, craft stores or online sites.

- **Muffin pans:** Available in mini, regular and jumbo for a variety of sizes of cupcakes and even in whimsical shapes like flowers, stars and hearts.
- **Paper baking cups:** Available in regular and mini in a variety of colors and designs.
- **Ice cream scoops:** Let you quickly make cupcakes all the same size. A #50 scoop is perfect for mini cupcakes, a #20 scoop is perfect for regular-size cupcakes, and a #8 scoop is perfect for jumbo cupcakes.

Sweet Baking Success

- Know your oven's true temperature. Most ovens run a little hot or cold, so invest in an oven thermometer and adjust the temperature control accordingly.
- Make sure your baking powder and baking soda are fresh—check the expiration date. These pantry staples can lose their leavening power over time.
- Measure well. Use a liquid measuring cup for liquid ingredients and the right size dry measuring cup for dry ingredients. When measuring flour or powdered sugar, fill your measuring cup with a spoon and level it off to avoid packing these ingredients down.
- Use a light touch when mixing the cupcake batter. Over mixing makes cupcakes tough.

Divide and Conquer

If you only have one 12-cup muffin pan and your recipe makes 24, fill and bake the first batch; cover and refrigerate the remaining batter. After the first batch of cupcakes have cooled in the pan for about ten minutes, move them to a cooling rack. Bake the rest of the batter, adding 1 or 2 minutes to the bake time (to make up for the batter being cold).

Mini size
2³/₄ x 1 inches

Regular size
2¹/₂ x 1¹/₄ inches

Jumbo size
3¹/₂ x 1³/₄ inches

frosting and decorating cupcakes

A cupcake is great topped with a smear of frosting—simple, easy and delicious. Add a few sprinkles and it's a party! But why stop there when there are so many great decorating ideas, from simple to extraordinary!

Frosting Basics

To frost with a spatula, place a generous dollop of frosting on the center of the cupcake, then spread toward the edges.

For a smooth finish, run the spatula edge over the top.

For fluffy frosting swirls, touch the frosting with the spatula and lift up.

To pipe swirled frosting, use a pastry bag fitted with a #6 star tip. Start at the outside edge, spiral up towards the center and pull tip up.

Decorating Essentials

A frosted cupcake can be adorned with many delightful decors, from colored sprinkles to sugar flowers or edible glitter.

- Pastry bags, or resealable food-storage plastic bags—snip a small corner off to create a simple piping bag.

- Decorating tips sold individually or in sets. They come in a variety of shapes and sizes to produce different designs with the frosting. Our recipes recommend various tips to use to frost the cupcakes.

- Decorating icing in assorted colors available in aerosol cans from your supermarket.

- Food colors available in liquid, gel or paste. Paste food color makes the most vivid color frosting.

- Assorted colored sugars, edible glitters and pearls.

- Assorted candy sprinkles in a wide variety of colors and shapes.

- Variety of premade decors made from sugar including flowers, hearts, stars and other decorative shapes.

Easy Ways to Decorate Cupcakes

- Dip tops of cupcakes into fluffy frosting; give a slight twist and pull up straight to create a nice peak.

- Instead of using frosting, place powdered sugar in a small strainer and tap the edge over the cupcake to cover evenly. Or, place a paper doily on top of unfrosted cupcakes, and sprinkle with powdered sugar.

- For a quick and easy frosting, mix a container of frozen whipped topping with flavored yogurt. Frost the cupcakes, and top with sprinkles or colored sugar for a festive touch.

- Top cupcakes with a dollop of whipped topping or scoop of ice cream and drizzle with chocolate or caramel ice cream topping.

Easy Finishing Touches for Frosted Cupcakes

Top cupcakes with one of these delightful choices just after frosting so they adhere well:

- Dip cupcakes in tinted coconut. To tint coconut, place it in a resealable food-storage plastic bag, add two or three drops of food coloring and shake well until evenly colored.

- Top with chocolate curls or shavings. To make curls, press a vegetable peeler over the surface of a chocolate bar. For shavings, run the chocolate over a coarse grater.

- Top with edible flowers, pearls or even bugs made from sugar.

- Top with a small shaped-chocolate candy or cookies such as animal crackers or gingerbread boys.

- Drizzle melted chocolate over frosting.

- Sprinkle with grated orange peel or top with orange zest strips created with a zester.

- Dip cupcakes into bowls of chopped nuts, colored sugar, sprinkles or finely-chopped candy. Or, just roll the cupcake edge in a plate of these toppings.

- Sprinkle with coarse decorating sugar or edible glitter. Use coordinating colors, or go for a nice contrast.

storing and toting cupcakes

Storing

Here are a few tips for keeping cupcakes fresh:

- Cool them completely before covering to keep the tops from becoming sticky, about 30 minutes.
- Frosted or unfrosted, cover cupcakes loosely with foil, plastic wrap or waxed paper.
- Store cupcakes with buttercream frosting at room temperature for up to two days.
- Refrigerate cupcakes with cream cheese or whipped cream toppings.
- Frost cupcakes with fluffy frosting on the day they'll be served.

Freezing

Get a head start; bake cupcakes ahead of time and freeze until you're ready to frost and serve. (Frosted cupcakes don't freeze very well as the frosting quality may change due to thawing.) Here are a few pointers for freezing cupcakes:

- Place cooled cupcakes in a single layer in airtight plastic containers or resealable freezer plastic bags. Unfrosted cupcakes can be kept frozen up to three months.
- Thaw cupcakes in the refrigerator or at room temperature. Loosen or remove wrapping before thawing.
- Frost cupcakes while they are still frozen; it will actually be easier since they have a nice hard surface.
- It is not recommended to freeze cupcakes with decorator icing, hard candies and colored sugars because the colors tend to run during thawing.

Paper Baking Cups

For great-looking cupcakes, use paper baking cups in the muffin pan. They're available in a wide range of styles, from plain white to animal prints. You can also find foil baking cups in various colors or even fancy tulip-shaped baking cups. Look for baking cups in your supermarket, dedicated baking stores, craft stores or online.

Cupcakes to Go

Toting cupcakes can be a challenge, but have no fear! Here are some handy tips for getting your cupcakes to the bake sale or party securely.

- Plastic cake carriers are ideal for packing cupcakes and will hold nearly a dozen cupcakes.

- A 13×9-inch pan will hold about one dozen standard cupcakes. Cover them loosely with foil.

- Serving plates will do in a pinch. Just remember to place toothpicks in each cupcake before loosely draping plastic wrap over them.

- Don't forget that old stand-by, the cardboard shirt box. Line it with waxed paper and cover the cupcakes with foil or plastic wrap.

chapter one

cupcake & frosting basics

yellow **cupcakes**

24 cupcakes   **PREP TIME: 15 Minutes**
START TO FINISH: 1 Hour 15 Minutes

2 1/3   cups all-purpose flour
2 1/2   teaspoons baking powder
  1/2   teaspoon salt
    1   cup butter or margarine, softened
1 1/4   cups sugar
    3   eggs
    1   teaspoon vanilla
  2/3   cup milk

1 Heat oven to 350°F. Place paper baking cup in each of 24 regular-size muffin cups. Grease and flour muffin cups, or spray with baking spray with flour.

2 In medium bowl, mix flour, baking powder and salt; set aside.

3 In large bowl, beat butter with electric mixer on medium speed 30 seconds. Gradually add sugar, about 1/4 cup at a time, beating well after each addition and scraping bowl occasionally. Beat 2 minutes longer. Add eggs, one at a time, beating well after each addition. Beat in vanilla. On low speed, alternately add flour mixture, about 1/3 of mixture at a time, and milk, about 1/2 at a time, beating just until blended.

4 Divide batter evenly among muffin cups, filling each about 2/3 full.

5 Bake 20 to 25 minutes or until golden brown and toothpick inserted in center comes out clean. Cool in pans 5 minutes. Remove cupcakes from pans; place on cooling racks to cool. Frost with desired frosting.

1 Cupcake: Calories 170; Total Fat 9g (Saturated Fat 5g; Trans Fat 0g); Cholesterol 45mg; Sodium 190mg; Total Carbohydrate 20g (Dietary Fiber 0g); Protein 2g **Exchanges:** 1 Starch, 1/2 Other Carbohydrate, 1 1/2 Fat **Carbohydrate Choices:** 1

Mini Cupcakes: Place mini paper baking cup in each of 24 mini muffin cups. Make batter as directed in recipe. Fill each cup until about 2/3 full. (Cover and refrigerate remaining batter until ready to bake; cool pan before reusing.) Bake 17 to 20 minutes or until golden brown and toothpick inserted in center comes out clean. Cool in pan 5 minutes. Remove cupcakes from pans; place on cooling racks to cool. Repeat with remaining batter to make an additional 48 mini cupcakes. Frost with desired frosting. About 72 mini cupcakes.

chocolate **cupcakes**

24 cupcakes **PREP TIME: 20 Minutes**
START TO FINISH: 1 Hour 15 Minutes

2	cups all-purpose flour
1 1/4	teaspoons baking soda
1	teaspoon salt
1/4	teaspoon baking powder
1	cup hot water
2/3	cup unsweetened baking cocoa
3/4	cup shortening
1 1/2	cups sugar
2	eggs
1	teaspoon vanilla

1 Heat oven to 350°F. Place paper baking cup in each of 24 regular-size muffin cups.

2 In medium bowl, mix flour, baking soda, salt and baking powder; set aside. In small bowl, mix hot water and cocoa until dissolved; set aside.

3 In large bowl, beat shortening with electric mixer on medium speed 30 seconds. Gradually add sugar, about 1/4 cup at a time, beating well after each addition and scraping bowl occasionally. Beat 2 minutes longer. Add eggs, one at a time, beating well after each addition. Beat in vanilla. On low speed, alternately add flour mixture, about 1/3 of mixture at a time, and cocoa mixture, about 1/2 at a time, beating just until blended.

4 Divide batter evenly among muffin cups, filling each about 2/3 full.

5 Bake 20 to 25 minutes or until golden brown and toothpick inserted in center comes out clean. Cool in pans 5 minutes. Remove cupcakes from pans; place on cooling racks to cool. Frost with desired frosting.

1 Cupcake: Calories 160; Total Fat 7g (Saturated Fat 2g; Trans Fat 1g);
Cholesterol 20mg; Sodium 180mg; Total Carbohydrate 22g (Dietary Fiber 1g);
Protein 2g **Exchanges:** 1/2 Starch, 1 Other Carbohydrate, 1 1/2 Fat
Carbohydrate Choices: 1 1/2

Mini Cupcakes: Place mini paper baking cup in each of 24 mini muffin cups. Make batter as directed in recipe. Fill each cup with until about 2/3 full. (Cover and refrigerate remaining batter until ready to bake; cool pan before reusing.) Bake 12 to 16 minutes or until toothpick inserted in center comes out clean. Cool in pan 5 minutes. Remove cupcakes from pans; place on cooling racks to cool. Repeat with remaining batter to make an additional 48 mini cupcakes. Frost with desired frosting. About 72 mini cupcakes.

white cupcakes

24 cupcakes   PREP TIME: 15 Minutes
START TO FINISH: 1 Hour 15 Minutes

2 3/4	cups all-purpose flour
3	teaspoons baking powder
1/2	teaspoon salt
3/4	cup shortening or butter
1 2/3	cups sugar
5	egg whites
2 1/2	teaspoons vanilla
1 1/4	cups milk

1 Heat oven to 350°F. Place paper baking cup in each of 24 regular-size muffin cups.

2 In medium bowl, mix flour, baking powder and salt; set aside.

3 In large bowl, beat shortening with electric mixer on medium speed 30 seconds. Gradually add sugar, about 1/3 cup at a time, beating well after each addition and scraping bowl occasionally. Beat 2 minutes longer. Add egg whites, one at a time, beating well after each addition. Beat in vanilla. On low speed, alternately add flour mixture, about 1/3 of mixture at a time, and milk, about 1/2 at a time, beating just until blended.

4 Divide batter evenly among muffin cups, filling each about 2/3 full.

5 Bake 18 to 20 minutes or until toothpick inserted in center comes out clean. Cool in pans 5 minutes. Remove cupcakes from pans; place on cooling racks to cool. Frost with desired frosting.

1 Cupcake: Calories 180; Total Fat 7g (Saturated Fat 2g; Trans Fat 1g); Cholesterol 0mg; Sodium 125mg; Total Carbohydrate 26g (Dietary Fiber 0g); Protein 2g **Exchanges:** 1/2 Starch, 1 Other Carbohydrate, 1 1/2 Fat **Carbohydrate Choices:** 2

Mini Cupcakes: Place mini paper baking cup in each of 24 mini muffin cups. Make batter as directed in recipe. Fill each cup until about 2/3 full. (Cover and refrigerate remaining batter until ready to bake; cool pan before reusing.) Bake 12 to 16 minutes or until toothpick inserted in center comes out clean. Cool in pan 5 minutes. Remove cupcakes from pans; place on cooling racks to cool. Repeat with remaining batter to make an additional 48 mini cupcakes. Frost with desired frosting. About 72 mini cupcakes.

lemon **cupcakes**

24 cupcakes   PREP TIME: 20 Minutes
START TO FINISH: 1 Hour 15 Minutes

2 $1/3$ cups all-purpose flour
2 $1/2$ teaspoons baking powder
$1/2$ teaspoon salt
1   cup butter or margarine, softened
1 $1/4$ cups sugar
3   eggs
2   tablespoons grated lemon peel
1   teaspoon vanilla
$2/3$ cup milk

1   Heat oven to 350°F. Place paper baking cup in each of 24 regular-size muffin cups or grease and flour muffin cups, or spray with baking spray with flour.

2   In medium bowl, mix flour, baking powder and salt; set aside.

3   In large bowl, beat butter with electric mixer on medium speed 30 seconds. Gradually add sugar, about $1/4$ cup at a time, beating well after each addition and scraping bowl occasionally. Beat 2 minutes longer. Add eggs, one at a time, beating well after each addition. Beat in lemon peel and vanilla. On low speed, alternately add flour mixture, about $1/3$ of mixture at a time, and milk, about $1/2$ at a time, beating just until blended.

4   Divide batter evenly among muffin cups, filling each about $2/3$ full.

5   Bake 20 to 25 minutes or until golden brown and toothpick inserted in center comes out clean. Cool in pans 5 minutes. Remove cupcakes from pans; place on cooling racks to cool. Frost with desired frosting.

1 Cupcake: Calories 170; Total Fat 9g (Saturated Fat 5g; Trans Fat 0g); Cholesterol 45mg; Sodium 190mg; Total Carbohydrate 20g (Dietary Fiber 0g); Protein 2g
Exchanges: 1 Starch, $1/2$ Other Carbohydrate, 1 $1/2$ Fat **Carbohydrate Choices:** 1

Mini Cupcakes: Place mini paper baking cup in each of 24 mini muffin cups. Make batter as directed in recipe. Fill each cup until about $2/3$ full. (Cover and refrigerate remaining batter until ready to bake; cool pan before reusing.) Bake 14 to 18 minutes or until golden brown and toothpick inserted in center comes out clean. Cool in pan 5 minutes. Remove cupcakes from pans; place on cooling racks to cool. Repeat with remaining batter to make an additional 48 mini cupcakes. Frost with desired frosting. About 72 mini cupcakes.

frosting palette

chocolate cream
cheese, page 21

fluffy white,
page 21

decorator
icing,
page 21

maple-nut
buttercream,
page 20

peanut butter
buttercream, page 20

fluffy cherry-nut,
page 21

orange
buttercream,
page 20

browned butter buttercream, page 20

lemon buttercream, page 20

fluffy butterscotch, page 21

fluffy peppermint, page 21

vanilla buttercream, page 20

creamy chocolate, page 20

cream cheese, page 20

vanilla buttercream
frosting

PREP TIME: 10 Minutes START TO FINISH: 10 Minutes

6 cups powdered sugar
²/₃ cup butter or margarine, softened
1 tablespoon vanilla
3 to 4 tablespoons milk

1 In large bowl, mix powdered sugar and butter with spoon or electric mixer on low speed. Stir in vanilla and 3 tablespoons of the milk.

2 Gradually beat in just enough remaining milk to make frosting smooth and spreadable. If frosting is too thick, beat in more milk, a few drops at a time. If frosting becomes too thin, beat in a small amount of powdered sugar. Generously frosts 24 cupcakes (about 3 ¹/₂ cups).

About 2 Tablespoons: Calories 140; Total Fat 4.5g (Saturated Fat 3g; Trans Fat 0g); Cholesterol 10mg; Sodium 30mg; Total Carbohydrate 26g (Dietary Fiber 0g); Protein 0g **Exchanges:** 1 ¹/₂ Other Carbohydrate, 1 Fat **Carbohydrate Choices:** 2

Browned Butter Buttercream Frosting: In 1-quart saucepan, heat ¹/₃ cup butter (do not use margarine or spreads) over medium heat just until light brown. Watch carefully because butter can brown and then burn quickly. Cool butter. Use browned butter instead of softened butter in recipe.

Lemon Buttercream Frosting: Omit vanilla. Substitute lemon juice for the milk. Stir in ¹/₂ teaspoon grated lemon peel.

Maple-Nut Buttercream Frosting: Omit vanilla. Substitute ¹/₂ cup maple-flavored syrup for the milk. Stir in ¹/₄ cup finely chopped nuts.

Orange Buttercream Frosting: Omit vanilla. Substitute orange juice for the milk. Stir in 2 teaspoons grated orange peel.

Peanut Butter Buttercream Frosting: Substitute peanut butter for the butter. Increase milk to ¹/₄ cup, adding more, if necessary, a few drops at a time.

creamy chocolate
frosting

PREP TIME: 10 Minutes START TO FINISH: 10 Minutes

¹/₂ cup butter or margarine, softened
3 oz unsweetened baking chocolate, melted, cooled
3 cups powdered sugar
2 teaspoons vanilla
3 to 4 tablespoons milk

1 In large bowl, mix butter and chocolate. Stir in powdered sugar. Beat in vanilla and milk until smooth and spreadable. If frosting is too thick, beat in more milk, a few drops at a time. If frosting becomes too thin, beat in a small amount of powdered sugar. Frosts 24 cupcakes (about 1 ¹/₄ cups).

About 2 Tablespoons: Calories 150; Total Fat 7g (Saturated Fat 4g; Trans Fat 0g); Cholesterol 15mg; Sodium 40mg; Total Carbohydrate 23g (Dietary Fiber 0g); Protein 0g **Exchanges:** 1 ¹/₂ Other Carbohydrate, 1 ¹/₂ Fat **Carbohydrate Choices:** 1 ¹/₂

cream cheese
frosting

PREP TIME: 10 Minutes START TO FINISH: 10 Minutes

1 package (8 oz) cream cheese, softened
¹/₄ cup butter or margarine, softened
1 teaspoon vanilla
2 to 3 teaspoons milk
4 cups powdered sugar

1 In large bowl, beat cream cheese, butter, vanilla and 2 teaspoons of the milk with electric mixer on low speed until smooth. beat in powdered sugar 1 cup at a time.

2 Gradually beat in just enough remaining milk to make frosting smooth and spreadable. If frosting is too thick, beat in more milk, a few drops at a time. If frosting becomes too thin, beat in a small amount of powdered sugar.

3 Leftover frosting can be tightly covered and refrigerated up to 5 days or frozen up to 1 month. Let stand 30 minutes at room temperature to soften; stir before using. Frosts 24 cupcakes (about 2 ¹/₂ cups).

About 2 Tablespoons: Calories 160; Total Fat 6g (Saturated Fat 3.5g; Trans Fat 0g); Cholesterol 20mg; Sodium 55mg; Total Carbohydrate 24g (Dietary Fiber 0g); Protein 0g **Exchanges:** ¹/₂ Starch, 1 Other Carbohydrate, 1 Fat **Carbohydrate Choices:** 1 ¹/₂

Chocolate Cream Cheese Frosting: Add 2 ounces unsweetened baking chocolate, melted and cooled 10 minutes, with the butter.

fluffy white frosting

PREP TIME: 25 Minutes
START TO FINISH: 1 Hour 5 Minutes

2 large egg whites
1/2 cup sugar
1/4 cup light corn syrup
2 tablespoons water
1 teaspoon vanilla

1 Let egg whites stand at room temperature 30 minutes. (Room temperature egg whites will have more volume when beaten than cold egg whites.) In medium bowl, beat egg whites with electric mixer on high speed just until stiff peaks form.

2 In 1-quart saucepan, stir sugar, corn syrup and water until well mixed. Cover; heat to rolling boil over medium heat. Uncover; boil 4 to 8 minutes, without stirring, to 242°F on candy thermometer or until small amount of mixture dropped into cup of very cold water forms a firm ball that holds its shape until pressed. For an accurate temperature reading, tilt saucepan slightly so mixture is deep enough for thermometer.

3 While beating constantly on medium speed, pour hot syrup very slowly in thin stream into egg whites. Add vanilla; beat on high speed about 10 minutes or until stiff peaks form.

4 Frosts 24 cupcakes. Leftover frosting can be tightly covered and refrigerated up to 2 days; do not freeze. Let stand 30 minutes at room temperature to soften; do not stir.

2 Tablespoons: Calories 30; Total Fat 0g (Saturated Fat 0g; Trans Fat 0g); Cholesterol 0mg; Sodium 5mg; Total Carbohydrate 7g (Dietary Fiber 0g); Protein 0g **Exchanges:** 1/2 Other Carbohydrate **Carbohydrate Choices:** 1/2

Fluffy Butterscotch Frosting: Substitute packed brown sugar for the sugar. Decrease vanilla to 1/2 teaspoon.

Fluffy Cherry-Nut Frosting: Stir in 1/4 cup cut-up candied cherries, 1/4 cup chopped nuts and, if desired, 6 to 8 drops red food color.

Fluffy Peppermint Frosting: Stir in 1/3 cup coarsely crushed hard peppermint candies or 1/2 teaspoon peppermint extract.

decorator icing

PREP TIME: 10 Minutes
START TO FINISH: 10 Minutes

1/2 cup butter or margarine, softened
1/4 cup shortening
1 teaspoon vanilla
1/8 teaspoon salt
4 cups powdered sugar
2 to 4 tablespoons milk or water

1 In large bowl, beat butter and shortening with electric mixer on medium speed until light and fluffy. Beat in vanilla and salt.

2 On low speed, beat in powdered sugar, 1 cup at a time, scraping down sides of bowl occasionally. Add 2 tablespoons milk; beat on high speed until light and fluffy. Gradually beat in just enough remaining milk to make frosting smooth and spreadable. Frosts 24 cupcakes (about 3 cups).

2 Tablespoons: Calories 140; Total Fat 6g (Saturated Fat 3g; Trans Fat 0.5g); Cholesterol 10mg; Sodium 40mg; Total Carbohydrate 20g (Dietary Fiber 0g); Protein 0g **Exchanges:** 1/2 Starch, 1 Other Carbohydrate, 1 Fat **Carbohydrate Choices:** 1

chocolate-sour cream cupcakes, page 42

chapter two

simply
delicious
cupcakes

chocolate whoopie **pie cupcakes**

24 cupcakes **PREP TIME: 30 Minutes** START TO FINISH: **1 Hour 25 Minutes**

CUPCAKES

Chocolate Cupcakes (page 15)

FILLING

1 cup fluffy white whipped ready-to-spread frosting (from 12-oz container)

³/₄ cup marshmallow creme

1 Make, bake and cool Chocolate Cupcakes as directed in recipe.

2 In small bowl, mix frosting and marshmallow creme. Cut cupcakes crosswise into halves. Frost each bottom half with about 1 tablespoon filling; replace tops of cupcakes.

1 Cupcake: Calories 210; Total Fat 9g (Saturated Fat 2.5g; Trans Fat 1.5g); Cholesterol 20mg; Sodium 190mg; Total Carbohydrate 29g (Dietary Fiber 1g); Protein 2g **Exchanges:** 1 Starch, 1 Other Carbohydrate, 1 ½ Fat **Carbohydrate Choices:** 2

sweet success tip

These cupcakes are a good dessert to pack for lunches because the frosting is inside the cupcake instead of on top.

use a cake mix

Substitute 1 box devil's food cake mix for the Chocolate Cupcakes. Make cake mix as directed on box for cupcakes. Continue as directed in recipe.

dried cherry and pistachio cupcakes

24 cupcakes **PREP TIME: 50 Minutes START TO FINISH: 1 Hour 50 Minutes**

CUPCAKES

Yellow Cupcakes (page 14)

$1/2$ cup butter or margarine, softened

$3/4$ cup packed brown sugar

$1/2$ cup granulated sugar

1 package (3 oz) cream cheese, softened

1 cup chopped dried cherries

$1/2$ cup chopped pistachio nuts

FROSTING

Vanilla Buttercream Frosting (page 20)

GARNISH

$3/4$ cup chopped dried cherries

$1/2$ cup chopped pistachio nuts

1 Make Yellow Cupcakes as directed in recipe except—use $1/2$ cup butter, $3/4$ cup brown sugar, $1/2$ cup granulated sugar. Beat cream cheese into batter with vanilla. Stir in chopped cherries and chopped pistachios. Bake and cool as directed.

2 Make Vanilla Buttercream Frosting as directed in recipe. Frost cupcakes. Garnish each cupcake with chopped cherries and pistachios.

1 Cupcake: Calories 370; Total Fat 13g (Saturated Fat 7g; Trans Fat 0g); Cholesterol 55mg; Sodium 160mg; Total Carbohydrate 60g (Dietary Fiber 1g); Protein 3g **Exchanges:** 1 Starch, 3 Other Carbohydrate, 2 $1/2$ Fat **Carbohydrate Choices:** 4

sweet success tip

Bake these cupcakes, but don't frost them. Place them in an airtight container and freeze them. A few hours before serving, remove them from the freezer, frost and decorate.

use a cake mix

Substitute 1 box white cake mix for the Yellow Cupcakes. Make cake mix as directed on box for cupcakes **except**—use 1 $1/4$ cups water, $1/3$ cup oil and 4 egg whites, and beat in 1 package (3 oz) cream cheese, softened. Toss 1 cup chopped dried cherries and $1/2$ cup chopped pistachio nuts with 1 tablespoon all-purpose flour; stir into batter. Bake 20 to 24 minutes. Cool as directed on box. For the frosting, substitute 1 container vanilla creamy ready-to-spread frosting. Garnish as directed in recipe.

chocolate-frosted cupcakes

12 cupcakes PREP TIME: **40 Minutes** START TO FINISH: **1 Hour 45 Minutes**

CUPCAKES

1 1/4 cups all-purpose flour
2/3 cup granulated sugar
1 1/2 teaspoons baking powder
1/4 teaspoon salt
1/2 cup fat-free (skim) milk
1/3 cup unsalted butter or no-trans-fat 68% vegetable oil spread stick, softened
2 teaspoons vanilla
3 egg whites

FROSTING

1 1/2 cups powdered sugar
1/4 cup unsweetened baking cocoa
2 tablespoons unsalted butter or no-trans-fat 68% vegetable oil spread stick, softened
2 teaspoons vanilla
1 to 3 tablespoons fat-free (skim) milk

1 Heat oven to 350°F. Place paper baking cup in each of 12 regular-size muffin cups.

2 In medium bowl, beat all cupcake ingredients except egg whites with electric mixer on low speed 30 seconds; beat on medium speed 1 minute. Add egg whites; beat on medium speed 1 minute. Divide batter evenly among muffin cups.

3 Bake 28 to 32 minutes or until toothpick inserted in center comes out clean and tops just begin to brown. Cool 2 minutes. Remove from pan; place on cooling rack to cool.

4 In medium bowl, mix powdered sugar, cocoa, 2 tablespoons butter, 2 teaspoons vanilla and 1 tablespoon of the milk with electric mixer on low speed. Gradually beat in just enough of remaining milk to make frosting smooth and spreadable. Frost cupcakes.

1 Cupcake: Calories 240; Total Fat 7g (Saturated Fat 4.5g; Trans Fat 0g); Cholesterol 20mg; Sodium 130mg; Total Carbohydrate 38g (Dietary Fiber 1g); Protein 3g **Exchanges:** 1 Starch, 1 1/2 Other Carbohydrate, 1 1/2 Fat **Carbohydrate Choices:** 2 1/2

sweet success tip

Feel free to serve these chocolate cupcakes with your favorite ice cream and candy sprinkles!

use a cake mix

Substitute 1 box white cake mix for the cupcakes above. Make cake mix as directed on box for cupcakes. For the frosting, substitute 1 container chocolate creamy ready-to-spread frosting. 24 cupcakes

malted milk **ball cupcakes**

24 cupcakes   **PREP TIME: 35 Minutes** START TO FINISH: **1 Hour 30 Minutes**

CUPCAKES

Yellow Cupcakes (page 14)

1   cup malted milk balls, crushed

1/4   cup natural-flavor malted milk powder

MALTED MILK FROSTING

1/4   cup butter or margarine, softened

2   cups powdered sugar

2   tablespoons natural-flavor malted milk powder

1   tablespoon unsweetened baking cocoa

2   tablespoons milk

GARNISH

2/3   cup malted milk balls, crushed

1   Make Yellow Cupcakes as directed in recipe except—add 1 cup malted milk balls and 1/4 cup malted milk powder. Bake and cool as directed.

2   In medium bowl, beat frosting ingredients with electric mixer on medium speed until smooth and spreadable. Frost cupcakes. Sprinkle with 2/3 cup malted milk balls.

1 Cupcake: Calories 260; Total Fat 12g (Saturated Fat 8g; Trans Fat 0g); Cholesterol 55mg; Sodium 220mg; Total Carbohydrate 36g (Dietary Fiber 0g); Protein 2g **Exchanges:** 1/2 Starch, 2 Other Carbohydrate, 2 1/2 Fat **Carbohydrate Choices:** 2 1/2

sweet success tip

Malted milk balls are easier to crush if they're frozen. Freeze them in a resealable freezer plastic bag for about 30 minutes. Then tap the bag with a rolling pin or meat mallet until the balls are coarsely crushed.

use a cake mix

Substitute 1 box yellow cake mix for the Yellow Cupcakes. Make cake mix as directed on box for cupcakes **except**—add 1 cup malted milk balls, crushed, and 1/4 cup natural-flavor malted milk powder. Bake and cool as directed on box. Frost as directed in recipe.

chocolate-orange **cupcakes**

24 cupcakes   PREP TIME: **50 Minutes** START TO FINISH: **1 Hour 50 Minutes**

CUPCAKES

Chocolate Cupcakes (page 15)

2   tablespoons grated orange peel

CHOCOLATE-ORANGE FROSTING

$1/2$ cup butter or margarine, softened

3   oz unsweetened baking chocolate, melted, cooled

3   cups powdered sugar

2   teaspoons vanilla

2   to 3 tablespoons orange juice

GARNISH

6   orange slice candies (wedges)

1   Make Chocolate Cupcakes as directed in recipe except—add orange peel with the vanilla. Bake and cool as directed.

2   In large bowl, mix butter and chocolate until blended. Stir in powdered sugar. Beat in vanilla and 2 tablespoons orange juice until smooth. If necessary, beat in additional orange juice, 1 teaspoon at a time, until frosting is spreadable. Frost cupcakes.

3   Cut each orange slice candy horizontally in half; cut each half equally into 6 pieces. Garnish each cupcake with 3 pieces of candy.

1 Cupcake: Calories 300; Total Fat 13g (Saturated Fat 6g; Trans Fat 1g); Cholesterol 30mg; Sodium 210mg; Total Carbohydrate 43g (Dietary Fiber 2g); Protein 2g **Exchanges:** 1 Starch, 2 Other Carbohydrate, 2 $1/2$ Fat **Carbohydrate Choices:** 3

sweet success tip

If you don't have orange slices, use orange sprinkles. Decorative Halloween cupcake liners could be used to serve these cupcakes for a Halloween party.

use a cake mix

Substitute 1 box devil's food cake mix for the Chocolate Cupcakes. Make cake mix as directed on box for cupcakes **except**—use $11/4$ cups water, $1/2$ cup vegetable oil, 3 eggs and 2 tablespoons grated orange peel. Bake and cool as directed in recipe. Frost and garnish as directed in recipe.

red velvet cupcakes **with marshmallow buttercream frosting**

24 cupcakes   **PREP TIME: 40 Minutes** START TO FINISH: **1 Hour 30 Minutes**

CUPCAKES

2 1/4   cups all-purpose flour

1/4   cup unsweetened baking cocoa

1   teaspoon salt

1/2   cup butter or margarine, softened

1 1/2   cups granulated sugar

2   eggs

1   bottle (1 oz) red food color (about 2 tablespoons)

1 1/2   teaspoons vanilla

1   cup buttermilk

1   teaspoon baking soda

1   tablespoon white vinegar

FROSTING

1   jar (7 to 7.5 oz) marshmallow creme

1   cup butter or margarine, softened

2   cups powdered sugar

DECORATIONS

Spearmint gumdrop leaves, if desired

Red cinnamon candies, if desired

Flaked coconut, if desired

1 Heat oven to 350°F. Place paper baking cup in each of 24 regular-size muffin cups. In small bowl, mix flour, cocoa and salt; set aside.

2 In large bowl, beat 1/2 cup butter and the granulated sugar with electric mixer on medium speed until mixed. Add eggs; beat 1 to 2 minutes or until light and fluffy. Stir in food color and vanilla. On low speed, alternately add flour mixture, 1/3 at a time, and buttermilk, 1/2 at a time, beating just until blended. Beat in baking soda and vinegar until well blended.

3 Divide batter evenly among muffin cups, filling each about 2/3 full.

4 Bake 20 to 22 minutes or until toothpick inserted in center comes out clean. Remove from pans to cooling racks to cool.

5 Remove lid and foil seal from jar of marshmallow creme. Microwave uncovered on High 15 to 20 seconds to soften. In large bowl, beat marshmallow creme and 1 cup butter with electric mixer on medium speed until smooth. Beat in powdered sugar until smooth. Spoon 1 rounded tablespoon frosting onto each cupcake, swirling frosting with back of spoon.

6 To decorate cupcakes, top cupcakes with flaked coconut. Split one green spearmint leaf candy in half horizontally and arrange on top of cupcakes for holly leaves. Add 3 red cinnamon candies for berries.

1 Frosted Cupcake (Undecorated): Calories 280; Total Fat 12g (Saturated Fat 8g; Trans Fat 0g); Cholesterol 50mg; Sodium 250mg; Total Carbohydrate 40g (Dietary Fiber 0g); Protein 2g **Exchanges:** 1/2 Starch, 2 Other Carbohydrate, 2 1/2 Fat **Carbohydrate Choices:** 2 1/2

use a cake mix

Substitute 1 box devil's food cake mix for the cupcakes above. Make cake mix as directed on box for cupcakes **except**—use 1 1/4 cups water, 1/2 cup vegetable oil and 3 eggs, and add 1 bottle (1 oz) red food color. Bake and cool as directed on box. For the frosting, substitute 1 container vanilla whipped ready-to-spread frosting mixed with 1 cup marshmallow creme. Frost and decorate as directed in recipe.

harvest apple cupcakes with cream cheese frosting

24 cupcakes   **PREP TIME: 1 Hour START TO FINISH: 2 Hours 15 Minutes**

CUPCAKES

1 1/2   cups sugar
1   cup vegetable oil
3   eggs
2   cups all-purpose flour
2   teaspoons ground cinnamon
1   teaspoon baking soda
1   teaspoon vanilla
1/2   teaspoon salt
3   cups chopped tart apples
1   cup coarsely chopped nuts

FROSTING

Cream Cheese Frosting
(page 20)

1 Heat oven to 350°F. Place paper baking cup in each of 24 regular-size muffin cups.

2 In large bowl, beat sugar, oil and eggs with electric mixer on low speed about 30 seconds or until blended. Add flour, cinnamon, baking soda, vanilla and the salt; beat on low speed 1 minute. Stir in apples and nuts.

3 Divide batter evenly among muffin cups, using about 1/2 cup batter for each.

4 Bake 30 to 35 minutes or until toothpick inserted in center of cupcake comes out clean. Cool 10 minutes; remove from pans to cooling racks to cool.

5 Make Cream Cheese Frosting as directed in recipe. Frost cupcakes. Store frosted cupcakes or any remaining frosting covered in refrigerator.

1 Cupcake: Calories 350; Total Fat 18g (Saturated Fat 5g; Trans Fat 0g); Cholesterol 40mg; Sodium 150mg; Total Carbohydrate 43g (Dietary Fiber 1g); Protein 3g **Exchanges:** 1 Starch, 2 Other Carbohydrate, 3 1/2 Fat **Carbohydrate Choices:** 3

sweet success tip

Be picky when picking your apples for this recipe. Cooking apples, such as Rome Beauty and Granny Smith, have a firm texture and will hold their shape when baked in these cupcakes.

use a cake mix

Substitute 1 box white cake mix for the cupcakes above. Place paper baking cup in each of 28 regular-size muffin cups. Make cake mix as directed on box for cupcakes **except**—add 2 teaspoons ground cinnamon with the egg whites. Stir in 3 cups finely chopped tart apples and 1 cup finely chopped nuts. Bake 29 to 33 minutes. For the frosting, substitute 1 container cream cheese creamy ready-to-spread frosting. 28 cupcakes

adorable applesauce **cupcakes**

24 cupcakes   PREP TIME: 1 Hour START TO FINISH: 2 Hours 5 Minutes

CUPCAKES

2 1/3 cups all-purpose flour

2 1/2 teaspoons baking powder

1/2 teaspoon salt

1/2 teaspoon cinnamon

1 cup butter or margarine, softened

1 1/4 cups sugar

3 eggs

1/2 cup unsweetened applesauce

1 teaspoon vanilla

1/2 cup apple juice

FROSTING

Vanilla Buttercream Frosting (page 20)

1/2 teaspoon red paste food color

DECORATIONS

12 thin pretzel sticks, broken into pieces

16 spearmint leaf gumdrops

12 gummy worm candies, cut in half, if desired

1 Heat oven to 350°F. Place paper baking cup in each of 24 regular-size muffin cups. Grease and flour muffin cups, or spray with baking spray with flour.

2 In medium bowl, mix flour, baking powder, salt and cinnamon; set aside.

3 In large bowl, beat butter with electric mixer on medium speed 30 seconds. Gradually add sugar, about 1/4 cup at a time, beating well after each addition and scraping bowl occasionally. Beat 2 minutes longer. Add eggs, one at a time, beating well after each addition. Beat in applesauce and vanilla. On low speed, alternately add flour mixture, about 1/3 of mixture at a time, and apple juice, about 1/2 at a time, beating just until blended.

4 Divide batter evenly among muffin cups, filling each about 2/3 full.

5 Bake 20 to 25 minutes or until golden brown and toothpick inserted in center comes out clean. Cool in pans 5 minutes. Remove cupcakes from pans; place on cooling racks to cool.

6 Make Vanilla Buttercream Frosting as directed in recipe (see page 20). Stir in food color paste. Frost cupcakes.

7 To decorate cupcakes, poke 1 pretzel piece into each cupcake for stem. Cut each gumdrop leaf into 3 slices. Poke 2 gumdrop leaves into top of each cupcake on either side of pretzel stem. Poke half of gummy worm into each cupcake.

1 Cupcake: Calories 350; Total Fat 14g (Saturated Fat 8g; Trans Fat 0.5g); Cholesterol 60mg; Sodium 220mg; Total Carbohydrate 54g (Dietary Fiber 0g); Protein 2g **Exchanges:** 1 1/2 Starch, 2 Other Carbohydrate, 2 1/2 Fat **Carbohydrate Choices:** 3 1/2

sweet success tip
Don't like unsweetened applesauce? Regular will taste great in these cupcakes too.

use a cake mix

Substitute 1 box yellow cake mix for the cupcakes above. Make cake mix as directed on box for cupcakes **except**—use 1 cup apple juice, 1/3 cup unsweetened applesauce and 3 eggs, and add 1/2 teaspoon ground cinnamon. Bake and cool as directed on box. For the frosting, substitute 1 container vanilla creamy ready-to-spread frosting mixed with 1/2 teaspoon red paste food color. Frost and decorate as directed in recipe.

lemon creme **cupcakes**

24 cupcakes   PREP TIME: **1 Hour** START TO FINISH: **2 Hours**

CUPCAKES

Yellow Cupcakes (page 14)

FILLING AND FROSTING

Vanilla Buttercream Frosting (page 20)

$^{1}/_{2}$ cup marshmallow creme

2   teaspoons grated lemon peel

4   teaspoons fresh lemon juice

DECORATIONS

$^{1}/_{4}$ cup star-shaped candy sprinkles

1   Make, bake and cool Yellow Cupcakes as directed in recipe.

2   With end of round handle of wooden spoon, make deep, $^{3}/_{4}$-inch-wide indentation in center of top of each cupcake, not quite to bottom (wiggle end of spoon in cupcake to make opening large enough).

3   Make Vanilla Buttercream Frosting. In small bowl, mix $^{3}/_{4}$ cup of the frosting and the marshmallow creme. Spoon into small resealable food-storage plastic bag; seal bag. Cut $^{3}/_{8}$-inch tip off one bottom corner of bag. Insert tip of bag into opening in each cupcake; squeeze bag to fill opening.

4   Into remaining Vanilla Buttercream Frosting, stir lemon peel and lemon juice. Frost cupcakes. Sprinkle with stars.

1 Cupcake: Calories 350; Total Fat 14g (Saturated Fat 9g; Trans Fat 0.5g); Cholesterol 60mg; Sodium 220mg; Total Carbohydrate 52g (Dietary Fiber 0g); Protein 2g **Exchanges:** 1 $^{1}/_{2}$ Starch, 2 Other Carbohydrate, 2 $^{1}/_{2}$ Fat **Carbohydrate Choices:** 3 $^{1}/_{2}$

sweet success tip

How much lemon do you need? One lemon will yield 2 to 3 tablespoons of lemon juice and 1½ to 3 teaspoons of grated lemon peel.

use a cake mix

Substitute 1 box yellow cake mix for the Yellow Cupcakes. Make cake mix as directed on box for cupcakes. Make indentations in cupcakes as directed in recipe. In small bowl, mix $^{3}/_{4}$ cup vanilla whipped ready-to-spread frosting and $^{1}/_{2}$ cup marshmallow creme. Fill cupcakes with filling as directed in recipe. For frosting, stir together 1 container vanilla whipped ready-to-spread frosting, 2 teaspoons grated lemon peel and 4 teaspoons fresh lemon juice. Frost cupcakes. Sprinkle with stars.

sunflower **cupcakes bouquet**

72 mini cupcakes PREP TIME: **1 Hour 35 Minutes** START TO FINISH: **1 Hour 55 Minutes**

CUPCAKES

White Cupcakes (page 16)

FROSTING

Decorator Icing (page 21)
Yellow food color

DECORATIONS AND SUPPLIES

72 black gummy raspberries
Green tissue paper
Green pail or clay pot
Green floral oasis
7 wooden skewers
7 pieces green licorice
7 candy spearmint leaves

1 Make, bake and cool 72 mini cupcakes using White Cupcakes.

2 Make Decorator Icing. Stir in food color, mixing to blend completely. Spoon icing into decorating bag fitted with open star tip #18.

3 On each cupcake, pipe 6 lines from the center of the cupcake, out to the edge, making an evenly spaced "spoke-like pattern" on each. With the same tip, start in the center and make a loop by going down one side of each spoke, turning at the edge of the cupcake and following the next spoke back into the center to make a flower petal. Repeat 5 times, ending with 6 petals. Place black gummy raspberry in center of each cupcake.

4 Place 2 sheets of tissue paper inside pail. Cut dry oasis to fit inside pail. Thread wooden skewer through green licorice. Thread spearmint leaf onto skewer and then cupcake. Repeat to make 6 additional flowers. Arrange flowers in pail. Place remaining cupcakes on platter.

1 Mini Cupcake: Calories 110; Total Fat 4.5g (Saturated Fat 1.5g; Trans Fat 0.5g); Cholesterol 0mg; Sodium 55mg; Total Carbohydrate 17g (Dietary Fiber 0g); Protein 1g **Exchanges:** $1/2$ Starch, $1/2$ Other Carbohydrate, 1 Fat **Carbohydrate Choices:** 1

sweet success tip

Seven of the cupcakes are used to make a cute bouquet, and the remaining cupcakes are arranged on a large platter. If you like, make additional bouquets and use as centerpieces for tables.

use a cake mix

Substitute 1 box white cake mix for the White Cupcakes. Make cake mix as directed on box for cupcakes. Fill 72 mini muffin cups $3/4$ full (about 1 heaping tablespoon each). Bake 10 to 15 minutes or until toothpick inserted in center of cupcake comes out clean. For frosting, use 2 containers vanilla creamy ready-to-spread frosting; stir in 1 cup powdered sugar and food color, mixing to blend completely. After piping icing on cupcakes, top with black gummy raspberries. Continue as directed in recipe.

snowball **cupcakes**

24 cupcakes   PREP TIME: **55 Minutes** START TO FINISH: **1 Hour 50 Minutes**

CUPCAKES

Chocolate Cupcakes (page 15)
1/2   cup sour cream
1   package (3 oz) cream cheese, cut into 24 cubes

FROSTING

1/2   cup sugar
2   tablespoons water
2   egg whites
1   jar (7 oz) marshmallow creme
1   teaspoon vanilla

GARNISH

2   cups flaked coconut

1 Make Chocolate Cupcakes as directed in recipe except—add sour cream with the vanilla. Place 1 cube cream cheese in center of each, pressing down into batter almost to center (top of cream cheese will still show). Bake and cool as directed in recipe.

2 In 2-quart stainless steel or other non-coated saucepan, mix sugar, water and egg whites. Cook over low heat about 4 minutes, beating continuously with electric hand mixer on high speed, until soft peaks form. Add marshmallow creme; beat until stiff peaks form. Remove saucepan from heat. Beat in vanilla.

3 Frost cupcakes. Sprinkle top of each with generous tablespoon coconut. Store covered in refrigerator.

1 Cupcake: Calories 270; Total Fat 12g (Saturated Fat 5g; Trans Fat 1g); Cholesterol 25mg; Sodium 220mg; Total Carbohydrate 36g (Dietary Fiber 1g); Protein 3g **Exchanges:** 1/2 Starch, 2 Other Carbohydrate, 2 1/2 Fat **Carbohydrate Choices:** 2 1/2

sweet success tip

Add sparkle to each snowball by sprinkling with edible glitter or decorator sugar.

use a cake mix

Substitute 1 box devil's food cake mix for the Chocolate Cupcakes. Make cake mix as directed on box for cupcakes **except**—use 2/3 cup water, 1/2 cup sour cream, 1/3 cup vegetable oil and 2 eggs. Place 1 cube cream cheese in center of each, pressing down into batter almost to center (top of cream cheese will still show). Bake 22 to 27 minutes. Cool as directed on box, frost and garnish cupcakes as directed in recipe.

chocolate–sour cream cupcakes

24 cupcakes **PREP TIME: 40 Minutes** START TO FINISH: **1 Hour 40 Minutes**

CUPCAKES

2	cups all-purpose flour
2/3	cup unsweetened baking cocoa
1 1/4	teaspoons baking soda
1	teaspoon salt
1/4	teaspoon baking powder
3/4	cup shortening
1 1/2	cups granulated sugar
2	eggs
1/2	cup sour cream
1	teaspoon vanilla
1	cup water

RICH CHOCOLATE BUTTERCREAM FROSTING

4	cups (1 lb) powdered sugar
1	cup butter or margarine, softened
3	to 4 tablespoons milk
1 1/2	teaspoons vanilla
3 oz	unsweetened baking chocolate, melted, cooled

1 Heat oven to 350°F. Place paper baking cup in each of 24 regular-size muffin cups. In medium bowl, stir together flour, cocoa, baking soda, salt and baking powder; set aside.

2 In large bowl, beat shortening with electric mixer on medium speed 30 seconds. Beat in granulated sugar, about 1/4 cup at a time. Beat 2 minutes longer. Beat in eggs, one at a time, beating well after each addition. Beat in sour cream and vanilla until well blended. On low speed, alternately add flour mixture, about 1/3 of mixture at a time, and water, about 1/2 at a time, beating just until blended.

3 Divide batter evenly among muffin cups, filling each about 2/3 full.

4 Bake 20 to 25 minutes or until toothpick inserted in center of cupcake comes out clean. Cool 5 minutes. Remove cupcakes from pans; place on cooling racks to cool.

5 In medium bowl, beat frosting ingredients with electric mixer on medium speed until smooth and spreadable. If necessary, stir in additional milk, 1 teaspoon at a time. Spoon frosting into decorating bag fitted with large star tip #6. Pipe frosting onto cupcakes or frost, as desired.

1 Cupcake: Calories 340; Total Fat 18g (Saturated Fat 9g; Trans Fat 1.5g); Cholesterol 40mg; Sodium 240mg; Total Carbohydrate 42g (Dietary Fiber 1g); Protein 2g **Exchanges:** 1 Starch, 2 Other Carbohydrate, 3 1/2 Fat **Carbohydrate Choices:** 3

sweet success tip

For a quick frosting, you can use chocolate creamy ready-to-spread frosting.

use a cake mix

Substitute 1 box chocolate fudge cake mix for the cupcakes above. Make, bake and cool cake mix as directed on box for cupcakes. Frost as directed in recipe.

chocolate chip cheesecake swirl cupcakes

24 cupcakes   PREP TIME: **30 Minutes** START TO FINISH: **1 Hour 30 Minutes**

FILLING

$1/2$ cup sugar

2   packages (3 oz each) cream cheese, softened

1   egg

1   cup semisweet chocolate chips (6 oz)

CUPCAKES

2 $1/4$ cups all-purpose flour

1 $2/3$ cups sugar

$1/4$ cup unsweetened baking cocoa

1 $1/4$ cups water

$1/2$ cup vegetable oil

2   tablespoons white vinegar

2   teaspoons baking soda

2   teaspoons vanilla

1   teaspoon salt

1 Heat oven to 350°F. Place paper baking cup in each of 24 regular-size muffin cups. In medium bowl, beat $1/2$ cup sugar and the cream cheese with electric mixer on medium speed until smooth. Beat in egg. Stir in chocolate chips; set aside.

2 In large bowl, beat cupcake ingredients with electric mixer on low speed 30 seconds, scraping bowl occasionally. Beat on high speed 3 minutes, scraping bowl occasionally. Reserve 1 $1/2$ cups batter.

3 Fill each muffin cup about $1/3$ full. Spoon 1 tablespoon filling onto batter in each cup. Top each with $1/2$ rounded tablespoon reserved batter.

4 Bake 30 to 35 minutes or until toothpick inserted between center and edge of cupcake comes out clean. Remove cupcakes from pan; place on cooling racks to cool. Store covered in refrigerator.

1 Cupcake: Calories 230; Total Fat 10g (Saturated Fat 3.5g; Trans Fat 0g); Cholesterol 15mg; Sodium 230mg; Total Carbohydrate 32g (Dietary Fiber 1g); Protein 2g **Exchanges:** $1/2$ Starch, 1 $1/2$ Other Carbohydrate, 2 Fat **Carbohydrate Choices:** 2

sweet success tip

These cupcakes with a cream cheese swirl are great for picnics. They can be made the day before so you can have them ready to serve to kids of all ages!

use a cake mix

Make filling as directed in recipe. Substitute 1 box devil's food cake mix for the cupcakes above. Make cake mix as directed on box for cupcakes. Reserve 1 $1/2$ cups batter. Fill muffin cups about $1/3$ full. Spoon 1 tablespoon filling onto batter in each cup. Top each with 1 rounded tablespoon reserved batter. Bake and cool as directed on box.

orange soda **cupcakes**

12 cupcakes PREP TIME: **15 Minutes** START TO FINISH: **1 Hour 10 Minutes**

2 cups all-purpose flour

³/₄ cup sugar

1 teaspoon baking powder

¹/₂ teaspoon baking soda

¹/₂ teaspoon salt

¹/₂ teaspoon grated orange peel

¹/₃ cup butter or margarine, softened

1 cup orange-flavored carbonated beverage (8 oz)

2 eggs

Powdered sugar, if desired

1 Heat oven to 350°F. Place paper baking cup in each of 12 regular-size muffin cups.

2 In medium bowl, beat all ingredients with electric mixer on low speed 30 seconds, scraping bowl occasionally. Beat on medium speed 2 minutes, scraping bowl occasionally. Divide batter evenly among muffin cups.

3 Bake 20 to 25 minutes or until toothpick inserted in center of cupcake comes out clean. Cool 5 minutes. Remove cupcakes from pan; place on cooling rack to cool. Sprinkle with powdered sugar or frost with desired frosting.

1 Cupcake: Calories 190; Total Fat 6g (Saturated Fat 3.5g; Trans Fat 0g); Cholesterol 50mg; Sodium 240mg; Total Carbohydrate 31g (Dietary Fiber 0g); Protein 3g **Exchanges:** 1 Starch, 1 Other Carbohydrate, 1 Fat **Carbohydrate Choices:** 2

sweet success tip

Like the idea of soda cupcakes but orange is not your favorite? Mix it up by substituting another flavor of soda that you like better!

use a cake mix

Substitute 1 box white cake mix for the cupcakes above. Make cake mix as directed on box for cupcakes **except**—use 1 ¹/₄ cups orange-flavored carbonated beverage, ¹/₃ cup vegetable oil, 3 egg whites, and add 1 teaspoon grated orange peel with the beverage. Bake and cool as directed on box. Sprinkle with powdered sugar or frost cupcakes. 24 cupcakes

peanut butter cupcakes with chocolate frosting

24 cupcakes   PREP TIME: **45 Minutes** START TO FINISH: **1 Hour 45 Minutes**

CUPCAKES

Yellow Cupcakes (page 14)

$^3/_4$ cup creamy peanut butter

FROSTING

Creamy Chocolate Frosting
(page 20)

$^1/_4$ cup creamy peanut butter

GARNISH

$^1/_3$ cup chopped peanuts

1 Make Yellow Cupcakes as directed in recipe except—decrease butter to $^3/_4$ cup and add $^3/_4$ cup peanut butter with the vanilla. Bake and cool as directed in recipe.

2 Make Creamy Chocolate Frosting as directed in recipe—except stir in $^1/_4$ cup peanut butter. Frost cupcakes. Sprinkle with peanuts; press lightly into frosting.

1 Cupcake: Calories 350; Total Fat 18g (Saturated Fat 8g; Trans Fat 0g); Cholesterol 55mg; Sodium 250mg; Total Carbohydrate 40g (Dietary Fiber 1g); Protein 5g **Exchanges:** 1 $^1/_2$ Starch, 1 Other Carbohydrate, 3 $^1/_2$ Fat **Carbohydrate Choices:** 2 $^1/_2$

use a cake mix

Substitute 1 yellow cake mix for the Yellow Cupcakes. Make cake mix as directed on box for cupcakes **except**—use 1 $^1/_4$ cups water, $^1/_4$ cup vegetable oil, 3 eggs and stir in $^3/_4$ cup creamy peanut butter. Bake 20 to 25 minutes or until toothpick inserted in center of cupcake comes out clean. For the frosting, substitute 1 container chocolate creamy ready-to-spread frosting and stir in $^1/_4$ cup creamy peanut butter. Frost cupcakes. Sprinkle with peanuts; press lightly into frosting.

confetti candy cupcakes

30 cupcakes　**PREP TIME: 55 Minutes** START TO FINISH: **3 Hours 15 Minutes**

CUPCAKES

Yellow Cupcakes (page 14)

1　cup coarsely chopped candy-coated chocolate candies (about 6.5 oz)

FUDGE FROSTING

1　cup granulated sugar

$1/2$　cup unsweetened baking cocoa

$1/2$　cup milk

$1/4$　cup butter or margarine

2　tablespoons light corn syrup

1　teaspoon vanilla

$1 1/2$　to 2 cups powdered sugar

GARNISH

Candy-coated chocolate candies (about $3/4$ cup)

1 Make Yellow Cupcakes as directed in recipe except—place paper baking cup in each of 30 regular-size muffin cups. Sprinkle batter in each cup with 1 heaping teaspoon chopped candies. Bake and cool as directed in recipe. (If baking cupcakes in batches, cover and refrigerate batter until ready to use.)

2 In 2-quart saucepan, mix 1 cup granulated sugar and the cocoa. Stir in $1/2$ cup milk, $1/4$ cup butter and the corn syrup. Heat to boiling over medium-high heat, stirring frequently. Boil 3 minutes, stirring occasionally. Remove from heat; beat in vanilla and enough powdered sugar with spoon until frosting is smooth and spreadable. Frost cupcakes. Garnish each with 5 candy-coated chocolate candies.

1 Cupcake: Calories 280; Total Fat 11g (Saturated Fat 7g; Trans Fat 0g); Cholesterol 45mg; Sodium 170mg; Total Carbohydrate 41g (Dietary Fiber 1g); Protein 2g **Exchanges:** 1 $1/2$ Starch, 1 Other Carbohydrate, 2 Fat **Carbohydrate Choices:** 3

sweet success tip

Make these cupcakes to share for the holidays. Use red and green candy-coated chocolate candies.

use a cake mix

Substitute 1 box yellow cake mix for the Yellow Cupcakes. Make cake mix as directed on box for cupcakes **except**—use 1 cup water, $1/3$ cup vegetable oil and 3 eggs. Sprinkle batter with $3/4$ cup finely chopped candy-coated chocolate candies. Bake and cool as directed on box. Frost and decorate as directed in recipe.

margarita **cupcakes**

24 cupcakes   PREP TIME: **45 Minutes** START TO FINISH: **1 Hour 45 Minutes**

CUPCAKES

- 3/4   cup crushed pretzels
- 2   tablespoons butter or margarine, melted
- 1   tablespoon sugar
     White Cupcakes (page 16)
- 2   teaspoons grated lime peel
- 1 1/4   cups nonalcoholic margarita mix

FROSTING

- 1 1/2   cups frozen (thawed) whipped topping
- 2   containers (6 oz each) Key lime pie low-fat yogurt
- 2   teaspoons grated lime peel

GARNISH

- 1/3   cup coarsely crushed pretzels

1 Heat oven to 350°F. Place paper baking cup in each of 24 regular-size muffin cups. In small bowl, mix 3/4 cup crushed pretzels, the butter and sugar. Spoon about 1 tablespoon pretzel mixture into each muffin cup.

2 Make White Cupcakes as directed in recipe except—substitute margarita mix for the milk and add grated lime peel with the vanilla. Bake and cool as directed in recipe.

3 In medium bowl, fold whipped topping, lime yogurt and 2 teaspoons lime peel until blended. Frost cupcakes. Sprinkle tops with crushed pretzels.

1 Cupcake: Calories 180; Total Fat 7g (Saturated Fat 3g; Trans Fat 0g); Cholesterol 5mg; Sodium 230mg; Total Carbohydrate 27g (Dietary Fiber 0g); Protein 2g **Exchanges:** 1 Starch, 1 Other Carbohydrate, 1 Fat **Carbohydrate Choices:** 2

sweet success tip
Just for fun, serve these cupcakes in Margarita glasses.

use a cake mix

Make pretzel mixture and spoon into muffin cups as directed in step 1. Substitute 1 box white cake mix for the White Cupcakes. Make cake mix as directed on box for cupcakes **except**—use 3/4 cup nonalcoholic margarita mix, 1/4 cup water, 1/3 cup vegetable oil, 2 teaspoons grated lime peel and 4 egg whites. Bake and cool as directed. Frost and garnish as directed in recipe.

streusel-topped strawberry-rhubarb cupcakes

24 cupcakes   PREP TIME: **1 Hour** START TO FINISH: **1 Hour 55 Minutes**

STREUSEL

- 1/2 cup all-purpose flour
- 3 tablespoons sugar
- 1/4 cup butter or margarine, cut into small pieces

CUPCAKES

- 14 to 15 fresh strawberries (9 oz)
- 1/4 cup milk
- 2 3/4 cups all-purpose flour
- 3 teaspoons baking powder
- 1/2 teaspoon salt
- 3/4 cup shortening
- 1 1/2 cups sugar
- 5 egg whites
- 2 1/2 teaspoons vanilla
- 12 drops red food color
- 1 cup finely chopped rhubarb

TOPPING

- 3/4 cup whipping cream
- 2 to 3 fresh strawberries, mashed (2 tablespoons)

GARNISH

- Fresh whole strawberries, cut into slices, if desired

1 Heat oven to 350°F. Place paper baking cup in each of 24 regular-size muffin cups, or grease and flour muffin cups, or spray with baking spray with flour. In small bowl, mix streusel ingredients with fork until crumbly; set aside.

2 In blender, place 14 strawberries and the milk. Cover; puree about 30 seconds or until almost smooth. Measure mixture; should equal 1 1/4 cups. If not, puree additional strawberry. Set aside.

3 In medium bowl, mix 2 3/4 cups flour, the baking powder and salt. In large bowl, beat shortening with electric mixer on medium speed 30 seconds. Gradually add 1 1/2 cups sugar, about 1/3 cup at a time, beating well after each addition and scraping bowl occasionally. Beat 2 minutes longer. Beat in egg whites, one at a time, beating well after each addition. Beat in vanilla and food color. On low speed, alternately add flour mixture, about 1/3 of mixture at a time, and strawberry mixture, about 1/2 at a time, beating just until blended. Stir in rhubarb.

4 Divide batter evenly among muffin cups, filling each about 2/3 full. Sprinkle each with about 2 teaspoons streusel mixture; press lightly into batter.

5 Bake 18 to 20 minutes or until toothpick inserted in center of cupcake comes out clean. Cool 5 minutes. Remove cupcakes from pans; place on cooling racks to cool.

6 In chilled small bowl, beat whipping cream with electric mixer on high speed until stiff peaks form. Fold mashed strawberries into whipped cream. Spoon cream mixture into decorating bag fittted with large star tip #6. Pipe or spread cream mixture onto each cupcake. Garnish with strawberry slice.

1 Cupcake: Calories 230; Total Fat 11g (Saturated Fat 4.5g; Trans Fat 1.5g); Cholesterol 15mg; Sodium 140mg; Total Carbohydrate 29g (Dietary Fiber 1g); Protein 3g **Exchanges:** 1 Starch, 1 Other Carbohydrate, 2 Fat **Carbohydrate Choices:** 2

use a cake mix

Substitute 1 box white cake mix for the cupcakes above. Prepare Streusel as directed in recipe. Puree about 10 strawberries and 3 tablespoons water as directed in recipe to make 1 cup puree. Make cake mix as directed on box for cupcakes **except**—use pureed strawberries, 1/3 cup vegetable oil and 3 egg whites. Toss 1 cup finely chopped rhubarb with 2 tablespoons flour; stir into batter. Sprinkle each cupcake with about 1/2 teaspoon streusel mixture. Bake and cool as directed on box. Frost and garnish as directed in recipe. 26 cupcakes

strawberry–cream **cheese cupcakes**

28 cupcakes **PREP TIME: 20 Minutes** START TO FINISH: **1 Hour 45 Minutes**

CUPCAKES

Yellow Cupcakes (page 14)

2 tablespoons plus 1 teaspoon strawberry spread

1 package (3 oz) cream cheese, cut into 28 pieces

FROSTING

Cream Cheese Frosting (page 20)

GARNISH

Sliced fresh small strawberries, if desired

1 Make Yellow Cupcakes as directed except—divide batter evenly among 28 muffin cups. Before baking, place strawberry spread in small bowl; stir until smooth. Place 1 piece cream cheese on top of each cupcake; press into batter slightly. Spoon 1/4 teaspoon strawberry spread on top of cream cheese in each cupcake. Bake 20 to 22 minutes. Cool as directed in recipe.

2 Make Cream Cheese Frosting. Frost cupcakes. Just before serving, garnish each cupcake with strawberry slices.

1 Cupcake: Calories 320; Total Fat 15g (Saturated Fat 9g; Trans Fat 0.5g); Cholesterol 65mg; Sodium 250mg; Total Carbohydrate 42g (Dietary Fiber 0g); Protein 3g **Exchanges:** 1 Starch, 2 Other Carbohydrate, 3 Fat **Carbohydrate Choices:** 3

sweet success tip
Cut cream cheese when it's cold because it's easier to cut.

green tea **and lemon cupcakes**

24 cupcakes PREP TIME: **1 Hour** START TO FINISH: **3 Hours**

CUPCAKES
- 3/4 cup boiling water
- 2 green tea bags
- Lemon Cupcakes (page 17)

GREEN TEA–LEMON FROSTING
- 1 package (8 oz) cream cheese, softened
- 1/4 cup butter, softened
- 2 teaspoons grated lemon peel
- 1 teaspoon vanilla
- 4 cups (1 lb) powdered sugar
- Reserved 1 to 2 teaspoons brewed strong green tea

GARNISH
- 24 fortune cookies, unwrapped
- Grated lemon peel, if desired

1 In 1-cup glass measuring cup, measure boiling water; add tea bags. Let steep 5 minutes. Squeeze liquid from tea bags into measuring cup. If necessary, add additional water to make 3/4 cup. Let tea stand until room temperature, about 1 hour.

2 Make Lemon Cupcakes as directed in recipe except—use 2/3 cup of the brewed tea for the milk. (Reserve remaining tea for frosting.) Bake and cool as directed.

3 Meanwhile, in medium bowl, beat cream cheese, butter, lemon peel and vanilla with electric mixer on low speed until smooth. Gradually beat in powdered sugar, 1 cup at a time, until smooth. Beat in 1 to 2 teaspoons of the reserved tea, 1 teaspoon at a time, until smooth and spreadable.

4 Spoon frosting into decorating bag fitted with large round tip #7. Pipe or spread about 2 tablespoons frosting on top of each cupcake. Just before serving, place fortune cookie on edge of frosting on each cupcake to resemble tea cup handle. Garnish with lemon peel. Store covered in refrigerator.

1 Cupcake: Calories 320; Total Fat 14g (Saturated Fat 8g; Trans Fat 0g); Cholesterol 60mg; Sodium 250mg; Total Carbohydrate 46g (Dietary Fiber 0g); Protein 3g **Exchanges:** 1 Starch, 2 Other Carbohydrate, 2 1/2 Fat **Carbohydrate Choices:** 3

sweet success tip
Green tea is made from leaves that are steamed and dried but not fermented, giving it a taste that is closer to the taste of a fresh leaf.

use a cake mix

Substitute 1 box lemon cake mix for the Lemon Cupcakes. Prepare tea as directed in step 1 except—use 1 1/4 cups water to make 1 1/4 cups tea. Make cake mix as directed on box for cupcakes **except**—use tea, 1/3 cup vegetable oil and 3 eggs. Bake and cool as directed on box. Frost and decorate as directed in recipe.

snickerdoodle **cupcakes**

24 cupcakes **PREP TIME: 40 Minutes** START TO FINISH: **1 Hour 35 Minutes**

CUPCAKES

    White Cupcakes (page 16)

1 teaspoon ground cinnamon

CINNAMON FROSTING

6 cups powdered sugar

2 teaspoons ground cinnamon

$^2/_3$ cup butter or margarine, softened

1 tablespoon vanilla

2 to 4 tablespoons milk

TOPPING

2 teaspoons granulated sugar

$^1/_2$ teaspoon ground cinnamon

1 Make White Cupcakes as directed in recipe except—add 1 teaspoon cinnamon with the flour. Bake and cool as directed.

2 Meanwhile, in large bowl, mix powdered sugar, 2 teaspoons cinnamon and the butter with electric mixer on low speed. Stir in vanilla and 2 tablespoons of the milk. Gradually beat in enough remaining milk, 1 teaspoon at a time, to make frosting smooth and spreadable.

3 Frost cupcakes. In small bowl, mix topping ingredients; sprinkle over frosted cupcakes.

1 Cupcake: Calories 350; Total Fat 12g (Saturated Fat 5g, Trans Fat 1.5g); Cholesterol 15mg; Sodium 160mg; Total Carbohydrate 56g (Dietary Fiber 0g); Protein 2g **Exchanges:** $^1/_2$ Starch, 3 Other Carbohydrate, $2^1/_2$ Fat **Carbohydrate Choices:** 4

use a cake mix

Substitute 1 box white cake mix for the White Cupcakes. Make cake mix as directed on box for cupcakes **except**—use 1 $^1/_4$ cups water, $^1/_3$ cup vegetable oil, 3 egg whites and $^1/_2$ teaspoon ground cinnamon. Bake and cool as directed on box. Frost and garnish as directed in recipe.

hazelnut-spice **cupcakes**

24 cupcakes **PREP TIME: 55 Minutes** START TO FINISH: **2 Hours 15 Minutes**

CUPCAKES

	Yellow Cupcakes (page 14)
1	teaspoon ground ginger
1	teaspoon ground nutmeg
1/2	teaspoon ground cloves
3/4	cup chopped skin-removed hazelnuts (filberts)

HAZELNUT-CHOCOLATE FROSTING

1 1/2	cups semisweet chocolate chips
1/2	cup butter (do not use margarine)
1/4	cup hazelnut spread with cocoa (from 13-oz jar)
1/3	cup whipping cream

GARNISH

Chopped hazelnuts (filberts), if desired

1 Make Yellow Cupcakes as directed in recipe except—add ginger, nutmeg and cloves with flour. Stir in hazelnuts. Bake and cool as directed.

2 Meanwhile, in 1 1/2-quart saucepan, heat frosting ingredients over low heat about 15 minutes, stirring occasionally, until chips are melted and mixture is smooth. Refrigerate about 20 minutes, stirring occasionally, until thickened.

3 Frost cupcakes. Sprinkle with chopped hazelnuts.

1 Cupcake: Calories 310; Total Fat 20g (Saturated Fat 11g; Trans Fat 0.5g); Cholesterol 60mg; Sodium 210mg; Total Carbohydrate 30g (Dietary Fiber 1g); Protein 3g **Exchanges:** 1 Starch, 1 Other Carbohydrate, 4 Fat **Carbohydrate Choices:** 2

sweet success tip

To remove the bitter brown skin from whole hazelnuts, heat them in a shallow pan at 350°F for 10 to 15 minutes or until the skins begin to flake. Place a handful of nuts at a time in a dish towel; fold the towel over the warm nuts and rub vigorously.

use a cake mix

Substitute 1 box yellow cake mix for the Yellow Cupcakes. Make cake mix as directed on box for cupcakes **except**—add 1 teaspoon ground ginger, 1 teaspoon ground nutmeg and 1/2 teaspoon ground cloves. Stir in 3/4 cup chopped skin-removed hazelnuts (filberts). Bake and cool as directed on box. Frost and garnish as directed in recipe.

brown sugar cupcakes with brown butter frosting

24 cupcakes **PREP TIME: 30 Minutes** START TO FINISH: **1 Hour 35 Minutes**

CUPCAKES

2 1/3 cups all-purpose flour

2 teaspoons baking powder

1/2 teaspoon baking soda

1/2 teaspoon salt

1 cup butter, softened

1 cup granulated sugar

1/4 cup dark brown sugar

3 eggs

2 teaspoons vanilla

2/3 cup milk

BROWN BUTTER FROSTING

1/2 cup butter (do not use margarine)

4 1/2 cups powdered sugar

6 to 8 tablespoons milk

1 Heat oven to 350°F. Place paper baking cup in each of 24 regular-size muffin cups, or grease and flour muffin cups, or spray with baking spray with flour.

2 In medium bowl, mix flour, baking powder, baking soda and salt. In large bowl, beat 1 cup butter on medium speed 30 seconds. Gradually add granulated sugar and dark brown sugar, about 1/4 cup at a time, beating well after each addition, scraping bowl occasionally. Beat 2 minutes longer. Beat in eggs, one at a time, beating well after each addition. Beat in vanilla.

3 On low speed, alternately add flour mixture, about 1/3 at a time, with milk, about 1/2 at a time, beating just until blended.

4 Divide batter evenly among muffin cups, filling each about 2/3 full.

5 Bake 18 to 22 minutes or until golden brown and toothpick inserted in center of cupcake comes out clean. Cool 5 minutes. Remove cupcakes from pans; place on cooling racks to cool.

6 In small saucepan, brown 1/2 cup butter over medium heat, stirring constantly, until light golden brown. Cool completely. In large bowl, beat browned butter, powdered sugar and 4 tablespoons of the milk with electric mixer on low speed. until blended. Beat in milk, 1 teaspoon at a time, until spreadable. Frost cupcakes.

1 Cupcake: Calories 300; Total Fat 13g (Saturated Fat 8g, Trans Fat 0g); Cholesterol 60mg; Sodium 210mg; Total Carbohydrate 43g (Dietary Fiber 0g); Protein 2g **Exchanges:** 1/2 Starch, 2 1/2 Other Carbohydrate, 2 1/2 Fat **Carbohydrate Choices:** 3

sweet success tip
Top each cupcake with toasted walnut or pecan halves.

gingerbread cupcakes with cream cheese frosting

18 cupcakes PREP TIME: **40 Minutes** START TO FINISH: **1 Hour 35 Minutes**

CUPCAKES

- 1/2 cup granulated sugar
- 1/2 cup butter or margarine, softened
- 1/2 cup molasses
- 2 eggs
- 2 cups all-purpose flour
- 1 teaspoon baking soda
- 1/2 teaspoon salt
- 1 1/2 teaspoons ground ginger
- 1/2 teaspoon ground cinnamon
- 1/2 teaspoon ground allspice
- 3/4 cup water

FROSTING

- 1 package (8 oz) cream cheese, softened
- 1/4 cup butter or margarine, softened
- 2 teaspoons grated lemon peel
- 1 teaspoon ground cinnamon
- 1 teaspoon vanilla
- 4 cups (1 lb) powdered sugar
- 1 to 2 teaspoons milk

1 Heat oven to 375°F. Place paper baking cup in each of 18 regular-size muffin cups.

2 In large bowl, beat granulated sugar, 1/2 cup butter, the molasses and eggs with electric mixer on medium speed, or mix with spoon. Stir in flour, baking soda, salt, ginger, 1/2 teaspoon cinnamon, allspice and water. Divide batter evenly among muffin cups, using about 1/4 cup batter for each.

3 Bake 15 to 18 minutes or until toothpick inserted in center comes out clean. Cool in pan 5 minutes. Remove from pans; place on cooling racks to cool.

4 Meanwhile, in medium bowl, beat cream cheese, 1/4 cup butter, lemon peel, 1 teaspoon cinnamon and vanilla with electric mixer on low speed until smooth. Gradually beat in powdered sugar, 1 cup at a time, until smooth. Beat in milk, 1 teaspoon at a time, until spreadable.

5 Spoon frosting into decorating bag fitted with large open tip #6. Pipe or spread a generous amount of frosting on top of each cupcake. Store covered in refrigerator.

1 Cupcake: Calories 320; Total Fat 13g (Saturated Fat 8g; Trans Fat 0g); Cholesterol 60mg; Sodium 240mg; Total Carbohydrate 49g (Dietary Fiber 0g); Protein 3g **Exchanges:** 1/2 Starch, 3 Other Carbohydrate, 2 1/2 Fat **Carbohydrate Choices:** 3

sweet success tip

Wondering what type of molasses to use? Either light or dark molasses can be used in the cupcake batter. Light molasses is lighter in both flavor and color, while dark molasses is thicker and less sweet.

use a cake mix

Substitute 1 box yellow cake mix for the cupcakes above. Make cake as directed on box for cupcakes **except**—use 1 cup water, 1/2 cup vegetable oil, 1/4 cup molasses, 3 eggs, 1 1/2 teaspoons ground ginger, 1/2 teaspoon ground cinnamon and 1/2 teaspoon ground allspice. Frost with 1 container cream cheese creamy ready-to-spread frosting.

boston cream **cupcakes**

24 cupcakes   **PREP TIME: 45 Minutes** START TO FINISH: **1 Hour 45 Minutes**

CUPCAKES

Yellow Cupcakes (page 14)

1 box (4-serving size) vanilla instant pudding and pie filling mix

1 ³/₄ cups milk

CHOCOLATE ICING

¹/₃ cup butter or margarine

2 oz unsweetened baking chocolate

1 ¹/₂ cups powdered sugar

1 teaspoon vanilla

¹/₃ cup hot water

1 Make, bake and cool Yellow Cupcakes as directed in recipe.

2 Meanwhile, make pudding and pie filling mix as directed on box except— use 1 ³/₄ cups milk.

3 Fill cupcakes following the directions on the opposite page.

4 In 1-quart saucepan, melt butter and chocolate over low heat, stirring occasionally. Stir in powdered sugar and vanilla. Stir in hot water until smooth. If necessary, stir in additional water, 1 teaspoon at a time, until icing is spreadable. With metal spatula or back of spoon, spread icing over tops of cupcakes. Refrigerate uncovered until serving time. Store covered in refrigerator.

1 Cupcake: Calories 280; Total Fat 13g (Saturated Fat 8g, Trans Fat 0g); Cholesterol 55mg; Sodium 280mg; Total Carbohydrate 38g (Dietary Fiber 0g); Protein 3g **Exchanges:** 1 Starch, 1¹/₂ Other Carbohydrate, 2¹/₂ Fat **Carbohydrate Choices:** 2¹/₂

use a cake mix

Substitute 1 box yellow cake mix for the Yellow Cupcakes. Make, bake and cool cake mix as directed on box for cupcakes. Fill and frost cupcakes as directed in recipe.

to fill cupcakes:

1. With melon baller, scoop out center of each cupcake, scooping almost to bottom of cupcake; discard pieces.

2. Spoon about 2 teaspoons pudding into center of cupcake.

banana-toffee cupcakes

24 cupcakes   PREP TIME: **50 Minutes** START TO FINISH: **1 Hour 55 Minutes**

CUPCAKES

Yellow Cupcakes (page 14)

2   ripe bananas, mashed (about 1 cup)

1   cup toffee bits (from 8-oz bag)

FROSTING

Creamy Chocolate Frosting (page 20)

GARNISH

$1/3$ cup toffee bits

1 Make Yellow Cupcakes as directed in recipe except—use paper baking cups in muffin cups, decrease butter to $3/4$ cup, add mashed bananas with the vanilla, decrease milk to $1/4$ cup, and stir in 1 cup of the toffee bits. Bake and cool as directed in recipe.

2 Make Creamy Chocolate Frosting as directed in recipe. Frost cupcakes. Sprinkle with remaining $1/3$ cup toffee bits.

1 Cupcake: Calories 320; Total Fat 15g (Saturated Fat 9g; Trans Fat 0g); Cholesterol 50mg; Sodium 190mg; Total Carbohydrate 45g (Dietary Fiber 0g); Protein 2g **Exchanges:** 1 Starch, 2 Other Carbohydrate, 3 Fat **Carbohydrate Choices:** 3

sweet success tip

Do a "taste test" before adding toffee bits to your recipe because they can become rancid. Store toffee bits in the freezer to prevent this from happening.

use a cake mix

Substitute 1 box yellow cake mix for the Yellow Cupcakes. In large bowl, beat cake mix, 2 very ripe medium bananas, mashed (about 1 cup), $1/2$ cup water, $1/4$ cup butter or margarine, softened, 1 teaspoon vanilla and 3 eggs with electric mixer on low speed 30 seconds. Beat on medium speed 2 minutes, scraping bowl occasionally. Toss 1 cup of the toffee bits with 2 tablespoons all-purpose flour; stir into batter. Stir in 1 cup of the toffee bits. Divide batter evenly among muffin cups, filling each about $2/3$ full. Bake 18 to 23 minutes or until toothpick inserted in center of cupcake comes out clean. Cool 10 minutes. Remove cupcakes from pans; place on cooling racks to cool. For the frosting, substitute 1 container chocolate ready-to-spread frosting. Sprinkle with $1/3$ cup toffee bits.

banana–chocolate chip cupcakes

24 cupcakes   PREP TIME: **40 Minutes** START TO FINISH: **1 Hour 35 Minutes**

CUPCAKES

Yellow Cupcakes (page 14)

2 very ripe medium bananas, mashed (about 1 cup)

$3/4$ cup miniature semisweet chocolate chips

FROSTING

Creamy Chocolate Frosting (page 20)

GARNISH

Banana-shaped candy, if desired

1 Make Yellow Cupcakes as directed in recipe except—decrease butter to $3/4$ cup, add 2 very ripe medium bananas, mashed (about 1 cup), decrease milk to $1/4$ cup, and stir in $3/4$ cup miniature semisweet chocolate chips. Bake and cool as directed in recipe.

2 Make Creamy Chocolate Frosting as directed in recipe. Frost cupcakes. Garnish each with banana-shaped candy.

1 Frosted Cupcake: Calories 300; Total Fat 13g (Saturated Fat 8g; Trans Fat 0g); Cholesterol 50mg; Sodium 200mg; Total Carbohydrate 43g (Dietary Fiber 1g); Protein 2g **Exchanges:** 1 Starch, 2 Other Carbohydrate, 2 $1/2$ Fat **Carbohydrate Choices:** 3

use a cake mix

Substitute 1 box yellow cake mix for the Yellow Cupcakes. In large bowl, beat cake mix, 2 very ripe medium bananas, mashed (about 1 cup), $1/2$ cup water, $1/4$ cup butter or margarine, softened, and 3 eggs with electric mixer on low speed 30 seconds. Beat on medium speed 2 minutes, scraping bowl occasionally. Toss $3/4$ cup miniature chocolate chips with $1 1/2$ tablespoons all-purpose flour; stir into batter. Divide batter evenly among muffin cups. Bake 18 to 22 minutes or until toothpick inserted in center comes out clean. Remove from pans; place on cooling racks to cool. For the frosting, substitute 1 container chocolate creamy ready-to-spread frosting.

ginger and peach **cupcakes**

24 cupcakes   PREP TIME: **45 Minutes** START TO FINISH: **1 Hour 45 Minutes**

CUPCAKES

2 1/3 cups all-purpose flour
2 1/2 teaspoons baking powder
 1/2 teaspoon salt
 1/4 teaspoon ground ginger
  1 cup butter or margarine, softened
1 1/4 cups sugar
  3 eggs
  1 teaspoon vanilla
  1 container (6 oz) harvest peach low-fat yogurt
  1 large peach, peeled, chopped (about 1 cup)
  1 tablespoon all-purpose flour

FROSTING

4 1/2 cups powdered sugar
  1 container (6 oz) harvest peach low-fat yogurt

GARNISH

  1 jar (2 oz) crystallized ginger, chopped

1 Heat oven to 350°F. Place paper baking cup in each of 24 regular-size muffin cups.

2 In medium bowl, mix 2 1/3 cups flour, baking powder, salt and ginger; set aside.

3 In large bowl, beat butter with electric mixer on medium speed 30 seconds. Gradually add sugar, about 1/4 cup at a time, beating well after each addition. Beat 2 minutes longer. Add eggs, one at a time, beating well after each addition. Beat in vanilla. On low speed, alternately add flour mixture, about 1/3 of mixture at a time, and yogurt, about 1/2 at a time, beating just until blended. In small bowl, toss peach with 1 tablespoon flour; fold into batter.

4 Divide batter evenly among muffin cups, filling each about 2/3 full.

5 Bake 20 to 25 minutes or until golden brown and toothpick inserted in center comes out clean. Cool in pans 5 minutes. Remove cupcakes from pans; place on cooling racks to cool.

6 Meanwhile, in small bowl, mix powdered sugar and 1 container peach yogurt until smooth and spreadable. Frost cupcakes. Sprinkle each with about 1/2 teaspoon chopped ginger.

1 Cupcake: Calories 280; Total Fat 9g (Saturated Fat 5g; Trans Fat 0g); Cholesterol 45mg; Sodium 190mg; Total Carbohydrate 48g (Dietary Fiber 0g); Protein 2g **Exchanges:** 1 1/2 Starch, 1 1/2 Other Carbohydrate, 1 1/2 Fat **Carbohydrate Choices:** 3

sweet success tip

If fresh peaches aren't available, you can substitute frozen peaches that are thawed and well-drained.

maple cornmeal cupcakes **with maple-butter frosting**

18 cupcakes   **PREP TIME: 45 Minutes** START TO FINISH: **1 Hour 45 Minutes**

CUPCAKES

1 1/2   cups all-purpose flour
1/3   cup yellow cornmeal
2   teaspoons baking powder
1/2   teaspoon salt
1/2   cup butter or margarine, softened
1   cup granulated sugar
1   teaspoon maple flavor
2   eggs
3/4   cup milk

FROSTING

4   cups powdered sugar
2   tablespoons butter or margarine, softened
2   teaspoons maple flavor
3   to 4 tablespoons milk

GARNISH

Maple leaf candy, if desired

1 Heat oven to 350°F. Place paper baking cup in each of 18 regular-size muffin cups.

2 In medium bowl, mix flour, cornmeal, baking powder and salt. In large bowl, beat 1/2 cup butter with electric mixer on medium speed 30 seconds. Gradually add granulated sugar, about 1/4 cup at a time, beating well after each addition, scraping bowl occasionally. Beat 2 minutes longer. Beat in 1 teaspoon maple flavor and eggs. On low speed, alternately add flour mixture, about 1/3 of mixture at a time, and 3/4 cup milk, about 1/2 at a time, beating just until blended.

3 Divide batter evenly among muffin cups, filling each about 2/3 full.

4 Bake 20 to 25 minutes or until golden brown and toothpick inserted in center of cupcake comes out clean. Cool 5 minutes. Remove cupcakes from pans; place on cooling racks to cool.

5 In medium bowl, beat frosting ingredients, adding enough milk, until frosting is smooth and spreadable. Frost cupcakes. Garnish each with maple leaf candy.

1 Cupcake: Calories 280; Total Fat 7g (Saturated Fat 4.5g; Trans Fat 0g); Cholesterol 40mg; Sodium 180mg; Total Carbohydrate 50g (Dietary Fiber 0g); Protein 2g **Exchanges:** 1 1/2 Starch, 2 Other Carbohydrate, 1 Fat **Carbohydrate Choices:** 3

sweet success tip
For another easy garnish idea, place a pecan half on each frosted cupcake.

caramel-carrot **cupcakes**

32 cupcakes   PREP TIME: **45 Minutes** START TO FINISH: **2 Hours 45 Minutes**

CUPCAKES

2 1/3 cups all-purpose flour
2 teaspoons baking powder
1/2 teaspoon baking soda
1/2 teaspoon salt
2 teaspoons ground cinnamon
1 cup butter, softened
1 1/4 cups granulated sugar
3 eggs
1 teaspoon vanilla
2/3 cup milk
3 cups shredded carrots (about 4 medium)
1 cup raisins
1 can (8 oz) crushed pineapple, well drained

CARAMEL FROSTING

1 cup butter
2 cups packed brown sugar
1/2 cup milk
2 teaspoons vanilla
5 cups powdered sugar
Pecan halves or chopped nuts, if desired

1 Heat oven to 350°F. Place paper baking cup in each of 24 regular-size muffin cups.

2 In medium bowl, mix flour, baking powder, baking soda, salt and cinnamon. In large bowl, beat 1 cup butter with electric mixer on medium speed 30 seconds. Gradually add granulated sugar, about 1/4 cup at a time, beating after each addition and scraping bowl occasionally. Beat 2 minutes longer. Add eggs, 1 at time, beating well after each addition. Beat in 1 teaspoon vanilla.

3 On low speed, alternately add flour mixture, about 1/3 at a time, and 2/3 cup milk, about 1/2 at a time, beating just until blended. Stir in carrots, raisins and pineapple.

4 Divide batter evenly among muffin cups, filling each about 2/3 full. (Cover and refrigerate remaining batter until ready to bake. Cool pan before reusing.)

5 Bake 20 to 25 minutes or until golden and toothpick inserted in center of cupcake comes out clean. Cool 5 minutes; remove from pans to cooling racks to cool.

6 Meanwhile, in 2-quart saucepan, melt 1 cup butter over medium heat. Stir in brown sugar. Heat to boiling, stirring constantly. Stir in 1/2 cup milk. Return to boiling; remove from heat. Stir in 2 teaspoons vanilla. Cool to lukewarm, about 30 minutes. Gradually stir in powdered sugar with whisk. Frost each cupcake with about 2 tablespoons frosting. Garnish with nuts.

1 Cupcake: Calories 330; Total Fat 12g (Saturated Fat 8g; Trans Fat 0g); Cholesterol 50mg; Sodium 190mg; Total Carbohydrate 53g (Dietary Fiber 1g); Protein 2g **Exchanges:** 1/2 Starch, 3 Other Carbohydrate, 2 1/2 Fat **Carbohydrate Choices:** 3 1/2

Mini Cupcakes: Prepare as directed above except—place mini paper baking cup in each of 24 mini muffin cups. Divide batter evenly among cups, filling each about 2/3 full. (Cover and refrigerate remaining batter until ready to bake. Cool pan before reusing.) Bake 17 to 20 minutes or until golden and toothpick inserted in center of cupcake comes out clean. Cool 5 minutes; remove from pans to cooling racks to cool. Frost. 96 mini cupcakes

double-coconut cupcakes

22 cupcakes   **PREP TIME: 50 Minutes** START TO FINISH: **2 Hours 5 Minutes**

FILLING

2 cups flaked coconut
1/2 cup sweetened condensed milk
    (from 14-oz can)

CUPCAKES

2 cups all-purpose flour
3/4 cup sugar
1/3 cup butter or margarine,
    softened
1 cup milk
1 teaspoon baking powder
1/2 teaspoon baking soda
1/2 teaspoon salt
2 eggs

FROSTING

Vanilla Buttercream Frosting
(page 20)

GARNISH

1 cup flaked coconut, toasted

1 Heat oven to 350°F. Place paper baking cup in each of 22 regular-size muffin cups. In small bowl, mix filling ingredients; set aside.

2 In medium bowl, beat cupcake ingredients with electric mixer on low speed 30 seconds, scraping bowl occasionally. Beat on medium speed 2 minutes, scraping bowl occasionally.

3 Divide batter evenly among muffin cups. Top batter in each cup with 1 rounded teaspoon filling.

4 Bake 20 to 25 minutes or until toothpick inserted between center and edge of cupcake comes out clean. Cool 10 minutes. Remove cupcakes from pan; place on cooling racks to cool.

5 Make Vanilla Buttercream Frosting as directed in recipe. Frost cupcakes. Dip tops of cupcakes into toasted coconut.

1 Cupcake: Calories 370; Total Fat 14g (Saturated Fat 10g; Trans Fat 0g); Cholesterol 45mg; Sodium 210mg; Total Carbohydrate 58g (Dietary Fiber 1g); Protein 3g **Exchanges:** 1 Starch, 3 Other Carbohydrate, 2 1/2 Fat **Carbohydrate Choices:** 4

sweet success tip

To toast the coconut, bake in a shallow pan at 350°F for 5 to 7 minutes, stirring occasionally, until golden brown. Watch closely, it browns quickly!

use a cake mix

Make filling as directed in recipe; set aside. Substitute 1 box yellow cake mix for the cupcakes above. Make cake mix as directed on box for cupcakes **except**—top batter in each cup with about 1 rounded teaspoon filling. Bake as directed on box. For the frosting, substitute 1 container vanilla ready-to-spread frosting. Continue as directed in recipe. 24 cupcakes

spiced pumpkin **cupcakes**

24 cupcakes **PREP TIME: 50 Minutes** START TO FINISH: **1 Hour 50 Minutes**

GARNISH

- 1/2 cup finely chopped pecans
- 3 tablespoons sugar

CUPCAKES

- 2 1/3 cups all-purpose flour
- 2 1/2 teaspoons baking powder
- 1 1/2 teaspoons pumpkin pie spice
- 1/2 teaspoon salt
- 1 cup butter or margarine, softened
- 1 1/4 cups sugar
- 3 eggs
- 1 cup (from 15-oz can) pumpkin (not pumpkin pie mix)
- 1 teaspoon vanilla
- 1/2 cup milk

FROSTING

Cream Cheese Frosting (page 20)

1 Heat oven to 350°F. Place paper baking cup in each of 24 regular-size muffin cups. Grease and flour muffin cups, or spray with baking spray with flour.

2 In 8-inch nonstick skillet, cook pecans and 2 tablespoons of the sugar over low heat about 8 minutes, stirring frequently, until sugar is melted. Spoon and spread pecans onto sheet of waxed paper. Sprinkle with remaining 1 tablespoon sugar; toss. Set aside.

3 In medium bowl, mix flour, baking powder, pumpkin pie spice and salt; set aside.

4 In large bowl, beat butter with electric mixer on medium speed 30 seconds. Gradually add sugar, about 1/4 cup at a time, beating well after each addition and scraping bowl occasionally. Beat 2 minutes longer. Add eggs, one at a time, beating well after each addition. Beat in pumpkin and vanilla. On low speed, alternately add flour mixture, about 1/3 of mixture at a time, and milk, about 1/2 at a time, beating just until blended.

5 Bake 20 to 25 minutes or until golden brown and toothpick inserted in center comes out clean. Cool in pans 5 minutes. Remove cupcakes from pans; place on cooling racks to cool.

6 Make Cream Cheese Frosting as directed in recipe. Frost cupcakes. Sprinkle edge of frosted cupcakes with sugar-coated pecans; press lightly into frosting.

1 Cupcake: Calories 330; Total Fat 15g (Saturated Fat 8g; Trans Fat 0g); Cholesterol 65mg; Sodium 230mg; Total Carbohydrate 43g (Dietary Fiber 1g); Protein 3g **Exchanges:** 1 Starch, 2 Other Carbohydrate, 3 Fat
Carbohydrate Choices: 3

use a cake mix

Substitute 1 box yellow cake mix for the cupcakes above. Make cake mix as directed on box for cupcakes **except**—use 1/2 cup water, 1/3 cup vegetable oil, 4 eggs, and add 1 cup (from 15-oz can) pumpkin (not pumpkin pie mix) and 1 1/2 teaspoons pumpkin pie spice. For the frosting, substitute 1 container cream cheese creamy ready-to-spread frosting. Frost and garnish as directed in recipe.

Spiced Caramel-Pear Cupcakes, page 126

chapter three

bake-sale
favorites

aztec chile-chocolate **cupcakes**

24 cupcakes PREP TIME: **40 Minutes** START TO FINISH: **2 Hours 20 Minutes**

CUPCAKES

Chocolate Cupcakes (page 15)

3   teaspoons ancho chili powder

1/8   teaspoon ground red pepper (cayenne)

CHOCOLATE SHARDS

1   bag (11.5 oz) milk chocolate chips (2 cups)

CINNAMON-CHOCOLATE FROSTING

1/2   cup butter or margarine, softened

3   oz unsweetened baking chocolate, melted, cooled

3   cups powdered sugar

1/2   teaspoon ground cinnamon

1   tablespoon instant espresso coffee powder or granules

3   to 4 tablespoons milk

2   teaspoons vanilla

1 Make Chocolate Cupcakes as directed in recipe except—add chili powder and ground red pepper with the flour. Bake and cool as directed in recipe.

2 Meanwhile, line cookie sheet with foil. In 1-quart saucepan, melt chocolate chips over low heat, stirring constantly, until smooth. Remove from heat. Spread chocolate to 1/8-inch thickness on foil-lined cookie sheet. Refrigerate about 30 minutes or until set. Break into pieces; reserve.

3 In large bowl, mix butter and cooled chocolate. Stir in powdered sugar and cinnamon. Stir espresso powder into 2 tablespoons milk until dissolved. With spoon, beat espresso mixture into powdered sugar mixture with vanilla. Beat in additional milk, 1 teaspoon at a time, until smooth and spreadable. Frost cupcakes. Garnish each with chocolate shards.

1 Cupcake: Calories 360; Total Fat 17g (Saturated Fat 8g; Trans Fat 1.5g); Cholesterol 30mg; Sodium 220mg; Total Carbohydrate 46g (Dietary Fiber 2g); Protein 3g **Exchanges:** 1 Starch, 2 Other Carbohydrate, 3 1/2 Fat **Carbohydrate Choices:** 3

sweet success tip

To complete the Mexican-inspired theme, serve with dulce de leche ice cream.

use a cake mix

Substitute 1 box devil's food cake mix for the Chocolate Cupcakes. Make cake mix as directed on box for cupcakes **except**—use 1 1/4 cups water, 1/2 cup vegetable oil, 3 eggs, 3 teaspoons ancho chili powder and 1/8 teaspoon ground red pepper (cayenne). Bake and cool as directed on box. For the frosting, substitute 1 container chocolate creamy ready-to-spread frosting mixed with 1/2 teaspoon ground cinnamon. Make Chocolate Shards; frost and garnish as directed in recipe.

surprise graduation **cupcakes**

24 cupcakes   PREP TIME: **35 Minutes** START TO FINISH: **2 Hours 5 Minutes**

CUPCAKES

   Chocolate Cupcakes (page 15)

24   milk chocolate candy drops or pieces, unwrapped

FROSTING AND DECORATION

3   cups powdered sugar

1/3   cup butter or margarine, softened

2   oz white chocolate baking bars, melted (from 6-oz package)

1   teaspoon vanilla

3   to 4 tablespoons milk

1/2   cup dark chocolate chips, melted

1   Make Chocolate Cupcakes as directed in recipe except—lightly press 1 milk chocolate candy drop or piece into center of each batter-filled muffin cup. Bake and cool as directed in recipe.

2   In medium bowl, beat powdered sugar, butter, melted white baking bar and vanilla with electric mixer on low speed until blended. Gradually beat in milk until smooth and creamy. Frost cupcakes. Pipe year with melted dark chocolate onto each cupcake.

1 Cupcake: Calories 300; Total Fat 13g (Saturated Fat 6g; Trans Fat 1g); Cholesterol 25mg; Sodium 200mg; Total Carbohydrate 43g (Dietary Fiber 1g); Protein 3g **Exchanges:** 1 Starch, 2 Other Carbohydrate, 2 1/2 Fat **Carbohydrate Choices:** 3

sweet success tip

For a quick-and-easy topping, sprinkle the cupcakes with the grad's school colors.

use a cake mix

Substitute 1 box devil's food cake mix for the Chocolate Cupcakes. Make cake mix as directed on box for cupcakes. Press 1 milk chocolate candy drop or piece into center of each batter-filled muffin cup. Frost and decorate as directed in recipe.

chocolate-espresso **cupcakes**

12 cupcakes   **PREP TIME: 15 Minutes** START TO FINISH: **1 Hour 15 Minutes**

1	cup all-purpose flour
1/2	cup unsweetened baking cocoa
1/2	teaspoon baking soda
1/4	teaspoon salt
2	egg whites
1	whole egg
1	cup granulated sugar
1/4	cup canola or vegetable oil
1/2	cup light chocolate soymilk
2	teaspoons instant espresso coffee granules
1 1/2	teaspoons vanilla
	Powdered sugar, if desired

1 Heat oven to 375°F. Lightly spray 12 regular-size muffin cups with cooking spray, or line with paper baking cups.

2 In medium bowl, mix flour, cocoa, baking soda and salt. In another medium bowl, beat egg whites, whole egg, granulated sugar and oil with electric mixer on medium-high speed 1 to 2 minutes or until well mixed. On low speed, alternately add flour mixture and soymilk, beating after each addition, until well blended. Add coffee granules and vanilla; beat on low speed 30 seconds. Divide batter evenly among muffin cups, filling each filling each about 2/3 full.

3 Bake 15 to 20 minutes or until toothpick inserted in center of cupcake comes out clean. Cool 10 minutes. Remove cupcakes from pan; place on cooling rack to cool.

4 Just before serving, sift powdered sugar over tops of cupcakes.

1 Cupcake: Calories 170; Total Fat 6g (Saturated Fat 1g; Trans Fat 0g); Cholesterol 20mg; Sodium 125mg; Total Carbohydrate 27g (Dietary Fiber 1g); Protein 3g **Exchanges:** 1/2 Starch, 1 1/2 Other Carbohydrate, 1 Fat **Carbohydrate Choices:** 2

Raspberry-Chocolate Cupcakes: Omit the vanilla and the espresso powder. Add 2 teaspoons raspberry extract with the soymilk. Serve with fresh raspberries.

chocolate candy **cupcakes**

18 cupcakes   PREP TIME: **55 Minutes** START TO FINISH: **2 Hours 10 Minutes**

FILLING

- 2 packages (3 oz each) cream cheese, softened
- 2 tablespoons powdered sugar
- 1 egg
- 2 chocolate-covered nougat, caramel and peanut candy bars (2.07 oz each), unwrapped, finely chopped

CUPCAKES

- 1 1/2 cups all-purpose flour
- 1 cup granulated sugar
- 1/3 cup unsweetened baking cocoa
- 1 teaspoon baking soda
- 1/2 teaspoon salt
- 1 cup buttermilk
- 1/3 cup vegetable oil
- 1 teaspoon vanilla

FROSTING

- 1/3 cup packed brown sugar
- 1/3 cup butter or margarine
- 3 tablespoons milk
- 1 1/2 cups powdered sugar
- 1 chocolate-covered nougat, caramel and peanut candy bar (2.07 oz), unwrapped, finely chopped, if desired

1 Heat oven to 350°F. Place paper baking cup in each of 18 regular-size muffin cups. In small bowl, beat cream cheese, 2 tablespoons powdered sugar and the egg with electric mixer on medium speed until smooth. With spoon, stir in 2 chopped candy bars; set aside.

2 In large bowl, mix flour, granulated sugar, cocoa, baking soda and salt. Add buttermilk, oil and vanilla; beat 2 minutes with electric mixer on medium speed. Divide batter evenly among muffin cups, filling each about 1/2 full. Spoon 1 tablespoon cream cheese mixture in center of batter in each cup.

3 Bake 23 to 30 minutes or until cream cheese mixture is light golden brown. Cool in pans 15 minutes. (Cupcakes will sink slightly in center.) Remove cupcakes from pans; place on cooling racks to cool.

4 Meanwhile, in 1 1/2-quart saucepan, cook brown sugar and butter over medium heat, stirring frequently, just until mixture boils. Remove from heat. Stir in milk. Cool 30 minutes. With spoon, beat 1 1/2 cups powdered sugar into brown sugar mixture until spreadable, adding 1 tablespoon additional powdered sugar at a time if necessary.

5 Frost cupcakes. Sprinkle with chopped candy bar.

1 Cupcake: Calories 290; Total Fat 13g (Saturated Fat 6g; Trans Fat 0g); Cholesterol 35mg; Sodium 220mg; Total Carbohydrate 40g (Dietary Fiber 1g); Protein 4g **Exchanges:** 1 Starch, 1 1/2 Other Carbohydrate, 2 1/2 Fat **Carbohydrate Choices:** 2 1/2

sweet success tip

Don't have buttermilk on hand? An easy substitute is 1 tablespoon vinegar or lemon juice plus enough milk to make 1 cup.

"our team" cupcakes

24 cupcakes   PREP TIME: 1 Hour START TO FINISH: 3 Hours 20 Minutes

CUPCAKES

Chocolate Cupcakes (page 15)

ICING AND DECORATIONS

Decorator Icing (page 21)

Assorted small candies

Candy sprinkles

Desired color decorating icing
(from 6.4-oz can)

1 Make, bake and cool Chocolate Cupcakes as directed in recipe.

2 Make Decorator Icing as directed in recipe.

3 Frost cupcakes. Decorate as desired with candies, sprinkles and canned decorating icing.

1 Cupcake: Calories 300; Total Fat 13g (Saturated Fat 5g; Trans Fat 1.5g); Cholesterol 30mg; Sodium 220mg; Total Carbohydrate 42g (Dietary Fiber 1g); Protein 2g **Exchanges:** 1 Starch, 2 Other Carbohydrate, 2 ½ Fat **Carbohydrate Choices:** 3

sweet success tip

Use paper baking cups that coordinate with your team's color theme.

Use a cake mix

Substitute 1 box devil's food cake mix for the Chocolate Cupcakes. Make cake mix as directed on box for cupcakes. For the frosting, substitute 1 container vanilla creamy ready-to-spread frosting. Frost and decorate as directed in recipe.

double chocolate–peanut butter cupcakes

12 cupcakes **PREP TIME: 20 Minutes** START TO FINISH: **1 Hour 10 Minutes**

3/4 cup granulated sugar

3 tablespoons creamy peanut butter

1/4 cup fat-free sour cream

1 egg

1 egg white

1 cup all-purpose flour

1/4 cup unsweetened baking cocoa

1/2 cup hot water

1/2 teaspoon baking soda

1/4 cup miniature semisweet chocolate chips

Powdered sugar, if desired

1 Heat oven to 350°F. Place paper baking cup in each of 12 regular-size muffin cups.

2 In large bowl, beat granulated sugar, peanut butter, sour cream, egg and egg white with electric mixer on medium speed until well blended. Beat in remaining ingredients except powdered sugar on low speed just until mixed.

3 Divide batter evenly among muffin cups.

4 Bake 15 to 20 minutes or until toothpick inserted in center of cupcake comes out clean. Remove cupcakes from pan; place on cooling rack to cool. Sprinkle tops with powdered sugar.

1 Cupcake: Calories 150; Total Fat 4g (Saturated Fat 1.5g; Trans Fat 0g); Cholesterol 20mg; Sodium 90mg; Total Carbohydrate 25g (Dietary Fiber 1g); Protein 4g **Exchanges:** 1/2 Starch, 1 Other Carbohydrate, 1 Fat **Carbohydrate Choices:** 1 1/2

sweet success tip

Make your cupcakes stand out at the next bake sale! Pick up fun foil or fancy, decorated paper baking cups sold at cake decorating or party supply stores.

use a cake mix

Substitute 1 box devil's food cake mix for the cupcakes above. Make cake mix as directed on box for cupcakes **except**—use 1 1/4 cups water, 3/4 cup creamy peanut butter, 1/4 cup vegetable oil, 3 eggs and add 1/2 cup miniature semisweet chocolate chips. Bake as directed on box. Cool in pans 10 minutes. Remove cupcakes from pans; place on cooling racks to cool. Sprinkle tops with powdered sugar. 24 cupcakes

chocolate-amaretto **cupcakes**

{ **Deborah Harroun Orem, Utah Taste and Tell** www.tasteandtellblog.com }

24 cupcakes **PREP TIME: 50 Minutes** START TO FINISH: **1 Hour 45 Minutes**

CUPCAKES

1 1/2   cups all-purpose flour
  3/4   cup unsweetened baking cocoa
   2   teaspoons baking soda
  1/4   teaspoon salt
  1/2   cup vegetable oil
1 1/4   cups granulated sugar
   4   eggs
   1   teaspoon vanilla
  3/4   cup milk

FROSTING

  3/4   cup milk
  1/4   cup all-purpose flour
  3/4   cup butter, softened
3 1/2   cups powdered sugar
   1   tablespoon amaretto or
        1/2 teaspoon almond extract

TOPPING

  1/2   cup semisweet chocolate chips,
        coarsely chopped
  1/4   cup chocolate syrup

1 Heat oven to 350°F. Place foil or paper baking cup in each of 24 regular-size muffin cups.

2 In medium bowl, mix 1 1/2 cups flour, the cocoa, baking soda and salt; set aside. In large bowl, beat oil and granulated sugar with electric mixer on medium speed. Add eggs, 1 at a time, beating well after each addition. Beat in vanilla. On low speed, alternately add flour mixture, about 1/3 at a time, and 3/4 cup milk, about 1/2 at a time, beating just until blended.

3 Divide batter evenly among muffin cups, filling each about 2/3 full.

4 Bake foil-lined cupcakes 13 to 17 minutes, paper-lined cupcakes 14 to 18 minutes, or until toothpick inserted in center of cupcake comes out clean. Cool 5 minutes; remove from pans to cooling racks to cool.

5 Meanwhile, in 1-quart saucepan, cook and stir 3/4 cup milk and 1/4 cup flour with whisk over medium heat until thick, about 2 minutes. Remove from heat; cool completely, about 1 hour.

6 In medium bowl, beat butter and powdered sugar with electric mixer on low speed until smooth. Add cooled milk mixture; beat until light and fluffy. Beat in amaretto. Add additional powdered sugar, if necessary, to achieve desired spreading consistency.

7 Frost cupcakes. Top each cupcake with chopped chocolate chips; drizzle with chocolate syrup.

1 Cupcake: Calories 300; Total Fat 13g (Saturated Fat 6g; Trans Fat 0g); Cholesterol 50mg; Sodium 190mg; Total Carbohydrate 42g (Dietary Fiber 1g); Protein 3g **Exchanges:** 1 Starch, 2 Other Carbohydrate, 2 1/2 Fat **Carbohydrate Choices:** 3

use a cake mix

Substitute 1 box devil's food cake mix for the cupcakes above. Make cake mix as directed on box for cupcakes. Frost and top cupcakes as directed in recipe.

chocolate cupcakes **with penuche filling**

24 cupcakes   PREP TIME: **50 Minutes** START TO FINISH: **2 Hours 10 Minutes**

CUPCAKES

Chocolate Cupcakes (page 15)

FILLING AND GARNISH

1   cup butter or margarine

2   cups packed brown sugar

1/2   cup milk

4   cups powdered sugar

1   oz grated semisweet baking
chocolate, if desired

1   Make, bake and cool Chocolate Cupcakes as directed in recipe.

2   Meanwhile, in 2-quart saucepan, melt butter over medium heat. Stir in brown sugar. Heat to boiling, stirring constantly. Reduce heat to low; boil and stir 2 minutes. Stir in milk. Heat to boiling. Remove from heat; pour mixture into medium bowl. Refrigerate until lukewarm, about 30 minutes.

3   Beat powdered sugar into cooled brown sugar mixture with electric mixer on low speed until smooth. If frosting becomes too stiff, stir in additional milk, 1 teaspoon at a time.

4   Using serrated knife, cut each cupcake in half horizontally, being careful not to break either half. Place 1 heaping tablespoon filling on each cupcake base. Replace rounded cupcake tops. Pipe or spoon frosting onto cupcake tops. Garnish with grated chocolate.

1 Cupcake: Calories 390; Total Fat 15g (Saturated Fat 7g; Trans Fat 1.5g); Cholesterol 40mg; Sodium 240mg; Total Carbohydrate 60g (Dietary Fiber 1g); Protein 2g **Exchanges:** 1/2 Starch, 3 1/2 Other Carbohydrate, 3 Fat **Carbohydrate Choices:** 4

sweet success tip

The word *penuche* comes from a Spanish word meaning "raw sugar" or "brown sugar." It is used to describe a fudgelike candy made from brown sugar, butter, milk or cream and vanilla.

use a cake mix

Substitute 1 box chocolate fudge cake mix for the Chocolate Cupcakes. Make cake mix as directed on box for cupcakes **except**—add 1 teaspoon vanilla. Bake and cool as directed on box. Fill and garnish cupcakes as directed in recipe.

minty fudge **cups**

24 cups   **PREP TIME: 30 Minutes** START TO FINISH: **1 Hour 20 Minutes**

TOPPING

1   package (4.67 oz) thin rectangular crème de menthe chocolate candies, unwrapped

FILLING

2/3   cup granulated sugar

1/3   cup unsweetened baking cocoa

2   tablespoons butter or margarine, softened

1   egg
    Reserved 1/2 cup coarsely chopped mints

FUDGE CUPS

1/4   cup butter or margarine, softened

1   package (3 oz) cream cheese, softened

3/4   cup all-purpose flour

1/4   cup powdered sugar

2   tablespoons unsweetened baking cocoa

1/2   teaspoon vanilla

1   container chocolate creamy ready-to-spread frosting

1   Heat oven to 350°F. If desired, place paper baking cup in each of 24 mini muffin cups. Coarsely chop mints.

2   In small bowl, beat all filling ingredients except mints with spoon until well mixed. Stir in 1/2 cup chopped mints. Reserve remaining chopped mints for topping.

3   In large bowl, beat 1/4 cup butter and the cream cheese with electric mixer on medium speed, or mix with spoon. Stir in flour, powdered sugar, 2 tablespoons cocoa and the vanilla.

4   Shape dough into 1-inch balls. Press each ball in bottom and up side of each muffin cup. Spoon about 2 teaspoons filling into each cup.

5   Bake 18 to 20 minutes or until almost no indentation remains when filling is touched lightly. Cool 5 minutes. Carefully remove from pan; place on cooling rack to cool. Frost cupcakes. Sprinkle with reserved chopped mints for topping.

1 Cup: Calories 190; Total Fat 9g (Saturated Fat 4.5g; Trans Fat 1g); Cholesterol 20mg; Sodium 90mg; Total Carbohydrate 26g (Dietary Fiber 1g); Protein 1g **Exchanges:** 1/2 Starch, 1 Other Carbohydrate, 2 Fat **Carbohydrate Choices:** 2

sweet success tip
Bake these little gems in decorative baking cups and package them as a gift for someone special.

cookies 'n cream **cupcakes**

24 cupcakes PREP TIME: **1 Hour** START TO FINISH: **2 Hours**

CUPCAKES
   Chocolate Cupcakes (page 15)

FILLING AND FROSTING
   Fluffy White Frosting (page 21)
   $1/2$ cup marshmallow creme

GARNISH
   10 creme-filled chocolate sandwich cookies, coarsely broken (about 1 cup)

1 Make, bake and cool Chocolate Cupcakes as directed in recipe.

2 With end of round handle of wooden spoon, make deep, $3/4$-inch-wide indentation in center of top of each cupcake, not quite to bottom (wiggle end of spoon in cupcake to make opening large enough).

3 Make Fluffy White Frosting as directed in recipe. In medium bowl, stir together $1/2$ cup of the frosting and the marshmallow creme. Spoon into small resealable food-storage plastic bag; seal bag. Cut $3/8$-inch tip off one bottom corner of bag. Insert tip of bag into each cupcake and squeeze bag to fill.

4 Frost cupcakes with remaining frosting. Garnish each with about 2 teaspoons broken cookies.

1 Cupcake: Calories 220; Total Fat 8g (Saturated Fat 2.5g; Trans Fat 1g); Cholesterol 20mg; Sodium 210mg; Total Carbohydrate 34g (Dietary Fiber 1g); Protein 2g **Exchanges:** 1 Starch, 1 $1/2$ Other Carbohydrate, 1 $1/2$ Fat **Carbohydrate Choices:** 2

sweet success tip
To easily scoop the marshmallow creme out of the jar, lightly spray a rubber spatula with cooking spray and you'll be surprised how easy it is!

use a cake mix

Substitute 1 box devil's food cake mix for the Chocolate Cupcakes. Make cake mix as directed on box for cupcakes. For the filling and frosting, substitute 1 container fluffy white whipped ready-to-spread frosting; use $1/2$ cup frosting with $1/2$ cup marshmallow creme for the filling, and frost cupcakes with the remaining frosting. Garnish as directed in recipe.

star-studded celebration cupcakes

36 cupcakes **PREP TIME: 1 Hour 10 Minutes** START TO FINISH: **1 Hour 20 Minutes**

GARNISH

3	(4 oz each) white chocolate baking bars, melted, if desired
1	4-oz bar sweet baking chocolate or semisweet baking chocolate

CUPCAKES

2	cups all-purpose flour
2	cups sugar
1 1/4	teaspoons baking soda
1	teaspoon salt
1/2	teaspoon baking powder
1	cup water
3/4	cup sour cream
1/4	cup shortening
1	teaspoon vanilla
2	eggs
4	oz unsweetened baking chocolate, melted, cooled

FROSTING

1	container creamy white or milk chocolate creamy ready-to-spread frosting

1 In medium microwaveable bowl, microwave white chocolate baking bars uncovered on Medium 1 1/2 to 2 minutes. Stir; microwave in 30-second increments, stirring after each, until chocolate is melted and smooth. Pour onto waxed paper-lined cookie sheets. Spread evenly to about 1/8 to 1/4-inch thickness. Refrigerate until slightly hardened, about 10 minutes. Repeat with sweet baking chocolate.

2 Lightly sprinkle white chocolate with baking cocoa, if desired. Press small star cutters, of desired sizes firmly into chocolate. Lift gently from waxed paper with spatula.

3 Heat oven to 350°F. Place paper baking cup in each of 36 regular-size muffin cups. In large bowl, beat cupcake ingredients with electric mixer on low speed 30 seconds, scraping bowl constantly. Beat on high speed 3 minutes, scraping bowl occasionally. Divide batter evenly among muffin cups, filling each about 1/2 full. (If baking cupcakes in batches, cover and refrigerate batter until ready to use; cool pans before reuse.)

4 Bake 20 to 25 minutes or until toothpick inserted in center of cupcake comes out clean. Remove from pans; place on cooling racks to cool.

5 Frost cupcakes. Garnish with chocolate cutouts.

1 Frosted Cupcake (Undecorated): Calories 180; Total Fat 6g (Saturated Fat 2.5g; Trans Fat 1g); Cholesterol 15mg; Sodium 150mg; Total Carbohydrate 29g (Dietary Fiber 0g); Protein 1g **Exchanges:** 1/2 Starch, 1 1/2 Other Carbohydrate, 1 Fat **Carbohydrate Choices:** 2

sweet success tip

You can also garnish these cupcakes with star sprinkles or other festive candy decors.

use a cake mix

Substitute 1 box devil's food cake mix for the cupcakes above. Make cake mix as directed on box. Frost and decorate cupcakes as directed in recipe. 24 cupcakes

mr. sun **cupcakes**

24 cupcakes   **PREP TIME: 1 Hour 15 Minutes** START TO FINISH: **2 Hours 20 Minutes**

CUPCAKES
Yellow Cupcakes (page 14)

FROSTING AND DECORATIONS
Yellow food color

1 container vanilla creamy ready-to-spread frosting

Sugar

48 large yellow, orange and/or red gumdrops (from 10-oz package)

Black decorating icing (from 4.25-oz tube)

Red decorating gel (from 0.68-oz tube)

1 Make, bake and cool Yellow Cupcakes as directed in recipe.

2 Stir 15 drops food color into frosting until bright yellow. Frost cupcakes.

3 Form sun rays following the directions on opposite page.

4 Using small writing tip on black icing tube, pipe sunglasses onto each cupcake. Using red gel, pipe smiling mouth onto each cupcake.

1 Frosted Cupcake (Undecorated): Calories 240; Total Fat 11g (Saturated Fat 6g; Trans Fat 1.5g); Cholesterol 45mg; Sodium 230mg; Total Carbohydrate 33g (Dietary Fiber 0g); Protein 2g **Exchanges:** 1 Starch, 1 Other Carbohydrate, 2 Fat **Carbohydrate Choices:** 2

sweet success tip

Roll and cut the sun rays ahead of time so kids can easily assemble the cupcakes. If you want brighter yellow frosting, try using gel food color instead of liquid.

use a cake mix

Substitute 1 box yellow cake mix for the Yellow Cupcakes. Make cake mix as directed on box for cupcakes. Frost and decorate cupcakes as directed in recipe.

1. Lightly sprinkle sugar on work surface and rolling pin. Roll 4 gumdrops at a time into flat ovals about 1/8-inch thick.

4. Arrange 8 gumdrop triangles around edge of each cupcake for sun rays.

2. Cut thin sliver off top and bottom of each oval to make rectangles.

3. Cut each rectangle in half crosswise to make 2 squares; cut each square diagonally in half to make 2 triangles.

goin' fishin' cupcakes

24 cupcakes   **PREP TIME: 1 Hour** START TO FINISH: **2 Hours**

CUPCAKES

Chocolate Cupcakes (page 15)

FROSTING

Vanilla Buttercream Frosting
(page 20)
Blue food color

FISHING POLES

24 cocktail straws

24 pieces dental floss

24 assorted chewy fruit-flavored
snack shark shapes (3 pouches)

1 Make, bake and cool Chocolate Cupcakes as directed in recipe.

2 Make Vanilla Buttercream Frosting as directed in recipe. Stir together frosting and 2 or 3 drops blue food color. Using metal spatula, frost cupcakes, pulling up on frosting so frosting looks like waves.

3 To make fishing poles, cut each straw to make one 3-inch piece. Cut dental floss into $3^1/_2$-inch lengths. Using needle, attach piece of dental floss to end of each straw to look like fish line. Attach 1 fruit snack to end of each piece of dental floss. Decorate each cupcake with a fishing pole.

1 Cupcake: Calories 330; Total Fat 12g (Saturated Fat 5g; Trans Fat 1.5g); Cholesterol 30mg; Sodium 210mg; Total Carbohydrate 52g (Dietary Fiber 1g); Protein 2g **Exchanges:** $^1/_2$ Starch, 3 Other Carbohydrate, $2^1/_2$ Fat **Carbohydrate Choices:** $3^1/_2$

sweet success tip

Keep the party theme going by serving blue raspberry punch with "fishy" ice cubes. Place 1 shark chewy fruit snack in each section of an ice-cube tray. Fill with ginger ale or water, and freeze until solid.

use a cake mix

Substitute 1 box devil's food cake mix for the Chocolate Cupcakes. Make cake mix as directed on box for cupcakes. For the frosting, substitute 1 container vanilla or butter cream creamy ready-to-spread frosting. Frost and decorate cupcakes as directed in recipe.

mini candy bar **cupcakes**

90 mini cupcakes   PREP TIME: **1 Hour** START TO FINISH: **1 Hour 40 Minutes**

7   bars (2.1 oz each) chocolate-covered crispy peanut-butter candy

   White Cupcakes (page 16)

   Creamy Chocolate Frosting (page 20)

1 Heat oven to 350°F. Place paper baking cup in each of 90 mini muffin cups. Finely chop enough candy (about 2 bars) to equal $3/4$ cup.

2 Make White Cupcakes as directed in recipe except—beat in $3/4$ cup chopped candy on low speed just until blended.

3 Divide batter evenly among mini muffin cups, filling each about $2/3$ full. (If baking cupcakes in batches, cover and refrigerate batter until ready to use; cool pans before reuse.)

4 Bake 12 to 16 minutes or until toothpick inserted in center of cupcake comes out clean. Cool 5 minutes. Remove cupcakes from pans; place on cooling racks to cool.

5 Make Creamy Chocolate Frosting as directed in recipe. Frost cupcakes. Coarsely chop remaining 5 bars of candy. Place candy pieces on frosting, pressing lightly into frosting.

1 Mini Cupcake: Calories 100; Total Fat 4g (Saturated Fat 1.5g; Trans Fat 0g); Cholesterol 0mg; Sodium 50mg; Total Carbohydrate 15g (Dietary Fiber 0g); Protein 1g **Exchanges:** 1 Other Carbohydrate, 1 Fat **Carbohydrate Choices:** 1

use a cake mix

Place paper baking cup in each of 72 mini muffin cups. Finely chop enough candy (about 2 bars) to equal $3/4$ cup. Substitute 1 box white cake mix for the White Cupcakes. Make cake mix as directed on box for cupcakes; beat in $3/4$ cup chopped candy on low speed. For the frosting, substitute 1 container milk chocolate whipped ready-to-spread frosting. Frost and decorate cupcakes as directed in recipe. 72 mini cupcakes

flower-power **cupcakes**

24 cupcakes **PREP TIME: 30 Min** **START TO FINISH: 1 Hr 30 Min**

CUPCAKES

White Cupcakes (page 16)

FROSTING AND DECORATIONS

Fluffy White Frosting (page 21)

Multicolored licorice twists

Candy sprinkles

1 Make, bake and cool White Cupcakes as directed in recipe.

2 Make Fluffy White Frosting as directed in recipe. Frost cooled cupcakes with frosting.

3 Cut licorice into desired size pieces. Create flower shapes with licorice; arrange on cupcakes. Sprinkle candy sprinkles in center of each flower.

1 Frosted Cupcake (Undecorated): Calories 180 (Calories from Fat 70); Total Fat 8g (Saturated Fat 2g, Trans Fat 1.5g); Cholesterol 0mg; Sodium 170mg; Total Carbohydrate 25g (Dietary Fiber 0g, Sugars 17g); Protein 1g **Exchanges**: 1/2 Starch, 1 Other Carbohydrate, 1 1/2 Fat **Carbohydrate Choices**: 1 1/2

sweet success tip

Arrange the cupcakes on a pedestal platter for a lovely table centerpiece.

use a cake mix

Substitute 1 box white cake mix for the White Cupcakes. Make cake mix as directed on box for cupcakes. For the frosting, substitute 1 container fluffy white ready-to-spread frosting. Frost and decorate as directed in recipe.

root beer **float cupcakes**

23 cupcakes PREP TIME: **1 Hour** START TO FINISH: **2 Hours**

CUPCAKES

23 flat-bottom ice cream cones
Yellow Cupcakes (page 14)

²/₃ cup root beer (measure liquid only—not foam)

FLUFFY ROOT BEER FROSTING

³/₄ cup granulated sugar

³/₄ cup packed brown sugar

¹/₃ cup cold root beer

¹/₄ teaspoon cream of tartar
Dash salt

2 egg whites

1 teaspoon vanilla

DECORATION

Root beer candies, coarsely crushed, if desired

46 straws, if desired

1 Heat oven to 350°F. Stand ice cream cones in muffin pans.

2 Make Yellow Cupcakes as directed in recipe except—substitute ²/₃ cup root beer for the milk. Divide batter evenly among ice cream cones, filling each with scant ¹/₄ cup batter.

3 Bake 20 to 25 minutes or until golden and toothpick inserted in center of cupcake comes out clean. Cool 5 minutes; remove cones from pans to cooling racks to cool.

4 Meanwhile, in heavy 3-quart saucepan, mix all frosting ingredients except vanilla. Beat with electric mixer on high speed 1 minute, scraping pan constantly. Place over low heat. Beat on high speed about 10 minutes or until stiff peaks form; remove from heat. Add vanilla. Beat on high speed 2 minutes or until fluffy.

5 Frost cupcakes. Decorate with root beer candies. Cut about 4 inches off bottom of each straw; discard. Poke 2 straws into each cupcake.

1 Cupcake: Calories 250; Total Fat 9g (Saturated Fat 5g; Trans Fat 0g); Cholesterol 50mg; Sodium 220mg; Total Carbohydrate 39g (Dietary Fiber 0g); Protein 3g **Exchanges:** 1 ¹/₂ Starch, 1 Other Carbohydrate, 1 ¹/₂ Fat **Carbohydrate Choices:** 2 ¹/₂

sweet success tip
You can also top the cupcakes with a variety of colored sprinkles.

use a cake mix

Substitute 1 box yellow cake mix for the Yellow Cupcakes. Make cake mix as directed on box for cupcakes **except**—use 1¹/₄ cups root beer (measure liquid only—not foam), ¹/₃ cup vegetable oil and 3 eggs. Stand 24 cones in muffin cups. Fill each ice cream cone about ¹/₂ full. Cover and refrigerate remaining batter. Bake 18 to 24 minutes. Remove to cooling rack. Cool as directed in recipe. Repeat with remaining batter and cones. For the frosting, substitute 1 container cream cheese creamy ready-to-spread frosting. Decorate as directed in recipe. 24 cones

mini raspberry-filled **chocolate cupcakes**

60 mini cupcakes   PREP TIME: **1 Hour** START TO FINISH: **1 Hour 35 Minutes**

1 box devil's food cake mix with pudding

Water, vegetable oil and eggs called for on cake mix box

$2/3$ cup seedless raspberry jam

1 cup fresh or frozen (thawed) raspberries

1 container fluffy white whipped ready-to-spread frosting

60 fresh raspberries (from three 6-oz containers)

1 Heat oven to 350°F. Place mini paper baking cup in each of 60 mini muffin cups.

2 Make cake mix as directed on box, using water, oil and eggs. Fill muffin cups about $3/4$ full.

3 Bake 10 to 15 minutes or until toothpick inserted in center of cupcake comes out clean. Cool 5 minutes; remove from pans to cooling racks to cool.

4 With end of round handle of wooden spoon, make deep, $1/2$-inch-wide indentation in center of top of each cupcake, not quite to bottom (wiggle end of spoon in mini cake to make opening large enough).

5 Spoon jam into small resealable food-storage plastic bag; seal bag. Cut $3/8$-inch tip off one bottom corner of bag. Insert tip of bag into opening in each cupcake; squeeze bag to fill opening.

6 In blender, place 1 cup raspberries. Cover; pulse 20 seconds or until pureed. Press puree through small strainer to remove seeds. Pour $1/4$ cup raspberry puree into medium bowl; stir in frosting until well mixed. Frost cupcakes. Garnish each with 1 raspberry.

1 Mini Cupcake: Calories 80; Total Fat 3g (Saturated Fat 1g; Trans Fat 0g); Cholesterol 10mg; Sodium 85mg; Total Carbohydrate 13g (Dietary Fiber 0g); Protein 0g **Exchanges:** 1 Other Carbohydrate, $1/2$ Fat **Carbohydrate Choices:** 1

sweet success tip
These little cupcakes would dazzle your guests served on a pedestal platter.

butternut squash **cupcakes**

24 cupcakes   **PREP TIME: 50 Minutes** START TO FINISH: **1 Hour 55 Minutes**

CUPCAKES

2 1/3	cups all-purpose flour
2 1/2	teaspoons baking powder
1 1/2	teaspoons pumpkin pie spice
1/2	teaspoon salt
1	cup butter or margarine, softened
1 1/4	cups sugar
3	eggs
1	cup mashed cooked butternut squash
2	teaspoons vanilla
1/2	cup milk
1/2	cup sweetened dried cranberries
1/2	cup chopped pecans

RUM BUTTERCREAM FROSTING

6	cups powdered sugar
2/3	cup butter or margarine, softened
3	teaspoons vanilla
1	tablespoon rum or 1 teaspoon rum extract plus 2 teaspoons milk
4	to 5 tablespoons milk
	Chopped pecans, if desired

1 Heat oven to 350°F. Place paper baking cup in each of 24 regular-size muffin cups. Grease and flour muffin cups, or spray with baking spray with flour.

2 In medium bowl, mix flour, baking powder, pumpkin pie spice and salt; set aside.

3 In large bowl, beat butter with electric mixer on medium speed 30 seconds. Gradually add sugar, about 1/4 cup at a time, beating well after each addition. Beat 2 minutes longer. Add eggs, one at a time, beating well after each addition. Beat in squash and vanilla. On low speed, alternately add flour mixture, about 1/3 of mixture at a time, and milk, beating just until blended. Stir in cranberries and pecans.

4 Divide batter evenly among muffin cups, filling each about 2/3 full.

5 Bake 20 to 25 minutes or until golden brown and toothpick inserted in center comes out clean. Cool in pans 5 minutes. Remove cupcakes from pans; place on cooling racks to cool.

6 Meanwhile, in medium bowl, mix powdered sugar and butter with electric mixer on low speed; stir in 3 teaspoons vanilla, the rum and 3 tablespoons of the milk. Gradually beat in enough remaining milk, 1 teaspoon at a time, to make frosting smooth and spreadable.

7 Frost cupcakes. Garnish with chopped pecans.

1 Cupcake: Calories 370; Total Fat 16g (Saturated Fat 9g, Trans Fat 0.5g); Cholesterol 60mg; Sodium 230mg; Total Carbohydrate 54g (Dietary Fiber 1g); Protein 3g **Exchanges:** 1 Starch, 2 1/2 Other Carbohydrate, 3 Fat **Carbohydrate Choices:** 3 1/2

use a cake mix

Substitute 1 box yellow cake mix for the cupcakes above. Make cake mix as directed on box for cupcakes **except**—use 1 cup mashed cooked butternut squash, 1/2 cup water, 1/3 cup vegetable oil and 4 eggs. Stir 1/2 cup sweetened dried cranberries and 1/2 cup chopped pecans into batter. Bake and cool as directed on box. Frost as directed in recipe.

lemon-blueberry **cupcakes**

28 cupcakes   PREP TIME: **50 Minutes** START TO FINISH: **1 Hour 50 Minutes**

CUPCAKES

Lemon Cupcakes (page 17)
1   cup fresh blueberries
1   tablespoon all-purpose flour

FROSTING

1 1/2   cups powdered sugar
3/4   cup unsalted butter, softened
1   teaspoon grated lemon peel
1/2   teaspoon kosher (coarse) salt
1 1/4   teaspoons vanilla
1   tablespoon milk

GARNISH

1   cup fresh blueberries
Lemon peel twists, if desired
Fresh mint leaves, if desired

1 Make Lemon Cupcakes as directed in recipe except—place paper baking cup in each of 28 regular-size muffin cups, toss 1 cup blueberries with 1 tablespoon flour, divide batter evenly among muffin cups, filling each about 1/2 full, and sprinkle berries over batter in each cup. Bake and cool as directed in recipe.

2 In medium bowl, beat frosting ingredients with electric mixer on high speed about 4 minutes or until smooth and well blended, adding more milk, 1 teaspoon at a time, if needed.

3 Frost cupcakes. Garnish with blueberries, lemon peel twists and mint leaves.

1 Cupcake: Calories 240; Total Fat 12g (Saturated Fat 8g; Trans Fat 0g); Cholesterol 55mg; Sodium 190mg; Total Carbohydrate 30g (Dietary Fiber 0g); Protein 2g **Exchanges:** 1/2 Starch, 1 1/2 Other Carbohydrate, 2 1/2 Fat **Carbohydrate Choices:** 2

sweet success tip

Coarse salt in these cupcakes was added for small bursts of saltiness to complement the sweetness of the other ingredients and to bring out the lemon flavor.

use a cake mix

Substitute 1 box lemon cake mix for the Lemon Cupcakes. Make lemon cake mix as directed on box **for cupcakes except**—use 3/4 cup water, 1/3 cup vegetable oil, 1 tablespoon grated lemon peel, 2 eggs, 1 package (3 oz) cream cheese, softened, and stir in 1 1/2 cups fresh blueberries. Bake 18 to 22 minutes or until tops are light golden brown. Frost and garnish cupcakes as directed in recipe. 24 cupcakes

strawberry colada **cupcakes**

{ **Christy Denney Weston, Florida** The Girl Who Ate Everything www.thegirlwhoateeverything.blogspot.com }

24 cupcakes PREP TIME: 50 Minutes START TO FINISH: 1 Hour 50 Minutes

CUPCAKES

1 1/2 cups fresh strawberries, hulled
1/2 cup canned coconut milk (not cream of coconut)
1 1/2 teaspoons coconut extract
1/2 teaspoon vanilla
2 cups cake flour
2 teaspoons baking powder
1/4 teaspoon salt
3/4 cup unsalted butter, softened
1 1/3 cups granulated sugar
1 whole egg
2 egg whites
1/4 cup well-drained crushed pineapple in unsweetened juice

FROSTING

1 cup butter or margarine, softened
3 1/2 cups powdered sugar
1 teaspoon coconut extract
1/2 teaspoon vanilla

GARNISH, IF DESIRED

Fresh strawberries
Toasted coconut

1 Heat oven to 350°F. Place paper baking cup in each of 24 regular-size muffin cups.

2 In blender, place 1 1/2 cups strawberries. Cover; puree about 30 seconds or until smooth. (Puree should measure about 1 cup; if not, puree additional berries.) Pour 2/3 cup puree into small bowl; stir in coconut milk, 1 1/2 teaspoons coconut extract and 1/2 teaspoon vanilla. Reserve remaining puree for frosting.

3 In medium bowl, mix flour, baking powder and salt; set aside. In large bowl, beat 3/4 cup butter and granulated sugar with electric mixer on medium speed 2 minutes or until light and fluffy. Add whole egg and egg whites, 1 at a time, beating well after each addition. On low speed, alternately add flour mixture, about 1/3 at a time, and strawberry-coconut milk mixture, about 1/2 at a time, beating just until blended. Stir in pineapple.

4 Divide batter evenly among muffin cups, filling each about 3/4 full.

5 Bake 18 to 22 minutes or until centers spring back when lightly touched. Cool 5 minutes; remove from pans to cooling racks to cool.

6 Meanwhile, in medium bowl, beat 1 cup butter with electric mixer on medium speed until light and fluffy. On low speed, beat in powdered sugar, about 1/2 cup at a time. Stir in 1 teaspoon coconut extract, 1/2 teaspoon vanilla and 3 tablespoons reserved strawberry puree just until blended (discard any remaining puree).

7 Frost each cupcake with generous tablespoon frosting. Garnish with strawberries and toasted coconut.

1 Cupcake: Calories 300; Total Fat 15g (Saturated Fat 9g; Trans Fat 0.5g); Cholesterol 45mg; Sodium 130mg; Total Carbohydrate 39g (Dietary Fiber 0g); Protein 1g **Exchanges:** 1/2 Starch, 2 Other Carbohydrate, 3 Fat **Carbohydrate Choices:** 2 1/2

sweet success tip

To toast coconut, cook in skillet over medium-low heat about 8 minutes, stirring frequently until browning begins, then stirring constantly until golden brown.

use a cake mix

Substitute 1 box yellow cake mix for the cupcakes above. Puree enough strawberries to make 3/4 cup. Make cake mix as directed on box for cupcakes **except**—use pureed strawberries, 1/2 cup canned coconut milk (not cream of coconut), 1 1/2 teaspoons coconut extract, 1/3 cup vegetable oil and 3 eggs. Stir 1/4 cup well-drained crushed pineapple in unsweetened juice into batter. Bake and cool as directed on box. For the frosting, substitute 1 container vanilla creamy ready-to-spread frosting mixed with 1/4 teaspoon coconut extract. Garnish as directed in recipe.

watermelon slice **cupcakes**

24 cupcakes **PREP TIME: 1 Hour 5 Minutes** START TO FINISH: **2 Hours**

CUPCAKES

2 1/3	cups all-purpose flour
2 1/2	teaspoons baking powder
1/2	teaspoon salt
1	package (0.3 oz) cherry or other red unsweetened soft drink mix
1	cup butter or margarine, softened
1 1/4	cups sugar
3	eggs
1	teaspoon vanilla
2/3	cup pureed watermelon (about 1 1/2 cups watermelon pieces)
3/4	cup miniature semisweet chocolate chips

ICING

Decorator Icing (page 21)
Green paste food color
Red paste food color

DECORATION

1/4 cup miniature semisweet chocolate chips

1 Heat oven to 350°F. Place paper baking cup in each of 24 regular-size muffin cups.

2 In medium bowl, mix flour, baking powder, salt and drink mix; set aside.

3 In large bowl, beat butter with electric mixer on medium speed 30 seconds. Gradually add sugar, about 1/4 cup at a time, beating well after each addition and scraping bowl occasionally. Beat 2 minutes longer. Add eggs, one at a time, beating well after each addition. Beat in vanilla. On low speed, alternately add flour mixture, about 1/3 of mixture at a time, and watermelon puree, about 1/2 at a time, beating just until blended. Stir in miniature chocolate chips.

4 Divide batter evenly among muffin cups, filling each with about 2/3 full.

5 Bake 20 to 25 minutes or until golden brown and toothpick inserted in center comes out clean. Cool in pans 5 minutes. Remove cupcakes from pans; place on cooling racks to cool.

6 Make Decorator Icing as directed in recipe. Tint 1 cup frosting with green paste food color. Place green frosting in decorating bag fitted with #19 star tip; set aside. Tint remaining frosting with red paste food color. Frost cupcakes with red frosting to within 1/2 inch from edge.

7 Pipe 1 row of green frosting around edge of each cupcake to look like watermelon rind. Decorate each with chocolate chips to look like seeds.

1 Cupcake: Calories 340; Total Fat 16g (Saturated Fat 9g; Trans Fat 1g); Cholesterol 55mg; Sodium 240mg; Total Carbohydrate 45g (Dietary Fiber 0g); Protein 2g **Exchanges:** 1 Starch, 2 Other Carbohydrate, 3 Fat **Carbohydrate Choices:** 3

use a **cake mix**

Substitute 1 box yellow cake mix for the cupcakes above. Puree enough watermelon to make 1 1/4 cups. Make cake mix as directed on box for cupcakes **except**—use pureed watermelon instead of water, 1/3 cup vegetable oil, 3 eggs and 1 package (0.3 oz) cherry or other red unsweetened soft drink mix. Stir 3/4 cup miniature chocolate chips into batter. Bake and cool as directed on box. Frost and decorate as directed in recipe.

lemon burst cupcakes

24 cupcakes   PREP TIME: **1 Hour 10 Minutes** START TO FINISH: **2 Hours 10 Minutes**

CUPCAKES

White Cupcakes (page 16)

FILLING

1   jar (10 to 12 oz) lemon curd

FROSTING AND DECORATIONS

Fluffy White Frosting (page 21)

1/4   cup yellow candy sprinkles

1/4   cup white candy sprinkles

1 Make, bake and cool White Cupcakes as directed in recipe.

2 With end of round handle of wooden spoon, make deep, 3/4-inch-wide indentation in center of top of each cupcake, not quite to bottom (wiggle end of spoon in cupcake to make opening large enough).

3 Spoon lemon curd into corner of resealable heavy-duty food-storage plastic bag. Cut about 1/4 inch off corner of bag. Gently push cut corner of bag into center of cupcake. Squeeze about 2 teaspoons lemon curd into center of each cupcake for filling, being careful not to split cupcake.

4 Make Fluffy White Frosting as directed in recipe. Frost cupcakes. To decorate, roll edge of each cupcake in candy sprinkles.

1 Cupcake: Calories 260; Total Fat 8g (Saturated Fat 2.5g; Trans Fat 1g); Cholesterol 10mg; Sodium 140mg; Total Carbohydrate 43g (Dietary Fiber 0g); Protein 3g **Exchanges:** 1 Starch, 2 Other Carbohydrate, 1 1/2 Fat **Carbohydrate Choices:** 3

sweet success tip

For a special occasion, sprinkle with coarse white decorator sugar.

use a cake mix

Substitute 1 box white cake mix for the White Cupcakes. Make cake mix as directed on box for cupcakes. Fill with lemon curd as directed in recipe. For the frosting, substitute 1 container fluffy white whipped ready-to-spread frosting. Frost and decorate cupcakes as directed in recipe.

somewhere over the rainbow **cupcakes**

{ **Christy Denney Weston, Florida The Girl Who Ate Everything** www.thegirlwhoateeverything.blogspot.com }

12 cupcakes   PREP TIME: 40 Minutes START TO FINISH: 1 Hour 40 Minutes

CUPCAKES

1 1/2 cups all-purpose flour
1 3/4 teaspoons baking powder
 1/2 cup butter, softened
 1 cup granulated sugar
 2 eggs
 1 teaspoon vanilla
 1 teaspoon coconut extract
 3/4 cup canned coconut milk (not cream of coconut)
   Yellow, green, red and blue liquid food color

FROSTING

1 1/2 cups unsalted butter or margarine, softened
 6 cups powdered sugar
   Dash salt
 5 tablespoons milk
 1/2 teaspoon vanilla
 1/4 teaspoon coconut extract
   Multicolored candy sprinkles, if desired

1 Heat oven to 350°F. Place paper baking cup in each of 12 regular-size muffin cups.

2 In small bowl, mix flour and baking powder; set aside. In medium bowl, beat 1/2 cup butter and the granulated sugar with electric mixer on medium speed 2 minutes or until light and fluffy. Add eggs, 1 at a time, beating well after each addition. Beat in 1 teaspoon vanilla and 1 teaspoon coconut extract. On low speed, alternately add flour mixture, 1/2 at a time, and coconut milk, 1/2 at a time, beating just until blended.

3 Measure about 3/4 cup batter into each of 5 small bowls. For yellow, stir about 6 drops yellow food color into batter in first bowl. Tint second bowl green, with 6 drops green food color; third bowl red, with about 8 drops red food color; fourth bowl blue, with about 10 drops blue food color; and fifth bowl purple, with about 8 drops red food color and 3 drops blue food color.

4 Spoon scant tablespoon of yellow batter into each cup; smooth to edge of baking cup with back of spoon. Repeat with green, red, blue and purple batters (fill cups to 3/4 full).

5 Bake 18 to 22 minutes or until toothpick inserted in center of cupcake comes out clean. Cool 5 minutes; remove from pan to cooling rack to cool.

6 In large bowl, beat 1 1/2 cups butter, the powdered sugar and salt with electric mixer on medium speed until light and fluffy. Beat in 4 tablespoons of the milk, 1/2 teaspoon vanilla and 1/4 teaspoon coconut extract. Add remaining milk, 1 teaspoon at a time, until frosting is smooth and spreadable. Beat until fluffy.

7 Pipe or frost about 1/4 cup frosting onto each cupcake. Sprinkle with multicolored sprinkles.

1 Cupcake: Calories 690; Total Fat 35g (Saturated Fat 22g; Trans Fat 1g); Cholesterol 115mg; Sodium 160mg; Total Carbohydrate 90g (Dietary Fiber 0g); Protein 3g **Exchanges:** 1 Starch, 5 Other Carbohydrate, 7 Fat **Carbohydrate Choices:** 6

sweet success tip

If your kids aren't in love with coconut, substitute vanilla flavoring for the coconut extract in the cake and frosting.

use a cake mix

Substitute 1 box white cake mix for the cupcakes above. Make cake mix as directed on box for cupcakes and follow steps 3 and 4 as directed in recipe. Bake and cool as directed on box. For the frosting, substitute 1 container vanilla creamy ready-to-spread frosting mixed with 1/4 teaspoon coconut extract. Frost and garnish as directed in recipe. 22 cupcakes

chocolate cupcakes **with white truffle frosting**

24 cupcakes   PREP TIME: **40 Minutes** START TO FINISH: **1 Hour 40 Minutes**

CUPCAKES

Chocolate Cupcakes (page 15)

FROSTING

1   cup white vanilla baking chips

1   container vanilla creamy ready-to-spread frosting

1   Make, bake and cool Chocolate Cupcakes as directed in recipe.

2   In medium microwavable bowl, microwave baking chips uncovered on Medium 4 to 5 minutes, stirring after 2 minutes. Stir until smooth; cool 5 minutes. Stir in frosting until well blended. Immediately frost cupcakes or pipe frosting onto cupcakes using a #9 round tip.

1 Cupcake: Calories 290; Total Fat 13g (Saturated Fat 5g; Trans Fat 2g); Cholesterol 20mg; Sodium 230mg; Total Carbohydrate 40g (Dietary Fiber 1g); Protein 2g **Exchanges:** 1/2 Starch, 2 Other Carbohydrate, 2 1/2 Fat **Carbohydrate Choices:** 2 1/2

sweet success tip

Change it up! Decorate these basic cupcakes any way you like with colored sugar, edible glitter or any other purchased decoration. If desired, tie ribbons around cupcakes.

use a cake mix

Substitute 1 box devil's food cake mix for the Chocolate Cupcakes. Make cake mix as directed on box for cupcakes. Frost cupcakes as directed in recipe.

spiced caramel-pear **cupcakes**

24 cupcakes   PREP TIME: **1 Hour 35 Minutes** START TO FINISH: **2 Hours 50 Minutes**

CUPCAKES

Yellow Cupcakes (page 14)
$1/2$ teaspoon ground cinnamon
1 cup chopped peeled pear (1 large)
1 tablespoon all-purpose flour

CARAMEL-SPICE FROSTING

$3/4$ cup butter or margarine
$1 1/2$ cups packed brown sugar
$1/2$ teaspoon ground cinnamon
$1/3$ cup milk
$3 1/2$ to 4 cups powdered sugar

SUGARED PEARS

39 caramels, unwrapped (from 14-oz package)
Yellow sanding sugar
Green decorating icing (from 6.4-oz can)

1 Make Yellow Cupcakes as directed in recipe except—stir cinnamon in with flour. Mix pear with 1 tablespoon flour; stir into batter. Bake and cool as directed.

2 Meanwhile, in 2-quart saucepan, melt $3/4$ cup butter over medium heat. Stir in brown sugar, $1/2$ teaspoon cinnamon and $1/3$ cup milk. Heat to boiling, stirring constantly. Remove from heat; cool to lukewarm, about 30 minutes.

3 On a small microwavable plate, microwave 6 caramels at a time on High 10 to 15 seconds or until softened. For each pear, mold $1 1/2$ caramels into a pear shape. Cut 1 caramel into 10 pieces; shape each into stem. With paring knife, make tiny slit in top of each pear; press stem into pear. Roll pears, but not stems, in yellow sanding sugar. Repeat with remaining caramels to make 24 pears.

4 Gradually stir powdered sugar into cooled brown sugar mixture until smooth and spreadable. Frost cupcakes. Onto each cupcake, pipe a few leaves with decorating icing. Top each with sugared pear.

1 Cupcake: Calories 360; Total Fat 14g (Saturated Fat 9g; Trans Fat 0.5g); Cholesterol 65mg; Sodium 230mg; Total Carbohydrate 56g (Dietary Fiber 0g); Protein 2g **Exchanges:** 1 $1/2$ Starch, 2 Other Carbohydrate, 2 $1/2$ Fat **Carbohydrate Choices:** 4

sweet success tip

Place these lovely cupcakes on a pedestal at the bake-sale and they'll sell quickly!

use a cake mix

Substitute 1 box white cake mix for the Yellow Cupcakes. Make cake mix as directed on box for cupcakes **except**—use $1 1/4$ cups water, $1/3$ cup vegetable oil, 3 egg whites and $3/4$ teaspoon ground cinnamon. Stir 1 cup finely chopped, peeled pears tossed with 1 tablespoon flour into batter. Bake 20 to 24 minutes. Cool as directed on box. Frost and garnish as directed in recipe.

piña colada **cupcakes**

24 cupcakes PREP TIME: **55 Minutes** START TO FINISH: **1 Hour 55 Minutes**

CUPCAKES

2 1/3 cups all-purpose flour

2 1/2 teaspoons baking powder

1/2 teaspoon salt

1 cup butter or margarine, softened 1 cup sugar

1 teaspoon coconut extract

1 teaspoon rum extract

1 can (8 oz) crushed pineapple in juice, undrained

1/4 cup milk

FLUFFY TROPICAL FROSTING

2 egg whites

1/2 cup sugar

1/4 cup light corn syrup

2 tablespoons water

1/2 teaspoon coconut extract

1/2 teaspoon rum extract

GARNISH

1 cup shredded coconut

use a cake mix

Substitute 1 box yellow cake mix for the cupcakes above. Make cake mix as directed on box for cupcakes **except**—use 1/3 cup vegetable oil, 1/4 cup water, 1 can (8 oz) crushed pineapple in juice, undrained, 1 teaspoon rum extract and 3 eggs. Bake and cool as directed. For the frosting, substitute 1 container vanilla whipped ready-to-spread frosting, and stir in 1 teaspoon coconut extract and 1 teaspoon rum extract. Frost and garnish cupcakes as directed in recipe.

1 Heat oven to 350°F. Place paper baking cup in each of 24 regular-size muffin cups.

2 In medium bowl, mix flour, baking powder and salt; set aside.

3 In large bowl, beat butter with electric mixer on medium speed 30 seconds. Gradually add sugar, about 1/4 cup at a time, beating well after each addition. Beat 2 minutes longer. Add eggs, one at a time, beating well after each addition. Beat in coconut and rum extract. Drain pineapple, reserving juice in small bowl. Stir in milk. On low speed, alternately add flour mixture, about 1/3 of mixture at a time, and milk mixture, about 1/2 at a time, beating just until blended. Stir in pineapple.

4 Divide batter evenly among muffin cups, filling each about 2/3 full.

5 Bake 20 to 25 minutes or until golden brown and toothpick inserted in center comes out clean. Cool in pans 5 minutes. Remove cupcakes from pans; place on cooling racks to cool.

6 Meanwhile, in small bowl, beat egg whites with electric mixer on high speed just until stiff peaks form.

7 In 1-quart saucepan, stir 1/2 cup sugar, the corn syrup and water until well mixed. Cover; heat to a rolling boil over medium heat. Uncover; boil 4 to 8 minutes, without stirring, to 242°F on candy thermometer or until small amount of mixture dropped into cup of very cold water forms a firm ball that holds its shape until pressed. For an accurate temperature reading, tilt the saucepan slightly so mixture is deep enough for thermometer.

8 Pour hot syrup very slowly in thin stream into beaten egg whites, beating constantly on medium speed. Add 1/2 teaspoon coconut extract and 1/2 teaspoon rum extract. Beat on high speed about 3 minutes or until stiff peaks form. Frost cupcakes. Dip tops of frosted cupcakes in coconut.

1 Cupcake: Calories 210; Total Fat 10g (Saturated Fat 6g; Trans Fat 0g); Cholesterol 45mg; Sodium 200mg; Total Carbohydrate 28g (Dietary Fiber 0g); Protein 2g **Exchanges:** 1/2 Starch, 1 1/2 Other Carbohydrate, 2 Fat **Carbohydrate Choices:** 2

sweet success tip
Decorate each cupcake with a paper umbrella to remind everyone of sitting on the beach.

peach bourbon **cupcakes**

{ **Lindsay Landis** Nashville, Tennessee **Love and Olive Oil** www.loveandoliveoil.com }

12 cupcakes   **PREP TIME: 45 Minutes** START TO FINISH: **1 Hour 45 Minutes**

CUPCAKES

3	medium peaches, peeled
1 1/4	cups all-purpose flour
1	teaspoon baking powder
1/4	teaspoon baking soda
1/2	teaspoon salt
1/3	cup butter or margarine, softened
1/2	cup granulated sugar
1	egg
1/4	cup milk
1	tablespoon bourbon
1/2	teaspoon vanilla
1	tablespoon all-purpose flour

FROSTING

1/4	cup butter or margarine, softened
3	to 4 cups powdered sugar
1	teaspoon bourbon
	Thin peach slices, if desired

1 Heat oven to 350°F. Place paper baking cup in each of 12 regular-size muffin cups.

2 Chop enough of the peaches to equal 3/4 cup; set aside. Cut remaining peaches into large pieces; place in blender. Cover; puree about 30 seconds or until smooth. Set aside.

3 In medium bowl, mix 1 1/4 cups flour, the baking powder, baking soda and salt. In large bowl, beat 1/3 cup butter with electric mixer on medium speed 30 seconds. Gradually add granulated sugar, about 1/4 cup at a time, beating well after each addition and scraping bowl occasionally. Beat 2 minutes longer. Add egg; beat well. Beat in 1 tablespoon bourbon and the vanilla.

4 On low speed, alternately add 1/3 of the flour mixture, the milk, 1/3 flour mixture, 1/2 cup of the reserved peach puree and remaining 1/3 flour mixture, beating just until blended. Toss reserved chopped peaches with 1 tablespoon flour; stir into batter.

5 Divide batter evenly among muffin cups, filling each about 3/4 full.

6 Bake 18 to 22 minutes or until toothpick inserted in center of cupcake comes out clean. Cool 5 minutes; remove from pans to cooling racks to cool.

7 Meanwhile, in medium bowl, beat 1/4 cup butter with electric mixer on medium speed 1 to 2 minutes or until fluffy. Add 1 1/2 cups of the powdered sugar, 1/2 cup at a time, beating until smooth. Beat in remaining 1/4 cup peach puree until combined. Add remaining powdered sugar, 1/2 cup at a time, beating until well incorporated. Add 1 teaspoon bourbon; beat on medium-high speed 2 to 3 minutes or until light and fluffy. Beat in additional powdered sugar, 1 tablespoon at a time, until frosting is smooth and spreadable. Spoon frosting into decorating bag fitted with large star tip #7. Pipe onto cupcakes in swirl design. Garnish with peach slice.

1 Cupcake: Calories 350; Total Fat 10g (Saturated Fat 6g; Trans Fat 0g); Cholesterol 40mg; Sodium 240mg; Total Carbohydrate 63g (Dietary Fiber 1g); Protein 2g **Exchanges:** 1 Starch, 3 Other Carbohydrate, 2 Fat **Carbohydrate Choices:** 4

This recipe was adapted from the original recipe from Lindsay Landis. The original recipe can be found on her blog at http://www.loveandoliveoil.com/peach-bourbon-cupcakes.

sweet success tip
Purchase the Marzipan peach garnish at a specialty food store or order it online. Or, just sprinkle orange decorator sugar over the cupcakes.

use a cake mix

Substitute 1 box white cake mix for the cupcakes above. Make cake mix as directed on box for cupcakes **except**—use 1 1/4 cups peach nectar, 1/3 cup vegetable oil, 3 eggs and 1 tablespoon bourbon. Bake and cool as directed on box. For the frosting, substitute 1 container vanilla creamy ready-to-spread frosting mixed with 1 teaspoon bourbon.

butterscotch cupcakes **with salty caramel frosting**

24 cupcakes   PREP TIME: **50 Minutes** START TO FINISH: **2 Hours 20 Minutes**

CUPCAKES

Yellow Cupcakes (page 14)
1 cup granulated sugar
2 teaspoons vanilla
3/4 cup butterscotch chips, coarsely chopped

CARAMEL FROSTING

1/2 cup butter or margarine
1 cup packed brown sugar
1/4 cup milk
3 1/2 cups powdered sugar

GARNISH

1/2 teaspoon kosher (coarse) salt

1 Make Yellow Cupcakes as directed in recipe except—use 1 cup sugar and 2 teaspoons vanilla. Stir butterscotch chips into batter. Bake and cool as directed.

2 Meanwhile, in 2-quart saucepan, melt 1/2 cup butter over medium heat. Stir in brown sugar with whisk. Heat to boiling, stirring constantly. Stir in 1/4 cup milk. Return to boiling. Remove from heat; cool until lukewarm, about 30 minutes. Gradually stir in powdered sugar. Frost cupcakes. Sprinkle each with kosher salt.

1 Cupcake: Calories 330; Total Fat 14g (Saturated Fat 9g; Trans Fat 0g); Cholesterol 60mg; Sodium 240mg; Total Carbohydrate 48g (Dietary Fiber 0g); Protein 2g **Exchanges:** 1 1/2 Starch, 1 1/2 Other Carbohydrate, 2 1/2 Fat **Carbohydrate Choices:** 3

sweet success tip
No kosher salt? Sprinkle chopped salted peanuts on the frosting instead.

orange-rosemary **cupcakes**

26 cupcakes　　PREP TIME: **50 Minutes** START TO FINISH: **1 Hour 50 Minutes**

CUPCAKES

　　Yellow Cupcakes (page 14)
2　tablespoons grated orange peel (2 medium)
1　teaspoon finely chopped fresh rosemary leaves

FROSTING

1/3　cup butter or margarine, softened
2　teaspoons grated orange peel
1/4　cup orange juice
4　cups powdered sugar
3　tablespoons whipping cream

GARNISH

　　Orange peel twists, if desired
　　Sprigs of fresh rosemary, if desired

1 Make Yellow Cupcakes as directed in recipe except—stir orange peel and rosemary in with the vanilla. Bake and cool as directed.

2 Meanwhile, in medium bowl, beat 1/3 cup butter with electric mixer on high speed until creamy. Beat in 2 teaspoons orange peel and the orange juice. On low speed, gradually beat in powdered sugar. Beat in whipping cream, 1 tablespoon at a time, until smooth and spreadable. Frost cupcakes. Using zester, cut strips from orange rind. Garnish cupcakes with orange peel twists and rosemary sprigs.

1 Cupcake: Calories 260; Total Fat 11g (Saturated Fat 7g; Trans Fat 0g); Cholesterol 50mg; Sodium 190mg; Total Carbohydrate 38g (Dietary Fiber 0g); Protein 2g **Exchanges:** 1/2 Starch, 2 Other Carbohydrate, 2 Fat **Carbohydrate Choices:** 2 1/2

sweet success tip
For an easy garnish, top cupcakes with candy orange slices.

use a cake mix

Substitute 1 box yellow cake mix for the Yellow Cupcakes. Make cake mix as directed on box for cupcakes **except**—use 1 1/4 cups water, 1/3 cup vegetable oil, 3 eggs, 2 tablespoons grated orange peel and 1 teaspoon finely chopped fresh rosemary leaves. Bake and cool as directed on box. Frost and garnish as directed in recipe.

autumn leaf **cupcakes**

24 cupcakes   PREP TIME: **50 Minutes** START TO FINISH: **2 Hours 30 Minutes**

CUPCAKES

Chocolate Cupcakes (page 15)

GARNISH AND FROSTING

½   cup semisweet chocolate chips, melted

½   cup butterscotch chips, melted
Creamy Chocolate Frosting (page 20)

1   Make, bake and cool Chocolate Cupcakes as directed in recipe.

2   Meanwhile, place 12-inch sheet of waxed paper on cookie sheet; mark an 8-inch square on waxed paper. Alternately place spoonfuls of melted chocolate and butterscotch on waxed paper. With small spatula, swirl together for marbled effect, spreading to an 8-inch square. Refrigerate until firm, about 30 minutes.

3   Remove chocolate-butterscotch square from refrigerator; let stand about 10 minutes or until slightly softened. Use 1 ½-inch leaf cookie cutter to make 24 leaf cutouts. Carefully remove cutouts from paper with spatula; place on another waxed paper–lined cookie sheet. Refrigerate until firm, about 5 minutes.

4   Make Creamy Chocolate Frosting as directed in recipe. Frost cupcakes. Garnish with leaf cutouts. Store loosely covered in refrigerator.

1 Cupcake: Calories 320; Total Fat 14g (Saturated Fat 7g; Trans Fat 1g); Cholesterol 30mg; Sodium 210mg; Total Carbohydrate 44g (Dietary Fiber 1g); Protein 2g **Exchanges:** 1 Starch, 2 Other Carbohydrate, 2 ½ Fat **Carbohydrate Choices:** 3

sweet success tip

Chocolate and butterscotch chips can easily be melted in the microwave, uncovered, on High for about 1 minute. Remember to stir after 30 seconds.

use a cake mix

Substitute 1 box devil's food cake mix for the Chocolate Cupcakes. Make cake mix as directed on box for cupcakes. For the frosting, substitute 1 container chocolate creamy ready-to-spread frosting. Frost and garnish as directed in recipe.

toasted almond **cupcakes**

{ **Bree Hester** Carmichael, California **Baked Bree** www.bakedbree.com }

About 28 cupcakes   PREP TIME: 50 Minutes START TO FINISH: **1 Hour 50 Minutes**

CUPCAKES

3	cups cake flour
1	tablespoon baking powder
1/2	teaspoon salt
1	cup butter or margarine, softened
2	cups granulated sugar
4	eggs
1/4	cup amaretto
3/4	cup milk

FROSTING

2	cups butter or margarine, softened
4 1/2	cups powdered sugar
6	tablespoons amaretto
1/4	cup whipping cream

GARNISH

1/2	cup sliced almonds, toasted*

1 Heat oven to 350°F. Place paper baking cup in each of 28 regular-size muffin cups. In medium bowl, stir together flour, baking powder and salt; set aside.

2 In large bowl, beat 1 cup butter and the granulated sugar with electric mixer on medium speed about 5 minutes or until light and fluffy. Add eggs, one at a time, beating well after each addition. Beat in 1/4 cup amaretto. On low speed, alternately add flour mixture, about 1/3 of mixture at a time, and milk, about 1/2 at a time, beating just until blended. Divide batter evenly among muffin cups.

3 Bake 20 to 24 minutes or until toothpick inserted in center of cupcake comes out clean. Cool 5 minutes. Remove cupcakes from pans; place on cooling racks to cool.

4 In another large bowl, beat 2 cups butter and the powdered sugar with electric mixer on medium speed until smooth. Add 6 tablespoons amaretto and the whipping cream; beat 5 minutes or until very fluffy. Spoon frosting into decorating bag fitted with large star tip #1. Pipe a swirl of frosting on top of each cupcake. Sprinkle each with toasted almonds.

1 Cupcake: Calories 410; Total Fat 22g (Saturated Fat 13g; Trans Fat 1g); Cholesterol 85mg; Sodium 250mg; Total Carbohydrate 48g (Dietary Fiber 0g); Protein 3g **Exchanges:** 1 Starch, 2 Other Carbohydrate, 4 1/2 Fat **Carbohydrate Choices:** 3

*To toast almonds: Spread almonds on cookie sheet and bake at 350°F for 5 to 7 minutes or until golden brown, stirring occasionally. Or, spread almonds in thin layer in microwave-safe pie pan. Microwave on High for 4 to 7 minutes or until golden brown, stirring frequently.

use a **cake mix**

Substitute 1 box yellow cake mix for the cupcakes above. Make cake mix as directed on box for cupcakes **except**—use 1 cup water, 1/4 cup amaretto, 1/3 cup vegetable oil and 3 eggs. Bake and cool as directed on box. Frost and garnish as directed in recipe.

Dreamy Sleepover Cupcakes, page 180

chapter four

kids'
party
cupcakes

chocolate malt cones

24 cupcake cones   **PREP TIME: 1 Hour 5 Minutes** START TO FINISH: **2 Hours 5 Minutes**

CUPCAKES

Chocolate Cupcakes (page 15)

24   flat-bottom ice cream cones

FROSTING

Fluffy White Frosting (page 21)

24   pirouette cookies (from 14-oz can)

24   maraschino cherries (from 10-oz jar), patted dry

1 Make Chocolate Cupcakes as directed in recipe except—divide batter evenly among cones, filling each with scant $1/4$ cup batter. Stand cones in muffin pan. Bake and cool as directed.

2 Meanwhile, make Fluffy White Frosting as directed in recipe. Frost cupcakes. Cut cookies in half crosswise to make 12 shorter cookies. Push into cupcakes to resemble straws. Garnish each cupcake with a cherry.

1 Cupcake Cone: Calories 280; Total Fat 10g (Saturated Fat 2.5g; Trans Fat 1.5g); Cholesterol 20mg; Sodium 250mg; Total Carbohydrate 43g (Dietary Fiber 2g); Protein 3g **Exchanges:** 1 Starch, 2 Other Carbohydrate, 2 Fat **Carbohydrate Choices:** 3

sweet success tip

You can also top these cones with cut colorful straws and colored sprinkles.

use a cake mix

Substitute 1 box devil's food cake mix for the cupcakes above. Make cake mix as directed on box for cupcakes **except**—use $1 1/4$ cups water, $1/2$ cup vegetable oil and 3 eggs. Stand 24 cones in muffin cups. Fill each ice cream cone $1/2$ full with batter. Cover and refrigerate remaining batter. Bake 21 to 26 minutes. Remove to cooling rack. Cool completely, about 30 minutes. For the frosting, substitute 1 container whipped fluffy white ready-to-spread frosting. Frost and garnish as directed in recipe. 30 to 36 cones

beary fun **cupcake cones**

24 cupcake cones PREP TIME: **55 Minutes** START TO FINISH: **1 Hour 55 Minutes**

CUPCAKE CONES

Chocolate Cupcakes (page 15)

24 flat-bottom ice cream cones

FROSTING

Vanilla Buttercream Frosting
(page 20)

Blue food color

DECORATIONS

Teddy bear–shaped graham
snacks

Gummy candy rings

Gum balls

Striped gum

1 Heat oven to 350°F. Make Chocolate Cupcakes as directed in recipe. Fill 12 ice cream cones with scant $1/4$ cup batter. Stand cones in muffin pan. Refrigerate remaining batter until ready to fill and bake remaining cones.

2 Bake 20 to 25 minutes or until toothpick carefully inserted in center of cupcake comes out clean. Cool completely. Repeat with remaining batter and cones.

3 Make Vanilla Buttercream Frosting as directed in recipe. Tint frosting with blue food color to look like water. Frost cupcake cone tops.

4 Use graham snacks for beach-going bears. Add candy rings for inner tubes, gum balls for beach balls and striped gum for inflatable floats.

1 Frosted Cupcake Cone (Undecorated): Calories 350; Total Fat 13g (Saturated Fat 5g; Trans Fat 1.5g); Cholesterol 30mg; Sodium 220mg; Total Carbohydrate 55g (Dietary Fiber 1g); Protein 2g **Exchanges:** $1/2$ Starch, 3 Other Carbohydrate, 2 $1/2$ Fat **Carbohydrate Choices:** 3 $1/2$

sweet success tip
Add cocktail parasols for the bears' beach scene.

use a cake mix

Substitute 1 box any non-swirl flavor cake mix for the Chocolate Cupcakes. Make cake mix as directed on box for cupcakes. Fill 12 flat-bottom ice cream cones about $1/2$ full of batter; stand cones in muffin pan. Refrigerate remaining batter until ready to fill and bake remaining cones. Bake 21 to 26 minutes or until toothpick carefully inserted in center of cupcake comes out clean. Cool completely. Repeat with remaining batter and cones. For the frosting, substitute 1 container any flavor whipped ready-to-spread frosting. Frost and decorate cones as directed in recipe. 30 to 36 cupcake cones

surprise cupcake **cones**

20 cupcake cones   PREP TIME: **55 Minutes** START TO FINISH: **3 Hours**

CUPCAKES
Yellow Cupcakes (page 14)

FROSTING
2   recipes of Fluffy White Frosting (page 21)
Red food color

DECORATIONS
1   cup candy-coated chocolate candies
20   flat-bottom ice cream cones
1/4   cup candy sprinkles

1 Heat oven to 350°F. Place paper baking cup in each of 20 regular-size muffin cups; place mini paper baking cup in each of 20 mini muffin cups. Make Yellow Cupcakes as directed in recipe; divide batter evenly among regular and mini muffin cups.

2 Bake mini cupcakes 17 to 20 minutes, regular cupcakes 20 to 25 minutes, or until toothpick inserted in center of cupcake comes out clean. Remove cupcakes from pans; place on cooling racks to cool.

3 If ice cream cone holder is unavailable, make a holder for the cones by tightly covering the tops of 2 empty square or rectangular pans (at least 2 to 2 1/2 inches deep) with heavy-duty foil. With sharp knife, cut 20 "stars" in foil, 3 inches apart, by making slits about 1 inch long.

4 Make 2 recipes of Fluffy White Frosting as directed in recipe. Tint with red food color to make pink frosting. Place about 2 teaspoons candies in each ice cream cone. Remove paper cups from cupcakes.

5 For each cone, frost top of 1 regular cupcake with frosting; turn upside down onto cone. Frost bottom (now the top) of cupcake. Place mini cupcake on frosted regular cupcake; frost side of regular cupcake and entire mini cupcake (it is easiest to frost from the cone toward the top). Sprinkle with candy sprinkles. Push cone through foil opening in cone holder; the foil will keep it upright.

1 Cupcake Cone: Calories 350; Total Fat 13g (Saturated Fat 8g; Trans Fat 0g); Cholesterol 60mg; Sodium 260mg; Total Carbohydrate 53g (Dietary Fiber 1g); Protein 4g **Exchanges:** 1 1/2 Starch, 2 Other Carbohydrate, 2 1/2 Fat **Carbohydrate Choices:** 3 1/2

sweet success tip
For extra pizzazz, top each "cone" with a maraschino cherry.

use a cake mix

Place paper baking cup in each of 18 regular-size muffin cups; place mini paper baking cup in each of 18 mini muffin cups. Substitute 1 box yellow cake mix for the Yellow Cupcakes. Make cake mix as directed on box for cupcakes. Divide batter evenly among regular and mini muffin cups. Bake mini cupcakes 11 to 13 minutes, regular cupcakes 17 to 22 minutes, or until toothpick inserted in center of cupcake comes out clean. Remove from pans; place on cooling racks to cool. For the frosting, substitute 3 containers strawberry whipped ready-to-spread frosting. Assemble, frost and decorate cupcake cones as directed in recipe. 18 cupcake cones

"just bugging you" cupcake cones

24 cupcake cones   PREP TIME: **1 Hour** START TO FINISH: **2 Hours 35 Minutes**

CUPCAKE CONES

Chocolate Cupcakes (page 15)

30 to 36 flat-bottom ice-cream cones

FROSTING

Vanilla Buttercream Frosting (page 20)

Food color

DECORATIONS

Small cookies or licorice candies

Miniature candy-coated chocolate baking bits

Small pieces black or red string licorice

1 Heat oven to 350°F. Make Chocolate Cupcakes as directed in recipe. Fill 12 cones each with scant $1/4$ cup batter. Stand cones in muffin pan. Refrigerate remaining batter until ready to fill and bake remaining cones.

2 Bake 20 to 25 minutes or until toothpick carefully inserted in center comes out clean. Cool completely, about 1 hour. Repeat with remaining batter and cones.

3 Make Vanilla Buttercream Frosting as directed in recipe. Divide frosting and tint with food color, as desired. Frost cupcake cone tops.

4 Use small cookies or licorice candies for bug or butterfly bodies, miniature candy-coated chocolate baking bits for eyes and small pieces of licorice for legs and antennae.

1 Frosted Cupcake Cone (Undecorated): Calories 290; Total Fat 13g (Saturated Fat 5g; Trans Fat 1.5g); Cholesterol 30mg; Sodium 210mg; Total Carbohydrate 42g (Dietary Fiber 1g); Protein 2g **Exchanges:** $1/2$ Starch, 2 $1/2$ Other Carbohydrate, 2 $1/2$ Fat **Carbohydrate Choices:** 3

sweet success tip

Look for colorful ice-cream cones for extra fun!

use a cake mix

Substitute 1 box devil's food cake mix for the Chocolate Cupcakes. Make cake mix as directed on box for cupcakes. Fill 12 cones about $1/2$ full of batter. Stand cones in muffin pan. Refrigerate any leftover batter until ready to fill and bake remaining cones. Bake and cool as directed. Repeat with remaining batter and cones. For the frosting, substitute 1 container any flavor whipped ready-to-spread frosting. Frost and decorate cupcakes as directed in recipe. 30 to 36 cupcake cones

mini cupcake **banana splits**

24 servings   **PREP TIME: 45 Minutes** START TO FINISH: **1 Hour 50 Minutes**

CUPCAKES

Yellow Cupcakes (page 14)

$3/4$ cup butter or margarine, softened

1 cup mashed very ripe bananas (2 medium)

$1/2$ cup milk

TOPPINGS

1 pint (2 cups) vanilla ice cream

1 pint (2 cups) chocolate ice cream

1 pint (2 cups) strawberry ice cream

$1 1/2$ cups chocolate-flavor syrup

$1 1/2$ cups strawberry topping

$1 1/2$ cups pineapple topping

$1 1/4$ cups chopped pecans

1 aerosol can whipped cream or whipped cream topping

24 maraschino cherries (from 10-oz jar), patted dry

1 Make, bake and cool mini version of Yellow Cupcakes except—use $3/4$ cup butter. Beat bananas in with the vanilla. Use $1/2$ cup milk.

2 To assemble cupcake banana splits, remove paper baking cups from cupcakes. Arrange 3 cupcakes in each serving dish. In each dish, place small scoop of vanilla ice cream on top of first cupcake, chocolate ice cream on second cupcake and strawberry ice cream on third cupcake.

3 Top chocolate ice cream with 1 tablespoon chocolate syrup, top strawberry ice cream with 1 tablespoon strawberry topping and top vanilla ice cream with 1 tablespoon pineapple topping. Sprinkle each serving with about 2 teaspoons pecans. Garnish each with whipped cream and a cherry.

1 Serving: Calories 460; Total Fat 16g (Saturated Fat 7g; Trans Fat 0g); Cholesterol 60mg; Sodium 220mg; Total Carbohydrate 75g (Dietary Fiber 2g); Protein 4g **Exchanges:** 1 $1/2$ Starch, 3 $1/2$ Other Carbohydrate, 3 Fat **Carbohydrate Choices:** 5

sweet success tip

Make as many servings as you need, then freeze remaining mini cupcakes for a later use.

use a cake mix

Place mini paper baking cup in each of 72 mini muffin cups. Substitute 1 box yellow cake mix for the Yellow Cupcakes. Make cake mix as directed on box for cupcakes **except**—use 1 cup mashed very ripe bananas (2 medium), $1/2$ cup water, $1/4$ cup butter or margarine, softened, 1 teaspoon vanilla and 3 eggs. Bake 11 to 17 minutes or until toothpick inserted in center of cupcake comes out clean. Cool completely. Assemble cupcake banana splits as directed in recipe.

dalmatian **cupcakes**

24 cupcakes   **PREP TIME: 40 Minutes** START TO FINISH: **1 Hour 40 Minutes**

FILLING

- 2 **packages (3 oz each) cream cheese, softened**
- 1/3 **cup sugar**
- 1 **egg**
- 1 **cup miniature or regular semisweet chocolate chips**

CUPCAKES

Chocolate Cupcakes (page 15)

FROSTING AND GARNISH

Vanilla Buttercream Frosting (page 20)

- 1/2 **cup miniature or regular semisweet chocolate chips**

1 Heat oven to 350°F. Place paper baking cup in each of 24 regular-size muffin cups.

2 In medium bowl, beat cream cheese, sugar and egg with electric mixer on medium speed until smooth. Stir in 1 cup chocolate chips; set aside.

3 Make Chocolate Cupcakes as directed in recipe. Top each with 1 heaping teaspoon filling.

4 Bake 20 to 25 minutes or until tops spring back when touched lightly. Cool 10 minutes. Remove cupcakes from pans; place on cooling racks to cool.

5 Make Vanilla Buttercream Frosting as directed in recipe. Frost cupcakes. Sprinkle tops with 1/2 cup chocolate chips. Store loosely covered in refrigerator.

1 Cupcake: Calories 430; Total Fat 18g (Saturated Fat 9g; Trans Fat 1.5g); Cholesterol 50mg; Sodium 240mg; Total Carbohydrate 62g (Dietary Fiber 1g); Protein 3g **Exchanges:** 1 Starch, 3 Other Carbohydrate, 3 1/2 Fat **Carbohydrate Choices:** 4

sweet success tip

How about a Dalmatian-themed party? Serve cupcakes with chocolate chip ice cream, play "pin the spot on the dog," and send kids home with a "doggie bag" full of dog-themed treats and prizes.

use a cake mix

Make filling as directed in step 2. Substitute 1 box devil's food cake mix for the Chocolate Cupcakes. Make cake mix as directed on box for cupcakes. Top batter in each cup with 1 heaping teaspoon filling. Bake and cool as directed in recipe. For the frosting, substitute 1 container vanilla creamy or whipped ready-to-spread frosting. Frost and decorate as directed in recipe.

crazy critter **cupcakes**

24 cupcakes   PREP TIME: **45 Minutes** START TO FINISH: **1 Hour 40 Minutes**

CUPCAKES

1 ^{2}/$_3$ cups all-purpose flour

1 ^{1}/$_2$ cups sugar

^{1}/$_2$ cup unsweetened baking cocoa

^{1}/$_2$ cup shortening

1 cup water

1 teaspoon baking soda

^{1}/$_2$ teaspoon baking powder

^{1}/$_2$ teaspoon salt

2 eggs

FROSTING AND DECORATIONS

1 container chocolate creamy ready-to-spread frosting

Assorted candies and cookies, if desired

1 tube (0.68 oz) black decorating gel, if desired

1 Heat oven to 400°F. Place paper baking cup in each of 24 regular-size muffin cups.

2 In large bowl, beat all cupcake ingredients with electric mixer on low speed 30 seconds, scraping bowl constantly. Beat on high speed 2 minutes, scraping bowl occasionally. Divide batter evenly among muffin cups, filling each about ^{1}/$_2$ full.

3 Bake 15 to 20 minutes or until toothpick inserted in center of cupcake comes out clean. Cool in pan 5 minutes. Remove from pans; place on cooling racks to cool.

4 Frost cupcakes. Decorate with candies and black gel to look like butterflies and ladybugs.

1 Frosted Cupcake (Undecorated): Calories 200; Total Fat 8g (Saturated Fat 2g; Trans Fat 2g); Cholesterol 20mg; Sodium 170mg; Total Carbohydrate 32g (Dietary Fiber 1g); Protein 1g **Exchanges:** ^{1}/$_2$ Starch, 1 ^{1}/$_2$ Other Carbohydrate, 1 ^{1}/$_2$ Fat **Carbohydrate Choices:** 2

sweet success tip

Have fun being creative with whatever candies you want to decorate these crazy critters!

use a cake mix

Substitute 1 box devil's food cake mix for the Chocolate Cupcakes. Make cake mix as directed on box for cupcakes. Frost and decorate as directed in recipe.

jungle animal cupcakes

24 cupcakes · PREP TIME: **55 Minutes** · START TO FINISH: **2 Hours 45 Minutes**

CUPCAKES

Yellow Cupcakes (page 14)

FROSTING

1 1/4 cups chocolate creamy ready-to-spread frosting (from 1-lb container)

Black food color

1 1/2 cups vanilla creamy ready-to-spread frosting (from two 1-lb containers)

Yellow food color

Red food color

LION DECORATIONS

1 1/2 cups caramel popcorn

12 brown miniature candy-coated chocolate baking bits

12 pretzel sticks

12 pieces Cheerios® cereal

TIGER DECORATIONS

12 brown miniature candy-coated chocolate baking bits

12 orange chewy fruit-flavored gumdrops (not sugar coated), cut in half crosswise, top halves discarded

MONKEY DECORATIONS

12 brown miniature candy-coated chocolate baking bits

6 miniature marshmallows, cut in half crosswise, pieces flattened

12 small round chocolate-covered creamy mints

ZEBRA DECORATIONS

6 round vanilla wafer cookies

24 brown miniature candy-coated chocolate baking bits

6 black chewy licorice-flavored gumdrops (not sugar coated), cut in half vertically

1 Make, bake and cool Yellow Cupcakes as directed in recipe.

2 In small bowl, mix 1/2 cup chocolate frosting with black food color to make black frosting. Place in resealable food-storage freezer plastic bag; cut small tip off one bottom corner of bag; set aside.

3 Lions and Tigers: In medium bowl, mix 1 cup vanilla frosting with enough yellow and red food colors to make orange. In small bowl, mix 1 tablespoon orange frosting with 3 tablespoons white vanilla frosting to make lighter orange for muzzles. Frost 12 cupcakes with darker orange frosting. For muzzle, spread or pipe small circle of lighter orange frosting on each cupcake.

4 For lions, place caramel corn around edges of cupcakes for mane. For eyes, add brown baking bits. For whiskers, break about 1/2-inch pieces off each end of pretzel sticks and insert in cupcakes. For ears, add cereal pieces. Using black frosting, pipe on mouth and nose.

5 For tigers, use black frosting to pipe on stripes, nose and mouth. For eyes, add brown baking bits. For ears, add gumdrop halves.

6 Monkeys: Frost 6 cupcakes with chocolate frosting. In small bowl, mix 1 tablespoon chocolate frosting and 2 tablespoons vanilla frosting to make light brown. For muzzle, spread or pipe circle of light brown on each cupcake that starts in middle and extends to edge; pipe small tuft of hair on opposite edge. For each eye, attach brown baking bit to marshmallow half with frosting; place on cupcakes. Using black frosting, pipe on nose and mouth. For ears, add mints.

7 Zebras: Cut small horizontal slit in top of 6 cupcakes near edge of paper cup. Insert edge of vanilla wafer cookie into each slit to create elongated face, adding small amount of vanilla frosting to cookie before inserting to help stick. Frost cupcakes with vanilla frosting. For muzzles, frost cookies with black frosting. Using black frosting, pipe on stripes and mane. Add brown baking bits for nostrils and eyes. For ears, add black gumdrop halves, cut sides down.

1 Frosted Cupcake (Undecorated): Calories 340; Total Fat 15g (Saturated Fat 7g; Trans Fat 3g); Cholesterol 45mg; Sodium 280mg; Total Carbohydrate 48g (Dietary Fiber 0g); Protein 2g **Exchanges:** 1 Starch, 2 Other Carbohydrate, 3 Fat **Carbohydrate Choices:** 3

use a cake mix

Substitute 1 box yellow cake mix for the Yellow Cupcakes. Make cake mix as directed on box for cupcakes. Frost and decorate as directed in recipe.

mr. mouse party **cupcakes**

8 cupcakes **PREP TIME: 30 Minutes** START TO FINISH: **1 Hour 30 Minutes**

CUPCAKES

Yellow Cupcakes (page 14)

TOPPING

8 scoops vanilla ice cream (about ¼ cup each)

16 miniature creme-filled chocolate sandwich cookies

Small candies

32 small pretzel sticks

1 Make, bake and cool Yellow Cupcakes as directed in recipe. Use 8 cupcakes for this recipe. (Wrap and freeze remaining cupcakes for later use.)

2 On cookie sheet, place scoops of ice cream about 3 inches apart. Decorate each ice cream scoop to resemble a mouse, using 2 cookies for ears, and small candies and pretzels for facial features and whiskers. Cover loosely with plastic wrap and freeze.

3 When ready to serve, place cupcakes on 8 dessert plates. Top each cupcake with decorated ice cream.

1 Cupcake: Calories 290; Total Fat 14g (Saturated Fat 8g; Trans Fat 0g); Cholesterol 60mg; Sodium 270mg; Total Carbohydrate 36g (Dietary Fiber 1g); Protein 4g **Exchanges:** 1 ½ Starch, 1 Other Carbohydrate, 2 ½ Fat **Carbohydrate Choices:** 2 ½

sweet success tip

String licorice works really well for whiskers instead of pretzels if you prefer.

use a cake mix

Substitute 1 box yellow cake mix for the Yellow Cupcakes. Make cake mix as directed on box for cupcakes. Continue as directed in recipe.

bug **cupcakes**

24 cupcakes PREP TIME: 50 Minutes START TO FINISH: 1 Hour 50 Minutes

CUPCAKES

White Cupcakes (page 16)

FROSTING AND DECORATIONS

2 containers (1 lb each) white creamy ready-to-spread frosting

Green and yellow paste or gel food color

Assorted candies (such as round mints, jelly beans, Jordan almonds, wafer candies, pieces from candy necklaces)

String licorice

White decorating icing (from 4.25-oz tube)

1 Make, bake and cool White Cupcakes as directed in recipe.

2 Tint frosting with green or yellow food color; frost cupcakes. Arrange candies on cupcakes to make bug heads, bodies and wings. In addition to candies, you can use whole marshmallows or sliced marshmallows sprinkled with colored sugar. Use pieces of licorice for antennae. For eyes, add dots of decorating icing.

1 Frosted Cupcake (Undecorated): Calories 320; Total Fat 12g (Saturated Fat 3g; Trans Fat 3.5g); Cholesterol 0mg; Sodium 200mg; Total Carbohydrate 51g (Dietary Fiber 0g); Protein 2g **Exchanges:** 1 1/2 Starch, 2 Other Carbohydrate, 2 Fat **Carbohydrate Choices:** 3 1/2

sweet success tip

For a kids' party, have the cupcakes already baked and frosted. Set out dishes of decorating candies and tubes of decorating gel, and let the kids create their own bugs.

use a cake mix

Substitute 1 box white cake mix for the White Cupcakes. Make cake mix as directed on box for cupcakes. Frost and decorate as directed in recipe.

chirping chick **cupcakes**

24 cupcakes **PREP TIME: 45 Minutes** START TO FINISH: **1 Hour 50 Minutes**

CUPCAKES

Yellow Cupcakes (page 14)

FROSTING AND DECORATIONS

2 containers (12 oz each) fluffy white whipped ready-to-spread frosting

Yellow food color

24 orange jelly beans

48 small orange candies

1 Make, bake and cool Yellow Cupcakes as directed in recipe.

2 Frost cupcakes with 1 container of frosting. Into other container of frosting, stir a few drops yellow food color.

3 Spoon 1 heaping teaspoonful yellow frosting onto center of each cupcake. To make beak, cut 1 orange jelly bean lengthwise to within $1/8$ inch of end; spread apart slightly. Press into yellow frosting. Add 2 orange candies for eyes.

1 Frosted Cupcake (Undecorated): Calories 290; Total Fat 14g (Saturated Fat 7g; Trans Fat 2g); Cholesterol 45mg; Sodium 210mg; Total Carbohydrate 38g (Dietary Fiber 0g); Protein 2g **Exchanges:** $1 1/2$ Starch, 1 Other Carbohydrate, $2 1/2$ Fat **Carbohydrate Choices:** $2 1/2$

sweet success tip

A pedestal platter topped with Easter grass and chirping chicks would make a perfect centerpiece for your table.

use a cake mix

Substitute 1 box yellow cake mix for the Yellow Cupcakes. Make cake mix as directed on box for cupcakes. Frost and decorate as directed in recipe.

creepy crawler **cupcakes**

24 cupcakes **PREP TIME: 40 Minutes** START TO FINISH: **1 Hour 40 Minutes**

CUPCAKES

Chocolate Cupcakes (page 15)

FROSTING AND DECORATIONS

1 container chocolate creamy ready-to-spread frosting

Candy rocks, if desired

24 gummy worms

1 Make, bake and cool Chocolate Cupcakes as directed in recipe.

2 Frost cupcakes. Sprinkle with candy rocks. Add gummy worms, gently pushing one end of worm into each cupcake.

1 Cupcake: Calories 260; Total Fat 10g (Saturated Fat 3g; Trans Fat 2g); Cholesterol 20mg; Sodium 230mg; Total Carbohydrate 41g (Dietary Fiber 1g); Protein 2g **Exchanges:** 1 Starch, 1 ½ Other Carbohydrate, 2 Fat **Carbohydrate Choices:** 3

sweet success tip

For a bake sale or a birthday bash, fill a new toy dump truck with cookie crumbs, gummy worms and decorated cupcakes.

use a cake mix

Substitute 1 box devil's food cake mix for the Chocolate Cupcakes. Make cake mix as directed on box for cupcakes. Frost and decorate as directed in recipe.

cupcake pet **parade**

24 cupcakes   PREP TIME: **1 Hour** START TO FINISH: **2 Hours**

CUPCAKES

Yellow Cupcakes (page 14)

FROSTING AND DECORATIONS

1   container vanilla creamy ready-to-spread frosting

1   tablespoon chocolate-flavored syrup

About 2 rolls chewy fruit snack , any flavor (from 5-oz box)

24   semisweet chocolate chips

16   large gumdrops

1   tube (0.68 oz) pink decorating gel

24   miniature candy-coated chocolate baking bits

8   miniature creme-filled chocolate sandwich cookies

1   tube (0.68 oz) black decorating gel

About 32 small gumdrops (from 10-oz package)

1   Make, bake and cool Yellow Cupcakes as directed in recipe.

2   For cats, stir together $1/2$ cup of the frosting and the chocolate syrup. Spread chocolate frosting over tops of 8 cupcakes. Cut small pieces of fruit snack for ears. Cut additional fruit snack into $1 \times 1/4$-inch strips for whiskers. Use chocolate chips for nose and eyes. Arrange on frosting to make cat faces.

3   For rabbits, spread half of the remaining vanilla frosting over tops of 8 cupcakes. Flatten large gumdrops with rolling pin; slightly fold and shape to form ears. Use pink gel to make inner ears. Cut fruit snack or flatten gumdrops and cut into $2 \times 1/4$-inch strips for whiskers. Use baking bits for eyes and nose. Arrange on frosting to make rabbit faces.

4   For dogs, spread remaining vanilla frosting over tops of remaining 8 cupcakes. Break or cut cookies in half; press 2 halves in each frosted cupcake for ears. Use black gel for spots or streaks on face. Use small gumdrops for eyes and nose. Flatten additional gumdrops for tongue. Arrange on frosting to make dog faces.

1 Cupcake: Calories 240; Total Fat 11g (Saturated Fat 6g; Trans Fat 1.5g); Cholesterol 45mg; Sodium 220mg; Total Carbohydrate 33g (Dietary Fiber 0g); Protein 2g **Exchanges:** 1 Starch, 1 Other Carbohydrate, 2 Fat **Carbohydrate Choices:** 2

sweet success tip

Planning a party for a pet lover? Celebrate with cupcakes decorated to look like cats, dogs and bunnies placed on a platter with green tinted coconut.

use a cake mix

Substitute 1 box yellow cake mix for the Yellow Cupcakes. Make as directed on box for cupcakes. Frost and decorate as directed in recipe.

chocolate moose **cupcakes**

14 cupcakes   PREP TIME: **1 Hour 15 Minutes** START TO FINISH: **2 Hours 5 Minutes**

CUPCAKES

1	cup milk
1/2	cup vegetable oil
1	egg
1 1/2	cups all-purpose flour
3/4	cup granulated sugar
1/3	cup unsweetened baking cocoa
1 1/2	teaspoons baking powder
1/2	teaspoon salt
3/4	cup chopped maraschino cherries, well drained

FROSTING

Creamy Chocolate Frosting (page 20)

DECORATIONS

14	peanut-shaped peanut butter sandwich cookies
14	small pretzel twists, cut lengthwise in half
	White and red decorating icing (from 6.4-oz cans)
28	blue candy-coated chocolate candies
28	brown candy-coated chocolate candies

1 Heat oven to 375°F. Place paper baking cup in each of 14 regular-size muffin cups, or grease bottoms only of muffin cups with shortening.

2 In medium bowl, beat milk, oil and egg with fork. Stir in remaining cupcake ingredients except cherries just until flour is moistened. Stir in cherries. Divide batter evenly among muffin cups (cups will be almost full).

3 Bake 18 to 20 minutes or until toothpick inserted in center of cupcake comes out clean. Cool 5 minutes; remove from pan to cooling racks to cool.

4 Meanwhile, make Creamy Chocolate Frosting as directed in recipe. Place 1/2 cup frosting in small microwavable bowl. Microwave uncovered on High 5 to 10 seconds or until frosting is melted and can be stirred smooth. Dip tops and sides of peanut butter cookies in melted frosting; place on waxed paper until hardened, about 15 minutes.

5 Frost cupcakes with remaining frosting. Press 1 coated cookie onto each cupcake so cookie extends over edge of cupcake to look like snout of moose. Poke 1 pretzel half into each cupcake, behind cookie, for antlers. Use white decorating icing to pipe on nostrils. Use red decorating icing to pipe on mouths. Attach blue candies for eyes and brown candies for ears.

1 Cupcake: Calories 490; Total Fat 21g (Saturated Fat 8g; Trans Fat 0g); Cholesterol 35mg; Sodium 300mg; Total Carbohydrate 70g (Dietary Fiber 2g); Protein 4g **Exchanges:** 1 1/2 Starch, 3 Other Carbohydrate, 4 Fat **Carbohydrate Choices:** 4 1/2

sweet success tip

For a fun party idea, make a centerpiece by placing the moose in a circle on a tray.

puffer fish **cupcakes**

24 cupcakes PREP TIME: **2 Hours 40 Minutes** START TO FINISH: **3 Hours 15 Minutes**

CUPCAKES

Chocolate Cupcakes (page 15)

FROSTING

1 ½ recipes of Vanilla Buttercream Frosting (page 20)

Blue paste food color

DECORATIONS

2 cups flaked coconut

Yellow and green liquid food color

24 vanilla creme-filled soft chocolate snack cakes

48 pieces Cheerios cereal

48 miniature candy-coated chocolate baking bits

24 candy-coated chocolate candies

24 orange slice candies (wedges)

1 Make, bake and cool Chocolate Cupcakes as directed in recipe.

2 Make Vanilla Buttercream Frosting as directed in recipe. Tint to desired blue color with paste food color. Reserve 2 ½ cups frosting for spreading on tops of snack cakes. Frost cupcakes with remaining frosting.

3 Place 1 cup coconut in each of 2 small bowls. To one bowl, add 2 to 3 drops yellow food color and 2 to 3 drops water; toss with fork until coconut reaches desired yellow color. Repeat with remaining bowl of coconut, using 2 drops yellow food color, 1 drop green food color and 2 to 3 drops water until coconut reaches desired yellow-green color. If desired, mix coconuts together in one bowl.

4 To decorate each cupcake, follow the directions on opposite page.

5 For fins, press 1 wedge on top of fish for dorsal fin. Press 1 small piece into each side of snack cake for side fins.

1 Cupcake: Calories 720; Total Fat 25g (Saturated Fat 14g; Trans Fat 0.5g); Cholesterol 70mg; Sodium 570mg; Total Carbohydrate 119g (Dietary Fiber 2g); Protein 5g **Exchanges:** 1 Starch, 7 Other Carbohydrate, 5 Fat **Carbohydrate Choices:** 8

use a **cake mix**

Substitute 1 box devil's food cake mix for the Chocolate Cupcakes. Make cake mix as directed on box for cupcakes. For the frosting, substitute 5 ½ cups from 2 containers vanilla creamy ready-to-spread frosting; tint with blue paste food color. Continue as directed in recipe.

1. Frost top and side of 1 snack cake with about 1½ tablespoons reserved frosting. Place on frosted cupcake; sprinkle with coconut.

2. For eyes, use 2 pieces of cereal; frost one side of each piece of cereal and place on snack cake. Attach 1 baking bit with frosting to each piece of cereal for eyes. Attach 1 chocolate candy for mouth.

3. Cut 1 orange slice horizontally into 2 thin wedges. Cut 1 of the wedges in half crosswise.

cupcake **sliders**

64 cupcake sliders   PREP TIME: **1 Hour 40 Minutes** START TO FINISH: **3 Hours 20 Minutes**

Yellow Cupcakes (page 14)

1	box (1lb 2.3 oz) fudge brownie mix
1/4	cup water
2/3	cup vegetable oil
2	eggs
1 1/2	cups flaked coconut
4	to 6 drops green food color
4	to 6 drops water
1	cup chocolate creamy ready-to-spread frosting (from 1-lb container)
64	orange juicy chewy fruit candies (from 14-oz package), unwrapped
16	rolls strawberry chewy fruit snacks in three-foot rolls, unwrapped (from 4.5-oz box)
2	tablespoons honey
1	to 2 teaspoons water
2	tablespoons sesame seed

1 Make, bake and cool mini version of Yellow Cupcakes as directed in recipe variation.

2 Make brownies as directed on box. Spread batter in 15 × 10 × 1-inch pan. Bake 22 to 26 minutes. Cool 20 minutes. With 1 1/2-inch round cutter, cut 64 brownie rounds for "burgers."

3 In medium bowl, toss coconut, green food color and 4 to 6 drops water with fork until coconut reaches desired color; set aside.

4 Remove paper baking cups from 64 cupcakes (reserve remaining cupcakes for another use). Cut each cupcake horizontally in half to make tops and bottoms of "buns." Place brownie rounds (burgers) on bottom halves of cupcakes (buns), using frosting to secure.

5 To make "cheese slices," on large plate, microwave about 8 juicy chewy fruit candies at a time on High 5 to 10 seconds to soften. Use bottom of measuring cup to flatten until each is about 1 3/4 inches in diameter. Secure to "burgers" with frosting. Repeat to make additional "cheese slices."

6 To make "ketchup," cut fruit snacks with kitchen scissors into about 1 3/4-inch irregular-edged circles (to resemble ketchup). Secure to "cheese" with frosting. Spread dab of frosting on "ketchup"; sprinkle each slider with scant 2 teaspoons coconut for "shredded lettuce."

7 In small bowl, mix honey and enough water until thin consistency. Brush honey mixture lightly over tops of "bun" tops; sprinkle each with sesame seed. Spread dab of frosting on cut sides of "bun" tops; secure to coconut, frosting-side down.

1 Cupcake Slider: Calories 190; Total Fat 8g (Saturated Fat 3.5g; Trans Fat 0g); Cholesterol 25mg; Sodium 135mg; Total Carbohydrate 27g (Dietary Fiber 0g); Protein 1g **Exchanges:** 1/2 Starch, 1 1/2 Other Carbohydrate, 1 1/2 Fat **Carbohydrate Choices:** 2

sweet success tip
Brownies can be baked ahead, but wait to cut out the "burgers" until ready to assemble so they don't dry out.

football cupcake **pull-aparts**

24 cupcakes PREP TIME: **50 Minutes** START TO FINISH: **1 Hour 50 Minutes**

CUPCAKES

Yellow Cupcakes (page 14)

FROSTING AND DECORATIONS

Creamy Chocolate Frosting
(page 20)

1/2 cup candy-coated chocolate
candies

1 tube (4.25 oz) white decorating
icing

1 Make, bake and cool Yellow Cupcakes as directed in recipe.

2 Make Creamy Chocolate Frosting as directed in recipe. Spoon frosting into decorating bag fitted with large star tip (size #5).

3 Arrange cupcakes in football shape using 15 of the 24 cupcakes. Pipe thick lines of frosting over football-cupcake shape; spread frosting with spatula to cover cupcakes. Pipe decorative border of frosting around edge of football. Sprinkle border with candy-coated chocolate candies. Pipe laces with white icing. Frost and decorate remaining cupcakes as desired, and serve alongside football.

1 Frosted Cupcake (Undecorated): Calories 280; Total Fat 14g (Saturated Fat 8g; Trans Fat 0g); Cholesterol 60mg; Sodium 210mg; Total Carbohydrate 38g (Dietary Fiber 0g); Protein 2g **Exchanges:** 1 1/2 Starch, 1 Other Carbohydrate, 2 1/2 Fat **Carbohydrate Choices:** 2 1/2

sweet success tip

Get in the team spirit! Use candy-coated chocolate candies that match your team or school colors.

use a cake mix

Substitute 1 box yellow cake mix for the Yellow Cupcakes. Make cake mix as directed on box for cupcakes. For the frosting, substitute 2 containers chocolate creamy ready-to-spread frosting. Arrange, frost and decorate as directed in recipe.

baseball **caps**

24 cupcakes   **PREP TIME: 1 Hour 5 Minutes** START TO FINISH: **2 Hours 5 Minutes**

CUPCAKES

Yellow Cupcakes (page 14)

FROSTING

2   recipes of Vanilla Buttercream Frosting (page 20)

Assorted food colors

DECORATIONS

Black shoestring licorice

Candy-coated fruit-flavored bite-size candies

Assorted fruit slice candies

1   tube (0.68 oz) decorating gel (any color), if desired

1   Make, bake and cool Yellow Cupcakes as directed in recipe.

2   Make 2 recipes of Vanilla Buttercream Frosting as directed in recipe. Divide frosting among small bowls for as many colors as desired; stir food color into each. Cut slice from top of each cupcake to make a flat surface. Turn cupcakes upside down. Frost cupcakes.

3   Starting at center of each cap, place pieces of licorice down sides for seams. Place 1 candy-coated fruit candy at center top. Use fruit slice candies for brims (trim fruit slices if necessary). Using gel, pipe team initial or child's name on caps.

1 Frosted Cupcake (Undecorated): Calories 510; Total Fat 19g (Saturated Fat 12g; Trans Fat 0.5g); Cholesterol 75mg; Sodium 260mg; Total Carbohydrate 80g (Dietary Fiber 0g); Protein 2g **Exchanges:** 1 Starch, 4 1/2 Other Carbohydrate, 3 1/2 Fat **Carbohydrate Choices:** 5

sweet success tip

Expand on the baseball theme by accompanying each cupcake with a baseball-size scoop of vanilla ice cream.

use a cake mix

Substitute 1 box yellow cake mix for the Yellow Cupcakes. Make cake mix as directed on box for cupcakes. For the frosting, substitute 3 containers vanilla creamy ready-to-spread frosting. Frost and decorate as directed in recipe.

kid-party **fun**

Few things are more fun or memorable for kids than a themed party. Whether it's a birthday party, school celebration or holiday gathering, here are some creative ideas to make planning your festivities a "piece of _cup_cake!"

Princess-for-a-Day Birthday Party

This party will appeal to all the little "fashionistas" out there! Prepare Fairy Princess Cupcakes (page 182) and display on a pedestal platter.

Decorations:

- Hang strings of fake pearls, feather boas or ribbons around the party space.
- Make a "red carpet" by taping red paper together to look like a red runner. Highlight the space with a spotlight or disco ball.

Games and activities:

- Play upbeat "fashion show" music.
- Supply a variety of dress-up clothes, borrowed from neighbors or purchased from second-hand stores. Divide up the clothes and guests between two teams. Have a relay, where the guests have to run over, put on all the dress-up clothes over their own clothes and run back. The first team to have all its members "dress up and down" wins.
- Have a fashion show: Let guests put together their own "designs" from the dress-up clothes at hand. Offer a variety of accessories, such as gloves, hats, glasses and jewelry. Each guest dresses up and "walks the red carpet" to show off their design.

Party favors:

- Little hand-held mirrors and brushes or a stick of lip gloss.

Cosmopolitan Cupcakes, page 296

Bewitching Black Cats, page 225

Baseball Caps, page 167

Howling Halloween Party

Perfect for a school celebration or neighborhood get-together, this party will be "spooky-fun!" Make Witch's Hat Cupcakes (page 222) or Skeleton Cupcakes (page 220).

Decorations:

- Hang orange and black streamers and cobwebs in the party space. Attach plastic spiders to the cobwebs.
- Play Halloween music or spooky sounds, available at party stores.

Games and activities:

- Have guests frost and decorate cupcakes with Halloween sprinkles and then eat their creations!
- Play "Monster Freeze." Turn on Halloween Music while guests dance. When the music stops, guests have to "freeze" in the position they were in when the music stopped.

Party favors:

- Glow-in-the-dark bouncy balls, Halloween pencils, erasers or wax lips, available at party stores or online.

Witch's Hat Cupcakes, page 222

Let's Play Ball Birthday Party!

Let the games begin! This party will make your birthday boy or girl feel like an MVP! Make Baseball Caps (page 167) in their favorite team colors. Let these cute cupcakes be a decoration during the party.

Decorations:

- Hang streamers, pennants and sports posters in the party space.
- Rename your home in honor of the birthday boy or girl! Festoon the front door with a banner proclaiming the new "stadium" name.
- Make signs for all the stadium hot spots—the backyard dugout, the snack bar where the party food is served and the souvenir stand with party favors for the guests to take home.
- Fill and hang a sports-themed piñata from a tree branch for outside fun.

Games and activities:

- As guests arrive, assign them to a team and then organize a ball game, complete with trophies.
- Supply inexpensive visors or baseball caps and an array of puff paints and art supplies for decorating them.

Party favors:

- Score points with sports fans by giving party favors like baseball cards, bouncy balls or chewing gum.

monster truck cupcake **pull-aparts**

24 cupcakes   PREP TIME: 1 Hour 5 Minutes START TO FINISH: 1 Hour 50 Minutes

CUPCAKES

Yellow Cupcakes (page 14)

ICING

Decorator Icing (page 21)

Green paste food color

DECORATIONS

2 chocolate or chocolate-frosted cruller doughnuts

Black decorating icing (from 6.4-oz can)

2 creme-filled chocolate sandwich cookies

6 large gumdrops

1 roll multicolored chewy fruit snack, unwrapped (from 4.5-oz box)

2 cinnamon candies

2 ring-shaped hard candies

1 colored plastic straw

1 Make, bake and cool Yellow Cupcakes as directed in recipe.

2 Meanwhile, make Decorator Icing as directed in recipe. Reserve ½ cup of icing; tint gray by mixing in small amount of black icing. Tint remaining icing with green (or desired color of truck) food color.

3 To assemble truck, place 23 cupcakes next to each other as shown in diagram. (Reserve remaining cupcake for another use.) Push cupcakes together slightly to frost truck, not just individual cupcakes. Frost truck-shaped cupcakes with colored icing. Frost window and bottom trim of truck using gray icing.

4 Press doughnuts against cupcakes for wheels. With small amount of black decorating icing, secure sandwich cookies to center of each doughnut to look like hubcaps. Attach 1 gumdrop to each cookie center with decorator icing.

5 Using black decorating icing, outline truck body and draw window. Peel backing from fruit snack roll. With scissors, cut flame decoration from roll; press onto cupcakes.

6 For each headlight, attach cinnamon candy to ring-shaped candy with small amount of decorating icing; press onto truck. Use gumdrops for lights on top of truck and taillights. Cut straw to desired length for roll bar; attach to truck.

1 Cupcake: Calories 340; Total Fat 14g (Saturated Fat 8g; Trans Fat 0.5g); Cholesterol 60mg; Sodium 230mg; Total Carbohydrate 50g (Dietary Fiber 0g); Protein 2g **Exchanges:** 1 Starch, 2 ½ Other Carbohydrate, 2 ½ Fat **Carbohydrate Choices:** 3

use a cake mix

Substitute 1 box yellow cake mix for the Yellow Cupcakes. Make cake mix as directed on box for cupcakes. For the frosting, substitute 1 container vanilla creamy ready-to-spread frosting. Tint 1 cup frosting with green paste food color. Frost and decorate as directed in recipe.

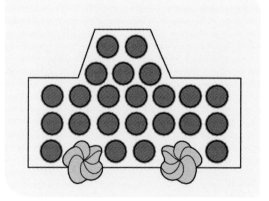

turtle-topped **cupcakes**

24 cupcakes   PREP TIME: **1 Hour 5 Minutes** START TO FINISH: **2 Hours 5 Minutes**

CUPCAKES

Yellow Cupcakes (page 14)

FROSTING

Vanilla Buttercream Frosting
(page 20)

DECORATIONS

2 packages (6.75 oz each) devil's
food cookie cakes

Green decorating icing (from
6.4-oz can)

48 small (1-inch) green chewy fruit-
flavored candies

1 Make, bake and cool Yellow Cupcakes as directed in recipe.

2 Make Vanilla Buttercream Frosting as directed in recipe. Frost cupcakes.

3 Press cookie cake in center on top of each cupcake. Use decorating icing to decorate cookies to resemble turtle shells.

4 For each turtle, microwave 2 green chewy chocolate candies on High 10 seconds or until warm enough to be pliable. Shape to form heads, tails and feet of turtles.

1 Cupcake: Calories 340; Total Fat 14g (Saturated Fat 8g; Trans Fat 0.5g); Cholesterol 60mg; Sodium 230mg; Total Carbohydrate 50g (Dietary Fiber 0g); Protein 2g **Exchanges:** 1 Starch, 2 ½ Other Carbohydrate, 2 ½ Fat **Carbohydrate Choices:** 3

use a cake mix

Substitute 1 box yellow cake mix for the Yellow Cupcakes. Make, bake and cool cake mix as directed on box for cupcakes. For the frosting, substitute 1 container vanilla creamy ready-to-spread frosting. Frost and decorate as directed in recipe.

tie-dyed **cupcakes**

24 cupcakes   PREP TIME: **15 Minutes** START TO FINISH: **1 Hour 25 Minutes**

White Cupcakes (page 16)
1   container (9 oz) confetti
    sprinkles

1 Make White Cupcakes as directed in recipe except—fill muffin cups $1/2$ full; top each with $1/4$ teaspoon sprinkles. Top with remaining batter; sprinkle each with $1/2$ teaspoon sprinkles.

2 Bake and cool as directed in recipe.

1 Cupcake: Calories 230; Total Fat 9g (Saturated Fat 3g; Trans Fat 1g); Cholesterol 0mg; Sodium 130mg; Total Carbohydrate 34g (Dietary Fiber 1g); Protein 3g **Exchanges:** 1 Starch, 1 $1/2$ Other Carbohydrate, 1 $1/2$ Fat **Carbohydrate Choices:** 2

sweet success tip

The brightly colored sprinkles melt into the cupcake batter, making a tie-dyed look inside and on top.

use a cake mix

Substitute 1 box white cake mix for the White Cupcakes. Make cake mix as directed on box for cupcakes **except**—fill cups $1/2$ full and top each with $1/4$ teaspoon sprinkles; then, top with remaining batter and sprinkle each with $1/2$ teaspoon sprinkles. Bake and cool as directed on box.

lucky charms **cupcakes**

24 cupcakes   PREP TIME: 45 Minutes START TO FINISH: **1 Hour 45 Minutes**

CUPCAKES

Yellow Cupcakes (page 14)

FROSTING AND DECORATIONS

Vanilla Buttercream Frosting
(page 20)

3   cups Lucky Charms® cereal
Green edible glitter

1 Make, bake and cool Yellow Cupcakes as directed in recipe.

2 Make Vanilla Buttercream Frosting as directed in recipe. Frost cupcakes. Top each cupcake with 2 tablespoons cereal; sprinkle with glitter.

1 Cupcake: Calories 340; Total Fat 14g (Saturated Fat 8g; Trans Fat 0.5g); Cholesterol 60mg; Sodium 220mg; Total Carbohydrate 50g (Dietary Fiber 0g); Protein 2g **Exchanges:** 1½ Starch, 2 Other Carbohydrate, 2½ Fat **Carbohydrate Choices:** 3

sweet success tip
Get the kids to help add the toppings to these fun cupcakes.

use a cake mix

Substitute 1 box yellow cake mix for the Yellow Cupcakes. Make cake mix as directed on box for cupcakes. For the frosting, substitute 1 container vanilla creamy ready-to-spread frosting. Frost and decorate as directed in recipe.

catchin' the rays **cupcakes**

24 cupcakes   **PREP TIME: 1 Hour 40 Minutes** START TO FINISH: **2 Hours 40 Minutes**

CUPCAKES

    Yellow Cupcakes (page 14)

FROSTING AND DECORATIONS

    Vanilla Buttercream Frosting (page 20)

    Blue paste food color

12 sticks striped fruit gum, unwrapped, cut in half

    Assorted colors decorating icing (from 6.4-oz cans)

24 teddy bear-shaped graham snacks (from 10-oz box)

24 large gumdrops (from 10-oz bag)

24 pretzel sticks

1 Make, bake and cool Yellow Cupcakes as directed in recipe.

2 Make Vanilla Buttercream Frosting as directed in recipe. Tint 1 cup frosting with blue food color. Frost one half of each cupcake top with blue frosting to look like water. Frost the other half of cupcake tops with remaining white frosting to look like sand.

3 Press 1 half piece of gum onto white-frosted half of each cupcake for "beach towel." Use decorating icing to add "swimsuits" and "sunglasses" to each bear-shaped snack. Attach 1 bear to each beach towel with small amount of decorating icing.

4 Flatten gumdrops into 1 1/2-inch circles. With scissors, make slits in edge of gumdrops to look like palm tree leaves. Press 1 gumdrop onto one end of each pretzel stick; poke 1 pretzel stick into each cupcake.

1 Cupcake: Calories 340; Total Fat 14g (Saturated Fat 8g; Trans Fat 0.5g); Cholesterol 60mg; Sodium 230mg; Total Carbohydrate 50g (Dietary Fiber 0g); Protein 2g **Exchanges:** 1 1/2 Starch, 2 Other Carbohydrate, 2 1/2 Fat **Carbohydrate Choices:** 3

sweet success tip

You can purchase cocktail umbrellas to place on the cupcakes for the bears at the beach!

use a cake mix

Substitute 1 box yellow cake mix for the Yellow Cupcakes. Make cake mix as directed on box for cupcakes. For the frosting, substitute 1 container vanilla creamy ready-to-spread frosting; tint 1 cup frosting with blue paste food color. Frost and decorate as directed in recipe.

game day cupcakes

24 cupcakes   PREP TIME: 1 Hour 25 Minutes START TO FINISH: 2 Hours 25 Minutes

CUPCAKES

Chocolate Cupcakes (page 15)

FROSTING

Fluffy White Frosting (page 21)
Paste food color

DECORATIONS

Star-shaped candy sprinkles

1 tube (4.25 oz) white decorating icing

24 milk chocolate-covered almonds (from 3-oz box)

4 rolls chewy fruit snacks, any flavor (from 5-oz box)

24 thin pretzel sticks

1 Make, bake and cool Chocolate Cupcakes as directed in recipe.

2 Make Fluffy White Frosting. To create your favorite team colors, divide $3/4$ cup frosting between 2 small bowls. Add desired food color to each bowl, and stir until thoroughly blended.

3 Frost cupcakes; sprinkle with stars. For footballs, pipe laces on almonds with decorating icing. Cut each fruit-flavored snack into 6 triangles. Wrap each triangle around one end of each pretzel for flag. Decorate each cupcake with a football and flag.

1 Cupcake: Calories 190; Total Fat 7g (Saturated Fat 2g; Trans Fat 1g); Cholesterol 20mg; Sodium 180mg; Total Carbohydrate 29g (Dietary Fiber 1g); Protein 2g **Exchanges:** $1/2$ Starch, $1 1/2$ Other Carbohydrate, $1 1/2$ Fat **Carbohydrate Choices:** 2

sweet success tip

For extra fun, make grass to look like a field. Shake 1 cup coconut and 3 drops green food color in tightly covered jar until evenly tinted. Then arrange cupcakes on the "field."

use a cake mix

Substitute 1 box devil's food cake mix for the Chocolate Cupcakes. Make cake mix as directed on box fir cupcakes. For the frosting, substitute 1 container fluffy white whipped ready-to-spread frosting. Frost and decorate as directed in recipe.

dreamy sleepover **cupcakes**

24 cupcakes PREP TIME: **2 Hours 40 Minutes** START TO FINISH: **3 Hours 40 Minutes**

CUPCAKES
Yellow Cupcakes (page 14)

FROSTING
Vanilla Buttercream Frosting
(page 20)

DECORATIONS
48 vanilla wafers

Assorted colors decorating
icing (from 6.4-oz cans)

12 rolls any flavor chewy fruit snack
rolls (from two 5-oz boxes)

Assorted candy sprinkles,
if desired

1 Make, bake and cool Yellow Cupcakes as directed in recipe.

2 Make Vanilla Buttercream Frosting as directed in recipe. Frost cupcakes.

3 On each cupcake, press 2 vanilla wafers, 1 for the head and 1 for the body. With decorator icing, decorate 1 wafer with facial features and hair. Cut 4 × 2 $^1/_2$-inch pieces from chewy fruit snack rolls; press onto cupcakes, covering other cookie, to look like a blanket. Decorate blankets with decorating icing and candy sprinkles.

1 Cupcake: Calories 340; Total Fat 14g (Saturated Fat 8g; Trans Fat 0.5g); Cholesterol 60mg; Sodium 230mg; Total Carbohydrate 50g (Dietary Fiber 0g); Protein 2g **Exchanges:** 1 Starch, 2 $^1/_2$ Other Carbohydrate, 2 $^1/_2$ Fat **Carbohydrate Choices:** 3

sweet success tip
Why not make these for a girl's sleepover party? Bake cupcakes ahead; place baked cupcakes and decorating items on plates for decorating. Let the creativity begin!

use a cake mix

Substitute 1 box yellow cake mix for the Yellow Cupcakes. Make cake mix as directed on box for cupcakes. For the frosting, substitute 1 container vanilla creamy ready-to-spread frosting. Frost and decorate as directed in recipe.

fairy princess cupcakes

Make magical dreams come true and create dreamy princess cupcakes! Make one of your favorite cupcakes from the basics chapter, and prepare Vanilla Buttercream Frosting on page 20. Tint frosting with pink paste food color. Pipe onto cupcakes using a #7 star tip, starting at outside edge and spiraling up towards the center.

Fairy Hats and Wands

Use sample-size ice-cream cones for fairy hat. Cut tassel for hat from chewy fruit snack rolls. For wand, roll gumdrop with rolling pin; cut out star shape with tiny cookie cutter or knife. Press gumdrop star onto pretzel stick. Sprinkle cupcakes with edible pearls.

Precious Necklaces

Top with candy sprinkles and rock candy. Make necklace with edible pearls, pressing into frosting. Use edible flower candy for necklace charm, adhering with water or a dab of frosting.

Princess Crowns

Top with candy sprinkles. To make each crown, microwave 3 yellow-colored chewy 1-inch candies about 10 seconds. Roll or press candies into 2 × 6-inch rectangle. Cut notches from one long side to resemble crown points; curve and insert into frosting. Brush crown with water to attach candy decors.

Frog Princes

For frogs, attach 2 small gumdrops halves to large gumdrop for eyes with toothpicks. Roll yellow gumdrop; cut to resemble crown and attach to large green gumdrop with toothpick. Using purchased tubes of black and white frosting, pipe on eyes. Using canned pink frosting, pipe on mouth. Attach 2 round green sprinkles for nostrils with frosting. Garnish as desired. Remove toothpicks before eating.

pirate's hidden treasure **cupcakes**

24 cupcakes **PREP TIME: 1 Hour 40 Minutes** START TO FINISH: **2 Hours 30 Minutes**

CUPCAKES

Chocolate Cupcakes (page 15)

24 miniature chocolate-covered peanut butter cup candies (from 12-oz bag), unwrapped

FROSTING

Vanilla Buttercream Frosting (page 20)

DECORATIONS

2 rolls chewy fruit snack (any red color) (from 4.5-oz box)

24 small ring-shaped candies or Cheerios cereal pieces

3 tablespoons miniature candy-coated semisweet chocolate baking bits

1 tablespoon semisweet chocolate chips

2 pieces black string licorice (each 34 inches long)

1 Heat oven to 350°F. Place paper baking cup in each of 24 regular-size muffin cups.

2 Make Chocolate Cupcakes as directed in recipe. Divide batter evenly among muffin cups, filling each about $2/3$ full. Place 1 candy in top of batter for each cupcake (candies will sink as cupcakes bake). Bake and cool as directed in recipe.

3 Make Vanilla Buttercream Frosting as directed in recipe. Frost cupcakes.

4 Cut 12-inch piece from 1 fruit snack roll; set aside. From remaining fruit snack, cut 24 (2-inch) pieces; cut crescent-shaped piece from each. Peel off paper backing; add 1 piece to each cupcake for top of kerchief.

5 Cut reserved fruit snack into 12 (1-inch) pieces; peel off paper backing. Cut each piece in half lengthwise. Twist each piece in middle; add to 1 end of crescent-shaped fruit snack on each cupcake, forming tie of kerchief. Add 1 piece of ring-shaped candy under each tie for earring. Use baking bits, chocolate chips and licorice to make facial features and eye patches.

1 Frosted Cupcake (Undecorated): Calories 350; Total Fat 14g (Saturated Fat 6g; Trans Fat 1g); Cholesterol 30mg; Sodium 220mg; Total Carbohydrate 54g (Dietary Fiber 1g); Protein 2g **Exchanges:** 1 1/2 Starch, 2 Other Carbohydrate, 2 1/2 Fat **Carbohydrate Choices:** 3 1/2

use a cake mix

Substitute 1 box chocolate fudge cake mix for the Chocolate Cupcakes. Make cake mix as directed on box for cupcakes. Divide batter evenly among muffin cups. Place 1 candy in top of batter for each cupcake (candies will sink as cupcakes bake). Bake and cool as directed on box. For the frosting, substitute 1 container vanilla creamy ready-to-spread frosting. Frost and decorate as directed in recipe. 24 cupcakes.

butterfly pull-apart **cupcakes**

24 cupcakes PREP TIME: **45 Minutes** START TO FINISH: **1 Hour 45 Minutes**

CUPCAKES

Yellow Cupcakes (page 14)

FROSTING AND DECORATIONS

1 container vanilla creamy ready-to-spread frosting

Red food color

Yellow food color

2/3 cup chocolate creamy ready-to-spread frosting (from 1-lb container)

Assorted spring-colored candies and sugar

1 Make, bake and cool Yellow Cupcakes as directed in recipe.

2 Place vanilla frosting in small bowl. Stir in 5 drops red food color and 5 drops yellow food color to make orange frosting; set aside.

3 On large serving tray or cookie sheet covered with foil, arrange 24 cupcakes as shown in diagram. Push cupcakes together slightly to frost entire body and antennae, not just individual cupcakes. Frost center body of butterfly and antennae with chocolate frosting.

4 Push cupcakes together slightly to frost entire wings, not just individual cupcakes. Frost remaining cupcakes with orange frosting for wings. Pipe chocolate frosting outline on wings, if desired. Decorate butterfly with candies and sugar.

1 Frosted Cupcake (Undecorated): Calories 270; Total Fat 12g (Saturated Fat 6g; Trans Fat 2g); Cholesterol 45mg; Sodium 240mg; Total Carbohydrate 37g (Dietary Fiber 0g); Protein 2g **Exchanges:** 1 1/2 Starch, 1 Other Carbohydrate, 2 Fat **Carbohydrate Choices:** 2 1/2

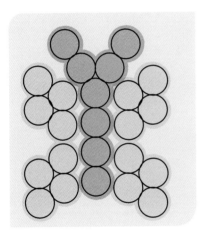

use a **cake mix**

Substitute 1 box yellow cake mix for the Yellow Cupcakes. Make cake mix as directed on box for cupcakes. Frost and decorate as directed in recipe.

campfire s'mores **cupcakes**

24 cupcakes **PREP TIME: 2 Hours 30 Minutes** START TO FINISH: **5 Hours 45 Minutes**

CUPCAKES

Chocolate Cupcakes (page 15)

DECORATIONS

20 individually wrapped red cinnamon hard candy disks (from 7-oz bag), unwrapped

20 individually wrapped yellow butterscotch hard candy disks (from 7-oz bag), unwrapped

60 pretzel sticks, broken in half

48 miniature marshmallows, toasted, if desired

24 toothpicks

MARSHMALLOW BUTTERCREAM FROSTING

1 jar (7 oz) marshmallow creme

1 cup butter or margarine, softened

2 cups powdered sugar

1/8 teaspoon lemon-yellow gel food color

1 Make, bake and cool Chocolate Cupcakes as directed in recipe.

2 Line 15 × 10 × 1-inch pan with foil; spray foil with cooking spray. Place unwrapped cinnamon and butterscotch candies in freezer plastic bag; with hammer or meat mallet, finely crush candies. Pour crushed candies into foil-lined pan; spread in thin layer. Bake at 350°F 6 to 8 minutes or until completely melted. Cool completely before handling.

3 Remove lid and foil seal from jar of marshmallow creme. Microwave uncovered on High 15 to 20 seconds to soften. In large bowl, beat marshmallow creme and butter with electric mixer on medium speed until smooth. Gradually beat in powdered sugar until smooth. Tint frosting with yellow food color. Frost cupcakes.

4 On each cupcake, arrange 5 pretzel pieces to look like logs of campfire. Break cooled sheets of melted candies into pointed shards. Insert candy pieces in tops of cupcakes around pretzels to look like flames.

5 Place 2 marshmallows on one end of each toothpick. Insert other end of toothpick into each cupcake.

1 Cupcake: Calories 350; Total Fat 15g (Saturated Fat 7g; Trans Fat 1.5g); Cholesterol 40mg; Sodium 280mg; Total Carbohydrate 50g (Dietary Fiber 1g); Protein 2g **Exchanges:** 1 Starch, 2 1/2 Other Carbohydrate, 3 Fat **Carbohydrate Choices:** 3

sweet success tip

Bake ahead and freeze the unfrosted cupcakes for up to 3 months; then frost and decorate when needed. Frozen cupcakes are also easier to frost!

use a cake mix

Substitute 1 box devil's food cake mix for the Chocolate Cupcakes. Make cake mix as directed on box for cupcakes. Continue as directed in recipe.

cream-filled **birthday cupcakes**

24 cupcakes   PREP TIME: **1 Hour 5 Minutes** START TO FINISH: **2 Hours 5 Minutes**

CUPCAKES

Yellow Cupcakes (page 14)

FILLING AND FROSTING

Vanilla Buttercream Frosting (page 20)

$1/2$ cup marshmallow creme

Paste food color

DECORATIONS

Candles

Assorted color gumballs

Multi-colored candy sprinkles

1 Make, bake and cool Yellow Cupcakes as directed in recipe.

2 Make Vanilla Buttercream Frosting as directed in recipe.

3 By slowly spinning end of round handle of wooden spoon back and forth, make deep, $3/4$-inch-wide indentation in center of top of each cooled cupcake, not quite to bottom. (Wiggle end of spoon in cupcake to make opening large enough.)

4 In small bowl, mix $1/2$ cup of the frosting and the marshmallow creme for filling. Spoon filling into small resealable food-storage plastic bag; seal bag. Cut $3/8$-inch tip off one bottom corner of bag. Insert tip of bag into opening in each cupcake; squeeze bag to fill opening.

5 Tint remaining frosting to desired color with food color. Arrange desired number of cupcakes together to form letters or numbers. Push cupcakes together slightly to frost letters or numbers, not just individual cupcakes. Frost letters or numbers with remaining frosting. (Any remaining cupcakes not used can be frosted and served as well.)

6 Arrange candles, gumballs and sprinkles on letters or numbers. Before eating, remove gumballs to enjoy separately from cupcakes.

1 Frosted Cupcake (Undecorated): Calories 340; Total Fat 14g (Saturated Fat 8g; Trans Fat 0.5g); Cholesterol 60mg; Sodium 230mg; Total Carbohydrate 52g (Dietary Fiber 0g); Protein 3g **Exchanges:** 1 Starch, 2 $1/2$ Other Carbohydrate, 2 $1/2$ Fat **Carbohydrate Choices:** 3 $1/2$

sweet success tip

Have the birthday boy or girl decide on the color of frosting and help decorate their special cupcake dessert.

use a cake mix

Substitute 1 box yellow cake mix for the Yellow Cupcakes. Make cake mix as directed on box for cupcakes. For the filling, in small bowl, mix $3/4$ cup vanilla whipped ready-to-spread frosting (from 12-oz container) and $1/2$ cup marshmallow creme. Fill as directed in recipe. For the frosting, substitute 1 container (1 lb) vanilla creamy ready-to-spread frosting; tint with desired food color. Decorate as directed in recipe.

Snow-Capped Gingerbread Train (page 246)

dazzling holiday cupcakes

new year's **mimosa cupcakes**

About 28 cupcakes PREP TIME: **55 Minutes** START TO FINISH: **1 Hour 50 Minutes**

CUPCAKES

White Cupcakes (page 16)
$3/4$ cup champagne or ginger ale
$1/2$ cup orange juice
1 teaspoon grated orange peel

FROSTING

6 cups powdered sugar
$1/2$ cup butter or margarine, softened
1 teaspoon grated orange peel
3 tablespoons champagne or ginger ale
2 to 3 tablespoons orange juice

GARNISH

Edible glitter or coarse white sparkling sugar

1 Heat oven to 350°F. Place paper baking cup in each of 28 regular-size muffin cups. Make White Cupcakes as directed in recipe except—substitute $3/4$ cup champagne or ginger ale and $1/2$ cup orange juice for the milk and add 1 teaspoon grated orange peel with the mix. Divide batter evenly among muffin cups. Bake and cool as directed in recipe.

2 Meanwhile, in large bowl, beat powdered sugar, butter, 1 teaspoon grated orange peel, 3 tablespoons champagne and 2 tablespoons orange juice with electric mixer on medium speed until smooth and creamy. If frosting is to stiff, stir in additional orange juice, 1 teaspoon at a time.

3 Spoon into decorating bag fitted with large star tip #5. Pipe frosting onto cupcakes. Sprinkle each with glitter. Store loosely covered in refrigerator.

1 Cupcake: Calories 280; Total Fat 9g (Saturated Fat 3.5g; Trans Fat 1g); Cholesterol 10mg; Sodium 130mg; Total Carbohydrate 48g (Dietary Fiber 0g); Protein 2g **Exchanges:** 1 $1/2$ Starch, 1 $1/2$ Other Carbohydrate, 1 $1/2$ Fat **Carbohydrate Choices:** 3

use a cake mix

Substitute 1 box white cake mix for the White Cupcakes. Make cake mix as directed on box **except**—use $3/4$ cup champagne or ginger ale, $1/2$ cup orange juice, $1/3$ cup vegetable oil, 3 egg whites and 1 teaspoon grated orange peel. Bake 15 to 20 minutes or until toothpick inserted in center of cupcake comes out clean. Frost and garnish as directed in recipe. 24 cupcakes

new year's party cupcakes

About 28 cupcakes   PREP TIME: **2 Hours 5 Minutes** START TO FINISH: **3 Hours 15 Minutes**

Yellow Cupcakes (page 14)

1 bag (12 oz) semisweet chocolate chips (2 cups)

2 teaspoons shortening

24 sample-size ice cream cones (about 1 inch wide at opening and 2 1/2 inches long)

24 frilled toothpicks

Vanilla Buttercream Frosting (page 20)

White decorating icing (from 6.4-oz can)

1 Make, bake and cool Yellow Cupcakes as directed in recipe.

2 Meanwhile, in small microwavable bowl, microwave chocolate chips and shortening uncovered on High 30 seconds. Stir; microwave about 30 seconds longer or just until mixture can be stirred smooth. Cool slightly. Dip ice cream cones in melted chocolate to coat; wipe off excess. Place point sides up on waxed paper–lined plate; insert frilled toothpick into point of each cone. Refrigerate while frosting cupcakes.

3 Make Vanilla Buttercream Frosting as directed in recipe. Frost cupcakes. Use decorating icing to decorate chocolate-coated cones; place 1 on each cupcake. With decorating icing, add "fringe" to edge of cone to look like party hat.

1 Cupcake: Calories 420; Total Fat 19g (Saturated Fat 11g; Trans Fat 0.5g); Cholesterol 60mg; Sodium 230mg; Total Carbohydrate 61g (Dietary Fiber 1g); Protein 3g **Exchanges:** 1 Starch, 3 Other Carbohydrate, 3 1/2 Fat **Carbohydrate Choices:** 4

use a cake mix

Substitute 1 box yellow cake mix for the Yellow Cupcakes. Make cake mix as directed on box for cupcakes. For the frosting, substitute 1 container vanilla creamy ready-to-spread frosting. Decorate as directed in recipe.

"from the heart" cupcakes

24 cupcakes **PREP TIME: 1 Hour** START TO FINISH: **2 Hours**

CUPCAKES

Chocolate Cupcakes (page 15)

FROSTING

1 cup white vanilla baking chips (6 oz)

1 container vanilla creamy ready-to-spread frosting

CHOCOLATE HEARTS

$\frac{1}{2}$ cup semisweet chocolate chips

$\frac{1}{2}$ teaspoon shortening

1 Make, bake and cool Chocolate Cupcakes as directed in recipe.

2 In medium microwavable bowl, microwave white baking chips uncovered on High 45 seconds. Stir; if necessary, microwave in 15-second increments, stirring after each, until chips are melted and smooth. Cool 5 minutes. Stir in frosting until well blended. Immediately frost cupcakes, or pipe frosting onto cupcakes.

3 Line cookie sheet with waxed paper. In 1-cup microwavable measuring cup, microwave chocolate chips and shortening uncovered on Medium 30 seconds. Stir; microwave in 10-second increments, stirring after each, until melted and smooth.

4 Place chocolate in small resealable food-storage plastic bag; seal bag. Cut off tiny corner of bag. Squeeze bag to pipe 24 heart shapes onto waxed paper. Refrigerate 10 minutes to set chocolate. Garnish each cupcake with a chocolate heart.

1 Cupcake: Calories 310; Total Fat 14g (Saturated Fat 5g; Trans Fat 2g); Cholesterol 20mg; Sodium 230mg; Total Carbohydrate 43g (Dietary Fiber 1g); Protein 3g **Exchanges:** 1 Starch, 2 Other Carbohydrate, 2 $\frac{1}{2}$ Fat **Carbohydrate Choices:** 3

sweet success tip

Add some variety! Make initials or free-form designs, using the melted chocolate.

use a cake mix

Substitute 1 box devil's food cake mix for the Chocolate Cupcakes. Make cake mix as directed on box for cupcakes. Continue as directed in recipe.

valentine parfait **cupcakes**

24 cupcakes   PREP TIME: **1 Hour** START TO FINISH: **2 Hours**

CUPCAKES

Chocolate Cupcakes (page 15)

FROSTING

Fluffy White Frosting (page 21)

DECORATIONS

1   cup semisweet or milk chocolate chips (6 oz)

2   teaspoons shortening

Heart-shaped candy sprinkles

1   Make, bake and cool Chocolate Cupcakes as directed in recipe.

2   Make Fluffy White Frosting as directed in recipe. Spoon frosting into decorating bag fitted with large round tip #7. Pipe dollop of frosting onto top of each cupcake.

3   In small microwavable bowl, microwave chocolate chips and shortening uncovered on High 1 minute, stirring once halfway through heating. Drizzle melted chocolate over frosted cupcakes. Sprinkle with candy sprinkles.

1 Cupcake: Calories 190; Total Fat 7g (Saturated Fat 2g; Trans Fat 1g); Cholesterol 20mg; Sodium 180mg; Total Carbohydrate 29g (Dietary Fiber 1g); Protein 2g **Exchanges:** $1/2$ Starch, $1 1/2$ Other Carbohydrate, $1 1/2$ Fat **Carbohydrate Choices:** 2

sweet success tip

Pick up Valentine candy sprinkles in the baking aisle, and sprinkle them on the cupcakes immediately after frosting. That way they are sure to stick!

use a cake mix

Substitute 1 box devil's food cake mix for the Chocolate Cupcakes. Make cake mix as directed on box for cupcakes. For the frosting, substitute 1 container fluffy white whipped ready-to-spread frosting. Frost and decorate as directed in recipe.

conversation **heart cupcakes**

24 cupcakes   PREP TIME: **1 Hour 10 Minutes** START TO FINISH: **2 Hours 5 Minutes**

Chocolate Cupcakes (page 15)

Vanilla Buttercream Frosting
(page 20)

Red colored sugar

Red decorating icing (from
6.4-oz can)

Valentine candy sprinkles

1 Make, bake and cool Chocolate Cupcakes as directed in recipe.

2 Make Vanilla Buttercream Frosting as directed in recipe. Frost cupcakes.

3 Lightly press heart-shaped cookie cutter into 1 frosted cupcake; remove. Dip cookie cutter into red colored sugar; lightly place cutter back on imprint on cupcake to transfer colored sugar. Repeat with remaining cupcakes.

4 With red icing, write messages inside hearts on some cupcakes. On other cupcakes, sprinkle with Valentine sprinkles.

1 Cupcake: Calories 330; Total Fat 12g (Saturated Fat 5g; Trans Fat 1.5g); Cholesterol 30mg; Sodium 210mg; Total Carbohydrate 52g (Dietary Fiber 1g); Protein 2g **Exchanges:** $1/2$ Starch, 3 Other Carbohydrate, 2 $1/2$ Fat **Carbohydrate Choices:** 3 $1/2$

sweet success tip

Use the opposite side of the heart cookie cutter for dipping into the frosting and sugar. Add conversation heart candies or Valentine sprinkles if you prefer not to write in the heart.

use a cake mix

Substitute 1 box devil's food cake mix for the Chocolate Cupcakes. Make cake mix as directed on box for cupcakes. Frost and decorate as directed in recipe.

shamrock mint **cupcakes**

24 cupcakes **PREP TIME: 1 Hour 10 Minutes** START TO FINISH: **2 Hours 10 Minutes**

CUPCAKES

Chocolate Cupcakes (page 15)

3/4 cup crème de menthe or mint baking chips (from 10-oz bag)

FROSTING AND DECORATIONS

Fluffy White Frosting (page 21)

1/2 teaspoon peppermint extract

24 large green gumdrops (from 10-oz bag)

1 Make Chocolate Cupcakes as directed in recipe except—stir baking chips into batter. Bake and cool as directed in recipe.

2 Make Fluffy White Frosting as directed in recipe except—stir peppermint extract into frosting with the vanilla until well blended. Frost cupcakes.

3 To decorate each cupcake, cut 1 gumdrop into 4 slices. Place 3 rounds on cupcake to make shamrock leaves. Press remaining round into thin strip; place below leaves for stem.

1 Cupcake: Calories 260; Total Fat 7g (Saturated Fat 2g; Trans Fat 1g); Cholesterol 20mg; Sodium 190mg; Total Carbohydrate 43g (Dietary Fiber 1g); Protein 2g **Exchanges:** 1 Starch, 2 Other Carbohydrate, 1 1/2 Fat **Carbohydrate Choices:** 3

sweet success tip

Not enough green for St. Patrick's Day? Color the frosting with a little green food color.

use a cake mix

Substitute 1 box chocolate fudge or devil's food cake mix for the Chocolate Cupcakes. Make cake mix as directed on box for cupcakes **except**—use 1 cup water, 1/2 cup vegetable oil and 3 eggs. Toss 3/4 cup crème de menthe baking chips (from a 10-oz bag) with 1 tablespoon all-purpose flour; stir into batter. Bake and cool as directed on box. For the frosting, substitute 1 container whipped fluffy white ready-to-spread frosting mixed with 1/4 teaspoon peppermint extract. Frost and garnish as directed in recipe.

bunny cupcakes

24 cupcakes   **PREP TIME: 1 Hour 25 Minutes** START TO FINISH: **2 Hours 25 Minutes**

CUPCAKES

Yellow Cupcakes (page 14)

FROSTING AND DECORATIONS

Vanilla Buttercream Frosting
(page 20)

Red food color

1   container fluffy white ready-to-
spread frosting

5   large marshmallows

Pink sugar

Candy decorations and
sprinkles, if desired

1   Make, bake and cool Yellow Cupcakes as directed in recipe.

2   Make Vanilla Buttercream Frosting as directed in recipe. Stir in red food color to make frosting pink. Frost cupcakes with pink frosting. Spoon 1 heaping teaspoonful fluffy white frosting on center of each cupcake.

3   To make ears, cut each large marshmallow crosswise into 5 pieces with kitchen scissors. Using scissors, cut through center of each marshmallow piece to within $1/4$ inch of edge. Separate to look like bunny ears; press 1 side of cut edges into pink sugar, flattening slightly. Arrange on each of the white icing mounds. Use candy decorations and sprinkles to make eyes, nose and whiskers.

1 Frosted Cupcake (Undecorated): Calories 250; Total Fat 12g (Saturated Fat 6g; Trans Fat 1.5g); Cholesterol 45mg; Sodium 210mg; Total Carbohydrate 31g (Dietary Fiber 0g); Protein 2g **Exchanges:** $1/2$ Starch, $1 1/2$ Other Carbohydrate, $2 1/2$ Fat **Carbohydrate Choices:** 2

use a cake mix

Substitute 1 box yellow cake mix for the Yellow Cupcakes. Make cake mix as directed on box for cupcakes. Frost and decorate as directed in recipe.

easter basket **cupcakes**

24 cupcakes PREP TIME: **1 Hour 10 Minutes** START TO FINISH: **2 Hours 10 Minutes**

CUPCAKES

    Yellow Cupcakes (page 14)

FROSTING AND DECORATIONS

    Fluffy White Frosting (page 21)

    Green-colored sour candy separated into 24 strips

    Jelly beans or other desired candies

1 Make, bake and cool Yellow Cupcakes as directed in recipe.

2 Make Fluffy White Frosting as directed in recipe. Frost cupcakes.

3 Insert ends of candy strips into cupcakes to make basket handles. Decorate with jelly beans and other candies.

1 Frosted Cupcake (Undecorated): Calories 200; Total Fat 9g (Saturated Fat 5g; Trans Fat 0g); Cholesterol 45mg; Sodium 200mg; Total Carbohydrate 27g (Dietary Fiber 0g); Protein 2g **Exchanges:** 1 Starch, 1 Other Carbohydrate, 1 ½ Fat **Carbohydrate Choices:** 2

sweet success tip

To make basket handles the same size, use the handle from the first basket to measure the length for the rest.

use a cake mix

Substitute 1 box yellow cake mix for the Yellow Cupcakes. Make cake mix as directed on box for cupcakes. For the frosting, substitute 1 container fluffy white whipped ready-to-spread frosting. Frost and decorate as directed in recipe.

may day **baskets**

24 cupcakes   **PREP TIME: 1 Hour 5 Minutes** START TO FINISH: **2 Hours 5 Minutes**

CUPCAKES

Yellow Cupcakes (page 14)

FROSTING AND DECORATIONS

Vanilla Buttercream Frosting
(page 20)

Red and blue berry twist licorice

Assorted small candies or
jelly beans

1 Make, bake and cool Yellow Cupcakes as directed in recipe.

2 Make Vanilla Buttercream Frosting as directed in recipe. Frost cupcakes.

3 Insert ends of licorice into cupcakes to make basket handles. Decorate with candies.

1 Frosted Cupcake (Undecorated): Calories 340; Total Fat 14g (Saturated Fat 8g; Trans Fat 0.5g); Cholesterol 60mg; Sodium 230mg; Total Carbohydrate 50g (Dietary Fiber 0g); Protein 2g **Exchanges:** 1 Starch, 2 1/2 Other Carbohydrate, 2 1/2 Fat **Carbohydrate Choices:** 3

sweet success tip

Rekindle the childhood tradition of giving May Day baskets. Why not make a batch of cupcakes and deliver them to your neighbors and friends?

use a cake mix

Substitute 1 box yellow cake mix for the Yellow Cupcakes. Make cake mix as directed on box for cupcakes. For the frosting, substitute 1 container any flavor creamy ready-to-spread frosting. Frost and decorate as directed in recipe.

lamb **cupcakes**

24 cupcakes **PREP TIME: 1 Hour 30 Minutes** START TO FINISH: **2 Hours 30 Minutes**

CUPCAKES

Yellow Cupcakes (page 14)

FROSTING

Fluffy White Frosting (page 21)

DECORATIONS

24 pastel-colored mint candy drops
(from 7-oz bag)

48 brown miniature candy-coated
chocolate baking bits
(from 12-oz bag)

12 large marshmallows, cut
in half diagonally

2 cups miniature marshmallows,
cut in half crosswise

1 Make, bake and cool Yellow Cupcakes as directed in recipe.

2 Meanwhile, make Fluffy White Frosting as directed in recipe. Frost cupcakes.

3 For each lamb muzzle, add 1 mint candy drop. For eyes, add 2 brown baking bits.

4 For ears, add 2 cut marshmallow halves, cut sides up. Place miniature marshmallow halves on face for wool.

1 Frosted Cupcake (Undecorated): Calories 240; Total Fat 9g (Saturated Fat 5g; Trans Fat 0g); Cholesterol 50mg; Sodium 210mg; Total Carbohydrate 37g (Dietary Fiber 0g); Protein 3g **Exchanges:** 1 Starch, 1 1/2 Other Carbohydrate, 1 1/2 Fat **Carbohydrate Choices:** 2 1/2

sweet success tip

To make these cupcakes even more special, bake them in decorative baking cups found at your favorite grocery or cake decorating store!

use a cake mix

Substitute 1 box yellow cake mix for the Yellow Cupcakes. Make cake mix as directed on box for cupcakes. For the frosting, substitute 1 container vanilla creamy ready-to-spread frosting. Frost and decorate as directed in recipe.

dark chocolate **chip–mascarpone cupcakes**

About 27 cupcakes   PREP TIME: **50 Minutes** START TO FINISH: **1 Hour 50 Minutes**

CUPCAKES

Chocolate Cupcakes (page 15)

$1/2$ cup mascarpone cheese (from 8-oz container)

$3/4$ cup dark chocolate chips, coarsely chopped

TOPPING AND GARNISH

2 packages (3 oz each) cream cheese, softened

$1/4$ cup mascarpone cheese (from 8-oz container)

$1/4$ cup powdered sugar

4 teaspoons Marsala wine or dark rum

$1 1/3$ cups whipping cream

2 teaspoons grated semisweet baking chocolate

1 Make Chocolate Cupcakes as directed in recipe except—add mascarpone cheese with the vanilla. Stir chocolate chips into batter. Bake and cool as directed.

2 In another large bowl, beat cream cheese and $1/4$ cup mascarpone cheese with electric mixer on medium speed until smooth and creamy. Beat in powdered sugar and wine.

3 In medium bowl, beat whipping cream until stiff peaks form. Fold whipped cream into cream cheese mixture. Spread topping on cupcakes, using about 2 heaping tablespoons on each. Sprinkle with grated chocolate.

1 Cupcake: Calories 250; Total Fat 16g (Saturated Fat 7g; Trans Fat 1g); Cholesterol 45mg; Sodium 180mg; Total Carbohydrate 24g (Dietary Fiber 1g); Protein 2g **Exchanges:** $1/2$ Starch, 1 Other Carbohydrate, 3 Fat **Carbohydrate Choices:** $1 1/2$

sweet success tip

For a special Mother's Day brunch, serve these cupcakes in a decorative cupcake stand.

use a cake mix

Substitute 1 box devil's food cake mix for the Chocolate Cupcakes. Make cake mix as directed on box for cupcakes **except**—use $3/4$ cup water, $1/2$ cup mascarpone cheese (from 8-oz container), $1/3$ cup vegetable oil and 3 eggs. Toss $3/4$ cup chopped dark chocolate chips with 1 tablespoon all-purpose flour; stir into batter. Bake and cool as directed on box. Frost and garnish as directed in recipe.

hole-in-one **father's day cupcakes**

24 cupcakes   **PREP TIME: 1 Hour** START TO FINISH: **1 Hour 45 Minutes**

Chocolate Cupcakes (page 15)

Vanilla Buttercream Frosting (page 20)

3 graham cracker squares, crushed

About 1/3 cup green candy sprinkles

24 colored straws

Colored paper

Tape

24 white gumballs or other round white candies

1 Make, bake and cool Chocolate Cupcakes as directed in recipe.

2 Make Vanilla Buttercream Frosting as directed in recipe. Frost cupcakes.

3 On one half of each cupcake, sprinkle about 1/2 teaspoon graham cracker crumbs for "sand." On other half of cupcake, sprinkle generous 1/2 teaspoon green sprinkles for "grass."

4 With scissors, cut straws into 3 1/2-inch lengths (discard any remaining pieces). Cut colored paper into flags; write a number on each flag, if desired. Tape each flag to one end of each straw piece; poke into cupcake. Gently press one gumball into each cupcake.

1 Cupcake: Calories 360; Total Fat 15g (Saturated Fat 9g; Trans Fat 0.5g); Cholesterol 60mg; Sodium 230mg; Total Carbohydrate 55g (Dietary Fiber 0g); Protein 2g **Exchanges:** 1/2 Starch, 3 Other Carbohydrate, 3 Fat **Carbohydrate Choices:** 3 1/2

sweet success tip

For a Father's Day party, arrange green Easter grass or green tinted coconut on a serving platter; add cupcakes.

use a cake mix

Substitute 1 box devil's food cake mix for the Chocolate Cupcakes. Make cake mix as directed on box for cupcakes. For the frosting, substitute 1 container vanilla creamy ready-to-spread frosting. Frost and decorate as directed in recipe.

fireworks cupcake **towers**

18 cupcake towers PREP TIME: **1 Hour 15 Minutes** START TO FINISH: **2 Hours 35 Minutes**

Yellow Cupcakes (page 14)
Vanilla Buttercream Frosting (page 20)
Red and blue paste food color
Candy decors, if desired

1 Make Yellow Cupcakes as directed in recipe except—place paper baking cup in each of 18 regular-size muffin cups and mini paper baking cup in each of 18 mini muffin cups. Divide batter evenly among muffin cups, filling each about 2/3 full.

2 Bake regular cupcakes 18 to 25 minutes, mini cupcakes 12 to 20 minutes, or until toothpick inserted in center of cupcake comes out clean. Cool 5 minutes; remove from pans; place on cooling racks to cool.

3 Meanwhile, make Vanilla Buttercream Frosting as directed in recipe. Place 1 1/2 cups frosting in decorating bag fitted with small round tip (#22). Frost each cupcake (regular and mini) with scant tablespoon frosting, making various length streamers. Divide remaining frosting between two bowls; tint frosting in one bowl red and the other blue.

4 Remove paper liners from mini cupcakes, if desired. Place 1 mini cupcake on top of each regular cupcake. Pipe blue and red frostings around base of mini cupcakes (on regular cupcakes) and on top of mini cupcakes, making various length streamers. Use any remaining white frosting to fill in streamers between red and blue ones. Decorate with candy decors, as desired.

1 Frosted Cupcake Tower (Undecorated): Calories 450; Total Fat 18g (Saturated Fat 11g; Trans Fat 0.5g); Cholesterol 80mg; Sodium 310mg; Total Carbohydrate 67g (Dietary Fiber 0g); Protein 3g **Exchanges:** 1 Starch, 3 1/2 Other Carbohydrate, 3 1/2 Fat **Carbohydrate Choices:** 4 1/2

sweet success tip

Make the cupcake towers into a centerpiece for your July 4th party. Add to the patriotic theme with plates, napkins and party decor to set the mood!

use a cake mix

Substitute 1 box yellow cake mix for the Yellow Cupcakes. Make cake mix as directed on box for cupcakes **except**—place paper baking cup in each of 18 regular-size muffin cups and mini paper baking cup in each of 18 mini muffin cups. Divide batter evenly among muffin cups. Bake regular cupcakes as directed on box; bake mini cupcakes 10 to 15 minutes. Cool as directed on box. Frost and decorate as directed in recipe.

stars and stripes **cupcakes**

24 cupcakes   PREP TIME: **55 Minutes** START TO FINISH: **1 Hour 50 Minutes**

CUPCAKES

White Cupcakes (page 16)
1/2 teaspoon almond extract
1 jar (10 oz) maraschino cherries (about 38 cherries), drained, finely chopped and patted dry

GLAZE

3 cups powdered sugar
3 to 4 tablespoons water
2 tablespoons light corn syrup
1/2 teaspoon almond extract

DECORATIONS

24 blue candy stars
Red decorating icing (from 4.25-oz tube)

1 Make White Cupcakes as directed in recipe except—stir in 1/2 teaspoon almond extract and chopped cherries. Bake and cool as directed in recipe.

2 In medium bowl, beat glaze ingredients with electric mixer on medium speed until smooth. Spoon over cupcakes, using back of spoon to spread. Let stand 10 minutes.

3 Place 1 candy star on each cupcake. Using writing tip, pipe icing in wavy stripes onto each cupcake to resemble flag.

1 Cupcake: Calories 250; Total Fat 7g (Saturated Fat 2g; Trans Fat 1g); Cholesterol 0mg; Sodium 130mg; Total Carbohydrate 45g (Dietary Fiber 0g); Protein 2g **Exchanges:** 1/2 Starch, 2 1/2 Other Carbohydrate, 1 1/2 Fat **Carbohydrate Choices:** 3

sweet success tip

When making the glaze, start with 3 tablespoons water. If the glaze is too stiff, add water, 1 teaspoon at a time, until the glaze is of desired consistency.

use a cake mix

Substitute 1 box white cake mix for the White Cupcakes. Make cake mix as directed on box for cupcakes **except**—use 1/2 cup sour cream, 1/2 cup vegetable oil, 1/2 teaspoon almond extract, 3 eggs; stir in 1 jar (10 oz) maraschino cherries (about 38), drained, finely chopped and patted dry. Bake 18 to 22 minutes or until toothpick inserted in center of cupcake comes out clean. Glaze and decorate as directed in recipe.

hairy heart **monster cupcakes**

24 cupcakes   PREP TIME: 50 Minutes START TO FINISH: 1 Hour 50 Minutes

CUPCAKES

Chocolate Cupcakes (page 15)

FROSTING AND DECORATIONS

1 can (6.4 oz) red decorating icing

1 can (6.4 oz) pink decorating icing

Valentine-shaped candy sprinkles

1 Make, bake and cool Chocolate Cupcakes as directed in recipe.

2 Remove paper baking cups from cupcakes; place cupcakes upside down on squares of waxed paper. Using star tip on cans of decorating icing, make rows of alternating colors of icing on each cupcake, starting at top of cupcake and ending at base of cupcake. Continue until entire cupcake is covered with icing.

3 Use candy sprinkles for eyes and mouth. Using waxed paper to lift cupcakes, place cupcakes on serving plate.

1 Frosted Cupcake (Undecorated): Calories 230; Total Fat 10g (Saturated Fat 4g; Trans Fat 1g); Cholesterol 20mg; Sodium 180mg; Total Carbohydrate 33g (Dietary Fiber 1g); Protein 2g **Exchanges:** ½ Starch, 1½ Other Carbohydrate, 2 Fat **Carbohydrate Choices:** 2

sweet success tip

Have the kids create their own monsters. Set out a variety of Valentine decors and let the fun begin!

use a cake mix

Substitute 1 box devil's food cake mix for the Chocolate Cupcakes. Make cake mix as directed on box for cupcakes. Frost and decorate as directed in recipe.

ghost cupcake cones

12 cupcake cones and 12 extra cupcakes   PREP TIME: **1 Hour** START TO FINISH: **1 Hour 35 Minutes**

CUPCAKES

Chocolate Cupcakes (page 15)
12 flat-bottom ice cream cones

FONDANT

2 cups powdered sugar
1 jar (7 oz) marshmallow creme

DECORATIONS

36 miniature semisweet chocolate chips (from 12-oz bag)

1 Heat oven to 350°F. Make cake batter for Chocolate Cupcakes as directed in recipe. Fill each cone with scant $1/4$ cup batter. Set remaining batter aside. Stand cones upright in muffin pan. Bake 15 to 20 minutes or until toothpick inserted in center comes out clean. Cool completely, about 30 minutes.

2 Place paper baking cup in each of 12 regular-size muffin cups. Use remaining batter to fill muffin cups about $2/3$ full. Bake and cool as directed in recipe. Save extra cupcakes for another use.

3 In medium bowl, place $1 1/2$ cups powdered sugar. Add marshmallow creme; stir, pressing mixture against side of bowl until it clumps together. Knead on work surface, gradually adding remaining $1/2$ cup powdered sugar until dough is smooth.

4 Lightly spray serving platter with cooking spray to prevent cupcakes from sticking to platter. Shape fondant into ghosts as directed on opposite page. Place 2 miniature chocolate chips on face for eyes and 1 for mouth (if necessary, moisten fondant with a little water so chips stick). Repeat with remaining cones, fondant and chips.

1 Cupcake Cone: Calories 310; Total Fat 8g (Saturated Fat 2g; Trans Fat 1g); Cholesterol 20mg; Sodium 190mg; Total Carbohydrate 58g (Dietary Fiber 1g); Protein 2g **Exchanges:** 1 Starch, 3 Other Carbohydrate, 1 1/2 Fat **Carbohydrate Choices:** 4

sweet success tip

If the fondant tears, just pinch it back together.

use a cake mix

Substitute 1 box devil's food cake mix for the Chocolate Cupcakes. Make cake as directed on box. Fill each cone with 2 tablespoons batter. Set remaining batter aside. Stand cones upright in muffin pan. Bake 15 to 20 minutes or until toothpick inserted in center comes out clean. Cool completely, about 30 minutes. Place paper baking cup in each of 18 regular-size muffin cups. Use remaining batter to fill muffin cups about $2/3$ full. Bake and cool as directed on box. Save for another use. Make fondant, assemble ghosts and decorate as directed in recipe. 12 cupcake cones and 18 extra cupcakes

to form ghosts:

1. Generously sprinkle powdered sugar on work surface and hands. On work surface, shape fondant into 12 balls (each 1½ inches in diameter).

2. Flatten each to 5½-inch round.

3. Turn 1 cone upside down, and place 1 fondant round over cone, draping fondant to form ghost body.

skeleton **cupcakes**

24 cupcakes **PREP TIME: 1 Hour** START TO FINISH: **2 Hours 15 Minutes**

Chocolate Cupcakes (page 15)

Creamy Chocolate Frosting (page 20)

24 yogurt-covered or white chocolate–covered pretzel twists

White decorating icing (from 6.4-oz can)

1 Make, bake and cool Chocolate Cupcakes as directed in recipe.

2 Make Creamy Chocolate Frosting as directed in recipe. Frost cupcakes.

3 Place 1 pretzel in center of each cupcake for chest of skeleton. Use decorating icing to draw and fill in head, arms, legs and feet of skeleton. To create eye sockets and mouth openings, insert toothpick into white icing in head; move toothpick in tiny circular motions to move icing away so chocolate frosting shows through.

1 Cupcake: Calories 280; Total Fat 14g (Saturated Fat 8g; Trans Fat 0g); Cholesterol 60mg; Sodium 220mg; Total Carbohydrate 38g (Dietary Fiber 0g); Protein 2g **Exchanges:** 1 1/2 Starch, 1 Other Carbohydrate, 2 1/2 Fat **Carbohydrate Choices:** 2 1/2

sweet success tip

Can't find white chocolate–covered pretzels? Make your own by dipping pretzels in melted white baking chocolate.

use a cake mix

Substitute 1 box devil's food cake mix for the Chocolate Cupcakes. Make cake mix as directed on box for cupcakes. For the frosting, substitute 1 container chocolate creamy ready-to-spread frosting. Frost and decorate as directed in recipe.

witch's hat **cupcakes**

24 cupcakes PREP TIME: **1 Hour** START TO FINISH: **2 Hours 40 Minutes**

CUPCAKES

Yellow Cupcakes (page 14)

FROSTING

2 recipes of Vanilla Buttercream Frosting (page 20)

Orange paste food color

DECORATIONS

24 fudge-striped shortbread cookies

24 chewy chocolate candies (from 6-oz bag), unwrapped

Star candy decors, if desired

1 Make, bake and cool Yellow Cupcakes as directed in recipe.

2 Make Vanilla Buttercream Frosting as directed in recipe. Tint frosting to desired shade of orange with food color. Place $1/2$ cup frosting in small resealable food-storage plastic bag; seal bag and set aside. Frost cupcakes with remaining orange frosting.

3 Place 1 cookie, striped side down, on each cupcake. Shape chocolate candies into cone shapes to resemble tops of hats; press onto cookies.

4 Cut tiny (about $1/8$-inch) tip off one bottom corner of bag of frosting. Pipe frosting around base of chocolate candy to resemble ribbon band. Decorate hat with star candy decors.

1 Cupcake: Calories 590; Total Fat 22g (Saturated Fat 13g; Trans Fat 1.5g); Cholesterol 75mg; Sodium 310mg; Total Carbohydrate 93g (Dietary Fiber 0g); Protein 3g **Exchanges:** 1 Starch, 5 Other Carbohydrate, 4 $1/2$ Fat **Carbohydrate Choices:** 6

Witch's Head Cupcakes: Make 2 recipes of Vanilla Buttercream Frosting; tint to desired shade of light orange. Place $1/2$ cup frosting in small resealable food-storage plastic bag; seal bag and set aside. Do not frost cupcakes. With ice cream scoop, scoop about $1/4$ cup of frosting onto each cupcake. (If frosting is too soft to hold shape, stir in additional powdered sugar.) Use pieces of string licorice for hair and assorted small candies for face, pressing lightly into frosting. Make hats as directed above; place on top of licorice hair.

use a cake mix

Substitute 1 box yellow cake mix for the Yellow Cupcakes. Make cake mix as directed on box for cupcakes. Continue as directed in recipe.

haunting halloween cupcakes

Halloween is all about treats to make little and big goblins howl with delight. Make one of your favorite cupcakes from the Basics chapter. Prepare Vanilla Buttercream Frosting on page 20 for all of these cupcakes except the cat; for the cat, use Creamy Chocolate Frosting on page 20. Frost and decorate to create your own goulish cupcakes!

Sparkly Pumpkins

Tint frosting with orange paste food color. Reserve ¾ cup. Frost cupcakes; sprinkle with orange decorator sugar. Use broken pretzels for stems. Pipe lines of reserved frosting onto cupcakes, using #4 round tip. Slice leaf-shaped gumdrop horizontally into strips for green part of stem. Use purchased green frosting to pipe vines using round tip.

Pumpkin Patch Graveyards

Make 2 recipes of frosting; tint 4½ cups with green paste food color. Use remaining frosting to frost cupcakes. Sprinkle centers of cupcakes with crushed chocolate wafer cookies for dirt. Pipe purchased black frosting onto peanut butter sandwich cookies for gravestones. Pipe reserved green frosting using #22 tip for grass.

Roaming Ghosts

Reserve ¼ cup frosting; tint remaining frosting with orange paste food color. Frost cupcakes. To make ghosts, stack 2 small gumdrops together with a dab of reserved frosting. Roll large white gumdrops with rolling pin; drape over stacked small gumdrops on cupcake. Press candy corn onto plastic pick for torch. Use purchased black frosting for ghost faces and writing using round tip.

Bewitching Black Cats

Immediately top chocolate-frosted cupcakes with chocolate sprinkles. For eyes, press chocolate-covered candies into frosting. Pipe slits on eyes with additional frosting using #3 tip. Add candy corn for ears, gumdrop for nose and red and black string licorice for whiskers and mouth.

mini pumpkin **cupcakes**

72 mini cakes   **PREP TIME: 1 Hour 25 Minutes** START TO FINISH: **2 Hours 15 Minutes**

CUPCAKES

   White Cupcakes (page 16)
2   teaspoons grated orange peel
6   to 8 drops red food color
6   to 8 drops yellow food color

FROSTING

   Vanilla Buttercream Frosting
   (page 20)
8   drops red food color
10 drops yellow food color

DECORATIONS

5   tubes (0.68 oz each) black
    decorating gel
5   rolls chewy fruit snack in
    3-foot rolls, any green variety
    (from 4.5-oz box), or small
    green candies

1 Make mini version of White Cupcakes as directed in recipe variation except—stir in orange peel, 6 to 8 drops red food color and 6 to 8 drops yellow food color until desired orange color. Bake and cool as directed in recipe.

2 Make Vanilla Buttercream Frosting as directed in recipe. Stir in 8 drops red food color and 10 drops yellow food color to make orange frosting. Frost mini cupcakes.

3 Using black gel, draw 2 triangles on each cupcake to look like pumpkin eyes, and draw a circle to look like a mouth. Cut fruit snack into 72 (1-inch) pieces; tightly roll each piece to make a stem for each pumpkin. Place stem at top of each pumpkin.

1 Mini Cake: Calories 110; Total Fat 4g (Saturated Fat 1.5g; Trans Fat 0g); Cholesterol 0mg; Sodium 55mg; Total Carbohydrate 19g (Dietary Fiber 0g); Protein 1g **Exchanges:** 1/2 Starch, 1 Other Carbohydrate, 1/2 Fat **Carbohydrate Choices:** 1

sweet success tip

For a more vivid pumpkin color, use paste food color instead of liquid in the frosting.

use a cake mix

Substitute 1 box white cake mix for the White Cupcakes. Place mini paper baking cup in each of 48 mini muffin cups. Make cake mix as directed on box for cupcakes **except**—add 2 teaspoons grated orange peel, 6 drops red food color and 8 drops yellow food color. Divide batter evenly among muffin cups, about 1 heaping tablespoon each. Bake 14 to 18 minutes or until toothpick inserted in center of cupcake comes out clean. Cool 5 minutes. Remove from pans; place on cooling racks to cool. For the frosting, substitute 1 container vanilla creamy ready-to-spread frosting, and stir in 6 drops red food color and 8 drops yellow food color. Frost cupcakes. Decorate with 3 tubes decorating gel and 3 rolls fruit snack as directed in recipe. 48 mini cupcakes

thanksgiving turkey cupcakes

24 cupcakes   **PREP TIME: 1 Hour 10 Minutes** START TO FINISH: **2 Hours 10 Minutes**

CUPCAKES

Yellow Cupcakes (page 14)

$^3/_4$ cup creamy peanut butter

FROSTING

Creamy Chocolate Frosting
(page 20)

DECORATIONS

4 oz vanilla-flavored candy
coating (almond bark)

4 oz semisweet baking chocolate

24 milk chocolate candy drops or
pieces, unwrapped

1 Make Yellow Cupcakes as directed in recipe except—decrease butter to $^3/_4$ cup and stir in peanut butter with the vanilla. Bake and cool as directed in recipe.

2 Make Creamy Chocolate Frosting as directed in recipe. Frost cupcakes.

3 Line cookie sheet with waxed paper. In separate small microwavable bowls, microwave candy coating and baking chocolate uncovered on High 30 to 60 seconds, stirring every 15 seconds, until melted and smooth. Place coating and chocolate in separate resealable food-storage plastic bags; snip off tiny bottom corner of each bag. Pipe coating and chocolate into feather shapes, about 3 inches long and 2 $^1/_2$ inches wide, as shown in photo. Refrigerate coating and chocolate about 5 minutes until set.

4 When set, peel feathers off waxed paper and insert into cupcakes. Place milk chocolate candy on each cupcake for head of turkey.

1 Cupcake: Calories 400; Total Fat 21g (Saturated Fat 11g; Trans Fat 0g); Cholesterol 55mg; Sodium 250mg; Total Carbohydrate 46g (Dietary Fiber 2g); Protein 6g **Exchanges:** 1 $^1/_2$ Starch, 1 $^1/_2$ Other Carbohydrate, 4 Fat **Carbohydrate Choices:** 3

use a cake mix

Substitute 1 box yellow cake mix for the Yellow Cupcakes. Make cake mix as directed on box for cupcakes **except**—add $^3/_4$ cup creamy peanut butter with the eggs. For the frosting, substitute 1 container chocolate creamy ready-to-spread frosting. Frost and decorate as directed in recipe.

hanukkah **dreidel cupcakes**

24 cupcakes   PREP TIME: **55 Minutes** START TO FINISH: **1 Hour 50 Minutes**

White Cupcakes (page 16)
1 cup milk
1 container (6 oz) French vanilla low-fat yogurt
Vanilla Buttercream Frosting (page 20)
Blue decorator sugar
24 caramels, unwrapped
12 pretzel sticks, cut in half
24 Hershey®'s Hugs® white and milk chocolates, unwrapped
Blue decorating icing (from 6.4-oz can)

1 Make White Cupcakes as directed in recipe except—use 1 cup milk and 1 container yogurt for the 1 1/4 cups milk. Divide batter evenly among muffin cups, filling each about 2/3 full.

2 Bake 18 to 20 minutes or until toothpick inserted in center of cupcake comes out clean. Cool 5 minutes; remove from pans to cooling racks to cool.

3 Make Vanilla Buttercream Frosting as directed in recipe. Reserve 1 tablespoon frosting for decorating. Frost cupcakes with remaining frosting. Sprinkle with blue decorator sugar.

4 In small microwavable bowl, microwave 6 caramels uncovered on High 5 to 10 seconds or just until slightly softened. Poke 1 pretzel half into each softened caramel to look like top of dreidel. Repeat with remaining caramels and pretzels. Attach chocolate to bottom of each caramel with small amount of reserved frosting.

5 Use blue icing to make decorations on 3 sides of dreidels. Place 1 dreidel on each frosted cupcake.

1 Cupcake: Calories 350; Total Fat 12g (Saturated Fat 5g; Trans Fat 1.5g); Cholesterol 15mg; Sodium 170mg; Total Carbohydrate 57g (Dietary Fiber 0g); Protein 3g **Exchanges:** 1/2 Starch, 3 1/2 Other Carbohydrate, 2 1/2 Fat **Carbohydrate Choices:** 4

HERSHEY'S and HUGS trademarks and trade dress are registered trademarks used under license.

use a cake mix

Substitute 1 box white cake mix for the White Cupcakes. Make cake mix as directed on box for cupcakes **except**—use 1 cup water, 1 container (6 oz) French vanilla low-fat yogurt, 1/3 cup vegetable oil and 3 egg whites. Bake and cool as directed on box. For the frosting, substitute 1 container vanilla creamy ready-to-spread frosting. Decorate as directed in recipe.

peppermint **twist cupcakes**

24 cupcakes   PREP TIME: **55 Minutes** START TO FINISH: **1 Hour 50 Minutes**

CUPCAKES
White Cupcakes (page 16)
1/4 teaspoon peppermint extract
Red paste food color

PEPPERMINT FROSTING
5 cups powdered sugar
1/2 cup butter or margarine, softened
1 teaspoon peppermint extract
6 to 8 tablespoons milk

GARNISH
Red liquid food color

1 Make White Cupcakes as directed in recipe except—spoon 1 1/2 cups cake batter into small bowl; stir in 1/4 teaspoon peppermint extract and paste food color to make red batter.

2 Into each muffin cup, spoon about 1 tablespoon white cake batter. Top with about 1 tablespoon red batter, then 1 tablespoon white batter. With table knife, draw an "S" in batter of each muffin cup to swirl batter.

3 Bake 18 to 20 minutes or until toothpick inserted in center of cupcake comes out clean. Cool 5 minutes; remove from pans to cooling racks to cool.

4 Meanwhile, in large bowl, beat powdered sugar, butter, 1 teaspoon peppermint extract and 6 tablespoons milk with electric mixer on medium speed until smooth. Beat in additional milk, 1 teaspoon at a time, until smooth and spreadable. Spread scant 2 tablespoons frosting on each cupcake.

5 With tiny paintbrush, "paint" liquid food color in swirl pattern on frosting on each cupcake.

1 Cupcake: Calories 310; Total Fat 11g (Saturated Fat 4.5g; Trans Fat 1.5g); Cholesterol 10mg; Sodium 160mg; Total Carbohydrate 51g (Dietary Fiber 0g); Protein 3g **Exchanges:** 1 Starch, 2 1/2 Other Carbohydrate, 2 Fat **Carbohydrate Choices:** 3 1/2

sweet success tip
For an easy decoration on the tops of these cupcakes, sprinkle with crushed peppermint candies.

use a cake mix

Substitute 1 box white cake mix for the White Cupcakes. Make cake mix as directed on box **except**—spoon 1 1/4 cups cake batter into small bowl; stir in 1/4 teaspoon peppermint extract and red food color. Into each muffin cup, spoon about 1 tablespoon white cake batter. Top with scant 1 tablespoon red batter, then 1 tablespoon white batter. With table knife, draw an "S" in batter of each muffin cup to swirl batter. Bake and cool as directed. For the frosting, substitute 1 container butter cream or vanilla creamy ready-to-spread frosting mixed with 1/4 teaspoon peppermint extract. Frost and decorate as directed in recipe.

poinsettia **cupcake wreath**

24 cupcakes   PREP TIME: **3 Hours 45 Minutes** START TO FINISH: **4 Hours 40 Minutes**

Yellow Cupcakes (page 14)
Decorator Icing (page 21)
60 colored chewy candies
(1 inch), (from 14-oz bag)
Green and yellow decorating
icing (from 6.4-oz cans)

1 Make, bake and cool Yellow Cupcakes as directed in recipe.

2 Make Decorator Icing as directed in recipe. Frost cupcakes.

3 In small microwavable bowl, microwave 2 candies uncovered on High 10 to 15 seconds or until warm enough to be pliable. Form petals following the directions on opposite page. Repeat with remaining candies.

4 On each cupcake, arrange 5 candy petals in shape of poinsettia. Using leaf tip, pipe green icing between some of the petals for leaves. With round tip and yellow icing, pipe dots in center of petals for stamen. To form wreath, arrange 12 cupcakes in circle on serving platter. Serve remaining cupcakes on another platter.

1 Cupcake: Calories 300; Total Fat 15g (Saturated Fat 8g; Trans Fat 1g); Cholesterol 60mg; Sodium 230mg; Total Carbohydrate 40g (Dietary Fiber 0g); Protein 2g **Exchanges:** ½ Starch, 2 Other Carbohydrate, 3 Fat **Carbohydrate Choices:** 2 ½

sweet success tip
Make flower petals up to 1 week ahead. Store in an airtight container, between sheets of waxed paper, at room temperature.

use a cake mix

Substitute 1 box yellow cake mix for the Yellow Cupcakes. Make cake mix as directed on box for cupcakes. For the frosting, substitute 1 container vanilla creamy ready-to-spread frosting. Decorate as directed in recipe.

to form petals:

1. Cut candies in half.

2. Form each half into flower petal, 1¼ inches long.

3. Use toothpick or paring knife to make marks on petals to look like veins.

almond-filled white christmas cupcakes

24 cupcakes   PREP TIME: **55 Minutes** START TO FINISH: **2 Hours 20 Minutes**

FILLING

- 1/2   cup finely chopped blanched almonds
- 1/4   cup granulated sugar
- 1/2   teaspoon grated lemon peel
- 1   egg white, slightly beaten

CUPCAKES

White Cupcakes (page 16)

WHITE CHOCOLATE-BUTTERCREAM FROSTING

- 1/2   cup whipping cream
- 4   oz white chocolate baking bars, chopped
- 1/3   cup white crème de cacao or cold brewed coffee
- 2   cups powdered sugar
- 1   cup butter or margarine, softened

GARNISH

White sanding sugar

1 Heat oven to 350°F. In small bowl, mix filling ingredients; set aside.

2 Make White Cupcakes as directed in recipe except—spoon about 1 1/2 teaspoons filling onto center of batter in each cup. Bake and cool as directed in recipe.

3 Meanwhile, in 1 1/2-quart saucepan, heat whipping cream and white chocolate over medium heat, stirring constantly, until chocolate is melted. Remove from heat; stir in crème de cacao. Refrigerate 30 minutes.

4 In medium bowl, beat powdered sugar and butter with electric mixer on medium speed, scraping bowl occasionally, until fluffy. Beat in chilled white chocolate mixture until smooth.

5 Frost cupcakes. Sprinkle each with sanding sugar.

1 Cupcake: Calories 360; Total Fat 19g (Saturated Fat 9g; Trans Fat 1.5g); Cholesterol 30mg; Sodium 190mg; Total Carbohydrate 43g (Dietary Fiber 0g); Protein 4g **Exchanges:** 1 1/2 Starch, 1 1/2 Other Carbohydrate, 3 1/2 Fat **Carbohydrate Choices:** 3

sweet success tip

Blanched almonds are almonds that have the skin removed. They can be found in the baking aisle of your supermarket.

use a cake mix

Substitute 1 box white cake mix for the White Cupcakes. Make filling as directed in recipe. Make cake mix as directed on box for cupcakes **except**—spoon about 1 1/2 teaspoons filling onto center of batter in each cup. Bake and cool as directed on box. Continue as directed in recipe.

holiday fruit **cupcakes with rum buttercream frosting**

About 28 cupcakes **PREP TIME: 25 Minutes START TO FINISH: 1 Hour 30 Minutes**

CUPCAKES

2 3/4	cups all-purpose flour
3	teaspoons baking powder
1/2	teaspoon salt
3/4	cup shortening
1 2/3	cups granulated sugar
5	egg whites
2	teaspoons vanilla
2	teaspoons rum extract
1 1/4	cups milk
1/2	cup finely chopped dried apricots
1/2	cup finely chopped sweetened dried pineapple
1/2	cup sweetened dried cherries or cranberries
1/2	cup chopped pecans

RUM BUTTERCREAM FROSTING

Vanilla Buttercream Frosting (page 20)

1   tablespoon dark rum or 1 teaspoon rum extract

DECORATIONS, IF DESIRED

Additional dried apricots, pineapple, cherries or cranberries

Additional pecans

1 Heat oven to 350°F. Place paper baking cup in each of 28 regular-size muffin cups. In medium bowl, stir together flour, baking powder and salt; set aside.

2 In large bowl, beat shortening with electric mixer on medium speed 30 seconds. Gradually add sugar, about 1/3 cup at a time, beating after each addition and scraping bowl occasionally. Beat 2 minutes longer. Add egg whites, 1 at a time, beating well after each addition. Beat in vanilla and rum extract. On low speed, alternately add flour mixture, about 1/3 of mixture at a time, and milk, about 1/2 at a time, beating just until blended. Stir in dried fruit and pecans.

3 Divide batter evenly among muffin cups, filling each about 2/3 full.

4 Bake 18 to 22 minutes or until toothpick inserted in center of cupcake comes out clean. Cool 5 minutes. Remove cupcakes from pans; place on cooling racks to cool.

5 Make Vanilla Buttercream Frosting as directed in recipe except— substitute dark rum for the vanilla. Frost cupcakes. Decorate with dried fruits and pecans.

1 Cupcake: Calories 330; Total Fat 12g (Saturated Fat 4.5g; Trans Fat 1g); Cholesterol 15mg; Sodium 140mg; Total Carbohydrate 53g (Dietary Fiber 1g); Protein 2g **Exchanges:** 1/2 Starch, 3 Other Carbohydrate, 2 1/2 Fat **Carbohydrate Choices:** 3 1/2

sweet success tip

If you don't want to purchase 3 different types of dried fruit, purchase two, and increase the amounts by 1/4 cup each in the cupcakes.

use a cake mix

Substitute 1 box white cake mix for the cupcakes above. In medium bowl, toss 1/2 cup finely chopped dried apricots, 1/2 cup finely chopped sweetened dried pineapple, 1/2 cup sweetened dried cherries or cranberries and 1/2 cup chopped pecans with 2 tablespoons all-purpose flour. Make cake mix as directed on box for cupcakes **except**—stir in dried fruit mixture and 1/2 teaspoon almond extract. Bake and cool as directed on box. For the frosting, substitute 1 container vanilla creamy ready-to-spread frosting mixed with 1/2 teaspoon rum extract. Frost and decorate as directed in recipe. 24 cupcakes

eggnog–poppy seed cupcakes

24 cupcakes   PREP TIME: **15 Minutes** START TO FINISH: **1 Hour 15 Minutes**

CUPCAKES

White Cupcakes (page 16)
1 teaspoon poppy seed
1/4 teaspoon nutmeg
1 1/4 cups eggnog

FROSTING AND GARNISH

Vanilla Buttercream Frosting (page 20)
2 to 4 tablespoons eggnog
3 teaspoons poppy seed

1 Make White Cupcakes as directed in recipe except—add 1 teaspoon poppy seed and the nutmeg with the flour and substitute 1 1/4 cups eggnog for the milk. Bake and cool as directed in recipe.

2 Make Vanilla Buttercream Frosting as directed in recipe except—use 2 to 4 tablespoons eggnog for the milk. Frost cupcakes. Sprinkle each with about 1/8 teaspoon poppy seed.

1 Cupcake: Calories 360; Total Fat 13g (Saturated Fat 6g; Trans Fat 1.5g); Cholesterol 25mg; Sodium 170mg; Total Carbohydrate 57g (Dietary Fiber 0g); Protein 3g **Exchanges:** 1 Starch, 3 Other Carbohydrate, 2 1/2 Fat **Carbohydrate Choices:** 4

sweet success tip

During the holidays, eggnog can be found in the dairy section of your favorite supermarket.

use a cake mix

Substitute 1 box white cake mix for the White Cupcakes. Make cake mix as directed on box for cupcakes **except**—use 1 1/4 cups eggnog, 1/3 cup vegetable oil, 3 egg whites, and stir 1 teaspoon poppy seed and 1/4 teaspoon ground nutmeg into the batter. Bake and cool as directed on box. For the frosting, substitute 1 container vanilla creamy ready-to-spread frosting. Frost and garnish as directed in recipe.

christmas pomegranate **cupcakes**

24 cupcakes   PREP TIME: **20 Minutes** START TO FINISH: **1 Hour 15 Minutes**

CUPCAKES

2 3/4 cups all-purpose flour

  3 teaspoons baking powder

1/2 teaspoon salt

3/4 cup shortening

1 2/3 cups granulated sugar

  5 egg whites

2 1/2 teaspoons vanilla

1 1/4 cups milk

  1 cup pomegranate seeds
(from 1 pomegranate)

FROSTING

Cream Cheese Frosting
(page 20)

GARNISH

  6 tablespoons pomegranate seeds
Fresh mint sprigs, if desired

1 Heat oven to 350°F. Place paper baking cup in each of 24 regular-size muffin cups, grease and flour muffin cups, or spray with baking spray with flour.

2 In medium bowl, stir together flour, baking powder and salt; set aside. In large bowl, beat shortening with electric mixer on medium speed 30 seconds. Gradually add sugar, about 1/3 cup at a time, beating after each addition and scraping bowl occasionally. Beat 2 minutes longer. Add egg whites, one at a time, beating well after each addition. Beat in vanilla. On low speed, alternately add flour mixture, about 1/3 of mixture at a time, and milk, about 1/2 at a time, beating just until blended. Stir in 1 cup pomegranate seeds.

3 Divide batter evenly among muffin cups, filling each about 2/3 full.

4 Bake 18 to 20 minutes or until toothpick inserted in center of cupcake comes out clean. Cool 5 minutes. Remove cupcakes from pans; place on cooling racks to cool.

5 Make Cream Cheese Frosting as directed in recipe. Frost cupcakes. Sprinkle each with 1 teaspoon pomegranate seeds. Place cupcakes on platter; surround with mint sprigs.

1 Cupcake: Calories 320; Total Fat 12g (Saturated Fat 5g; Trans Fat 1.5g); Cholesterol 15mg; Sodium 170mg; Total Carbohydrate 48g (Dietary Fiber 0g); Protein 3g **Exchanges:** 1 Starch, 2 Other Carbohydrate, 2 1/2 Fat **Carbohydrate Choices:** 3

sweet success tip

To uncover the brilliant ruby red pomegranate seeds, cut a pomegranate in half and use a spoon to remove the seeds. Discard any of the light-colored membrane that may stick to the seeds.

use a cake mix

Substitute 1 box white cake mix for the cupcakes above. Make cake mix as directed on box for cupcakes **except**—use 1 cup water, 1/3 cup vegetable oil and 3 egg whites. Toss 1 cup pomegranate seeds with 2 tablespoons all-purpose flour; stir into batter. Bake and cool as directed on box. For the frosting, substitute 1 container vanilla creamy ready-to-spread frosting. Frost and garnish as directed in recipe.

very merry holiday ornament cupcakes

These whimsical cupcakes are sure to delight guests and provide merriment for the holidays. Make one of your favorite cupcakes from the basics chapter; prepare Vanilla Buttercream frosting on page 20. Frost the cupcakes and after decorating, complete the ornament topping by inserting a piece of string licorice and a foil wrapped chocolate-covered candy.

Distinguished Diamonds

Prepare 1½ recipes of frosting. Pipe frosting using #4 round tip to make parallel diagonal lines, about ½-inch apart. Pipe lines at a diagonal in the opposite direction, over first lines, forming diamond pattern; sprinkle with decorator sugar. Press red candy sprinkles into frosting where lines intersect.

Dazzling Swirls

Sprinkle with decorator sugar. Pipe purchased green and red frosting to make swirls, using small round tip, in a tight zig-zag pattern, gradually making wider zig-zags toward edge of cupcakes.

Merry Stripes

Sprinkle with decorator sugar. Make stripes on cupcakes using red string licorice. Or you can make stripes with colored canned frosting. Press red candy sprinkles onto stripes using dab of frosting on toothpick for "glue".

Squiggle And Dots

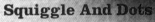

Sprinkle with decorator sugar. Pipe purchased green frosting, using small round tip, across cupcake in squiggly line. Press red candy-coated fruit-flavored chewy candies into frosting.

snowman **cupcakes**

24 cupcakes   **PREP TIME: 1 Hour 25 Minutes** START TO FINISH: **2 Hours 20 Minutes**

CUPCAKES
   White Cupcakes (page 16)

FROSTING
   Fluffy White Frosting (page 21)

DECORATIONS
   White decorator sugar crystals
 1 bag (16 oz) large marshmallows
   Pretzel sticks
   Chewy fruit snack rolls in 3-foot rolls, any red or orange flavor (from 4.5-oz box)
   Assorted candies (such as gumdrops, gummy ring candies, peppermint candies, chocolate chips, pastel mint chips, candy decors, string licorice)

1 Make, bake and cool White Cupcakes as directed in recipe.

2 Make Fluffy White Frosting as directed in recipe. Set aside $1/4$ cup frosting. Frost cupcakes with remaining frosting.

3 Sprinkle frosting with sugar crystals. Stack 2 or 3 marshmallows on each cupcake, using $1/2$ teaspoon frosting between marshmallows to attach.

4 For arms, break pretzel sticks into pieces $1 1/2$ inches long. Press 2 pieces into marshmallow on each cupcake. Cut 1-inch mitten shapes from fruit snack. Attach mittens to pretzels. For scarves, cut fruit snack into $6 \times 1/4$-inch pieces; wrap and tie around base of top marshmallows. For hats, stack candies, using frosting to attach. For earmuffs, use piece of string licorice and candies, using frosting to attach. For faces and buttons, attach desired candies with small amounts of frosting.

1 Frosted Cupcake (Undecorated): Calories 210; Total Fat 7g (Saturated Fat 2g; Trans Fat 1g); Cholesterol 0mg; Sodium 135mg; Total Carbohydrate 33g (Dietary Fiber 0g); Protein 3g **Exchanges:** 1 Starch, 1 Other Carbohydrate, 1 $1/2$ Fat **Carbohydrate Choices:** 2

sweet success tip
There are lots of clever ways to decorate snow people. Check your pantry for colorful candies you might have on hand and create your own snow creatures!

use a cake mix

Substitute 1 box white cake mix for the White Cupcakes. Make cake mix as directed on box for cupcakes. For the frosting, substitute 1 container fluffy white ready-to-spread frosting; set aside $1/4$ cup frosting. Frost and decorate as directed in recipe.

rudolph **cupcakes**

24 cupcakes   **PREP TIME: 1 Hour 5 Minutes** START TO FINISH: **2 Hours 5 Minutes**

CUPCAKES

Chocolate Cupcakes (page 15)

FROSTING AND DECORATIONS

Creamy Chocolate Frosting
(page 20)

Chocolate candy sprinkles

24   large pretzel twists

24   miniature marshmallows

24   red cinnamon candies

24   small green gumdrops

1 Make, bake and cool Chocolate Cupcakes as directed in recipe.

2 Make Creamy Chocolate Frosting as directed in recipe. Frost cupcakes. Sprinkle candy sprinkles over tops of cupcakes.

3 For each cupcake, cut pretzel twist in half; arrange on cupcake for reindeer antlers. Cut miniature marshmallow in half; arrange on cupcake for eyes. Center gumdrop below marshmallow halves for nose. Place red cinnamon candy below gumdrop for mouth.

1 Frosted Cupcake (Undecorated): Calories 280; Total Fat 12g (Saturated Fat 5g; Trans Fat 1g); Cholesterol 30mg; Sodium 200mg; Total Carbohydrate 39g (Dietary Fiber 1g); Protein 2g **Exchanges:** ½ Starch, 2 Other Carbohydrate, 2 ½ Fat **Carbohydrate Choices:** 2 ½

sweet success tip

Save time during the holidays! Freeze these cupcakes in an airtight freezer container up to 4 months. Decorate the frozen cupcakes; they'll thaw while you're decorating.

use a cake mix

Substitute 1 box devil's food cake mix for the Chocolate Cupcakes. Make cake mix as directed on box for cupcakes. For the frosting, substitute 1 container chocolate creamy ready-to-spread frosting. Frost and decorate as directed in recipe.

snow-capped **gingerbread train**

10 regular cupcakes and 18 mini cupcakes   PREP TIME: **1 Hour 5 Minutes** START TO FINISH: **2 Hours**

CUPCAKES AND FROSTING

Gingerbread Cupcakes with Cream Cheese Frosting (page 66)

DECORATIONS

Assorted candies (such as candy-coated chocolate pieces, round chewy caramels in milk chocolate, chewy fruit snacks, licorice twists, hard round peppermint candies, fruit-flavored ring-shaped hard candies and gumdrops)

Pretzel sticks

Sample-size cones

1 Heat oven to 350°F. Grease and flour 10 regular-size muffin cups, or spray with baking spray with flour. Place mini paper baking cup in each of 18 mini muffin cups.

2 Make Gingerbread Cupcakes as directed in recipe except—fill regular and mini muffin cups about $2/3$ full of batter.

3 Bake regular cupcakes 15 to 18 minutes, mini cupcakes 11 to 15 minutes, or until toothpick inserted in center of cupcake comes out clean. Cool 5 minutes; remove from pans to cooling racks to cool.

4 Make Cream Cheese Frosting as directed in Gingerbread Cupcakes recipe; reserve $1/2$ cup frosting for decorating. Frost cupcakes with remaining frosting leaving one regular size cupcake unfrosted. Place 5 regular cupcakes on serving platter. Cut unfrosted cupcake in half; place upside down at front of train as shown. Attach mini cupcakes to both sides of train with frosting and connect with pretzel sticks. Add additional cupcakes to front and back of train as shown. Decorate with candies, pretzel sticks and cone, as desired (attaching with frosting as needed). Serve any remaining cupcakes, as desired.

1 Frosted Cupcake (Undecorated): Calories 320; Total Fat 13g (Saturated Fat 8g; Trans Fat 0g); Cholesterol 60mg; Sodium 240mg; Total Carbohydrate 49g (Dietary Fiber 0g); Protein 3g **Exchanges:** $1/2$ Starch, 3 Other Carbohydrate, 2 $1/2$ Fat **Carbohydrate Choices:** 3

sweet success tip

Use cream cheese ready-to-spread frosting instead of the homemade. You'll still get rave reviews for these sensational sweets!

gnome's homes cupcakes

18 regular cupcakes and 18 mini cupcakes   PREP TIME: **1 Hour 30 Minutes** START TO FINISH: **4 Hours 5 Minutes**

Chocolate Cupcakes (page 15)

Creamy Chocolate Frosting
(page 20)

Assorted candies (such as
chewy fruit candies, suckers,
sugar decors, candy sprinkles,
chocolate-covered almonds,
if desired

Green decorator icing, if desired

1   Make Chocolate Cupcakes as directed in recipe except—grease and flour
18 regular-size muffin cups, or spray with baking spray with flour, and place
mini paper baking cup in each of 18 mini muffin cups. Divide batter evenly
among muffin cups, filling each about $2/3$ full.

2   Bake regular cupcakes 18 to 25 minutes, mini cupcakes 12 to 20 minutes,
or until toothpick inserted in center of cupcake comes out clean. Cool in pans
5 minutes. Remove cupcakes from pans; place on cooling racks to cool.

3   Meanwhile, make Creamy Chocolate Frosting as directed in recipe.
Remove paper liners from mini cupcakes. Frost and decorate regular and mini
cupcakes to resemble village of tiny homes with assorted candies and icing.

1 Frosted Cupcake (Undecorated): Calories 300; Total Fat 13g (Saturated Fat 5g; Trans Fat 1.5g); Cholesterol
30mg; Sodium 220mg; Total Carbohydrate 42g (Dietary Fiber 1g); Protein 2g **Exchanges:** 1 Starch, 2 Other
Carbohydrate, 2 $1/2$ Fat **Carbohydrate Choices:** 3

sweet success tip

Create a holiday "Gnome Village"; use red and green colored candies to
decorate. Use coconut to resemble snow and chocolate-covered raisins or
candy rocks for boulders.

use a cake mix

Substitute 1 box chocolate cake mix for the Chocolate Cupcakes. Make cake
mix as directed on box for cupcakes **except**—place paper baking cup in
each of 18 regular-size muffin cups and mini paper baking cup in each of
18 mini muffin cups. Divide batter evenly among muffin cups. Bake regular
cupcakes as directed on box; bake mini cupcakes 10 to 15 minutes. Cool as
directed on box. Frost and decorate as directed in recipe.

red velvet elf cupcakes

24 cupcakes   **PREP TIME: 1 Hour 10 Minutes** START TO FINISH: **2 Hours 20 Minutes**

CUPCAKES

2 1/4	cup all-purpose flour
1/4	cup unsweetened baking cocoa
1	teaspoon baking soda
1	teaspoon salt
1/2	cup butter or margarine, softened
1 1/4	cups sugar
2	eggs
1	bottle (1 oz) red food color (about 2 tablespoons)
1 1/2	teaspoons vanilla
1	cup buttermilk

FROSTING

Cream Cheese Frosting (page 20)

DECORATIONS

6	dried apricot halves
6	rolls chewy fruit snacks, any flavor (from 5-oz box)
24	small red gum drops (from 10-oz package), cut in half
48	semisweet chocolate chips (from 8-oz package)
1	tube (7 oz) red decorating cookie icing

1 Heat oven to 350°F. Place paper baking cup in each of 24 regular-size muffin cups. In small bowl, stir together flour, cocoa, baking soda and salt; set aside.

2 In large bowl, beat butter and sugar with electric mixer on medium speed until mixed. Add eggs; beat 1 to 2 minutes or until light and fluffy. Beat in food color and vanilla. On low speed, alternately add flour mixture, about 1/3 at a time, and buttermilk, about 1/2 at a time, beating just until blended. Divide batter evenly among muffin cups, filling each 2/3 full.

3 Bake 20 to 25 minutes or until toothpick inserted in center of cupcake comes out clean. Cool 5 minutes. Remove cupcakes from pans; place on cooling racks to cool.

4 Make Cream Cheese Frosting as directed in recipe. Reserve 1 tablespoon frosting; frost cupcakes with remaining frosting.

5 Cut each apricot half into 8 pieces; place 2 pieces on each side of cupcakes for ears. Cut each fruit snack into 4 triangles. Place 1 triangle on top of each cupcake, folding pointed end over to form hat. Attach 1 gumdrop to pointed end of hat, using reserved frosting. Use remaining gumdrops for nose and chocolate chips for eyes. Pipe red decorating cookie icing for mouth.

1 Cupcake: Calories 250; Total Fat 9g (Saturated Fat 6g; Trans Fat 0g); Cholesterol 45mg; Sodium 230mg; Total Carbohydrate 39g (Dietary Fiber 0g); Protein 3g **Exchanges:** 1 Starch, 1 1/2 Other Carbohydrate, 1 1/2 Fat **Carbohydrate Choices:** 2 1/2

Butterfly Cupcake Petits Fours (page 278)

chapter six

special-occasion cupcakes

pistachio **fudge cups**

24 cups   **PREP TIME: 25 Minutes** START TO FINISH: **45 Minutes**

CRUST

1/4	cup butter or margarine, softened
1	package (3 oz) cream cheese, softened
3/4	cup all-purpose flour
1/4	cup powdered sugar
2	tablespoons unsweetened baking cocoa
1/2	teaspoon vanilla

FILLING

2/3	cup granulated sugar
2/3	cup chopped pistachio nuts
1/3	cup unsweetened baking cocoa
2	tablespoons butter or margarine, softened
1	egg

1 Heat oven to 350°F. In large bowl, beat 1/4 cup butter and the cream cheese with electric mixer on medium speed, or mix with spoon. Stir in remaining crust ingredients until well blended and dough forms.

2 Divide dough into 24 equal pieces. Press each piece in bottom and up side of ungreased mini muffin cup.

3 In medium bowl, mix filling ingredients until well blended. Spoon about 2 teaspoons filling into each cup.

4 Bake 18 to 20 minutes or until almost no indentation remains when filling is touched lightly. Cool 5 minutes. Loosen from muffin cups with tip of knife. Remove from pans; place on cooling rack to cool.

1 Cup: Calories 90; Total Fat 6g (Saturated Fat 3g; Trans Fat 0g); Cholesterol 20mg; Sodium 35mg; Total Carbohydrate 6g (Dietary Fiber 1g); Protein 2g **Exchanges:** 1/2 Starch, 1 Fat **Carbohydrate Choices:** 1/2

Coconut Fudge Cups: Use 2/3 cup flaked coconut in place of the pistachio nuts.

chocolate-raspberry **cupcakes**

24 cupcakes   PREP TIME: 1 Hour START TO FINISH: 1 Hour 50 Minutes

CUPCAKES
- 24   foil baking cups
  Chocolate Cupcakes (page 15)

FROSTING
- 5   oz semisweet chocolate
- $1/3$ cup milk
- 3   tablespoons instant espresso powder
- $3/4$ cup shortening
- $3/4$ cup butter or margarine, softened
- $1 1/2$ teaspoons vanilla
- $1/8$ teaspoon coarse (kosher) salt
- 5   cups powdered sugar

FILLING
- 1   cup seedless raspberry jam

GARNISH
  Extra-fine edible glitter or decorator sugar crystals, if desired

1   Heat oven to 350°F. Remove and discard paper liners from inside foil baking cups; place foil baking cup in each of 24 regular-size muffin cups.

2   Make, bake and cool Chocolate Cupcakes as directed in recipe. Meanwhile, in small microwaveable bowl, microwave chocolate on High 1 minute 30 seconds, stirring every 30 seconds, until chocolate can be stirred smooth; set aside.

3   In microwavable measuring cup, microwave milk on High 30 to 45 seconds until very warm. Stir in espresso powder until dissolved. Cool to room temperature, about 10 minutes.

4   In large bowl, mix shortening and butter with electric mixer on medium speed, about 30 seconds, until smooth. Add cooled chocolate, vanilla, salt and milk mixture; beat on medium speed until smooth. On low speed and scraping bowl occasionally, gradually add powdered sugar until frosting is thick and smooth. Set aside.

5   Spoon jam into decorating bag fitted with round tip #6 (opening about $1/8$ inch in diameter). Insert tip in center of cooled cupcake, about halfway down. Gently squeeze decorating bag, pulling upwards until cupcake swells slightly and filling comes to the top.

6   Spoon frosting into decorating bag fitted with round tip #1 (opening about $1/2$ inch in diameter). Generously pipe frosting in circular motion, leaving $1/4$-inch border around cupcake. Dust with edible glitter.

1 Cupcake: Calories 440; Total Fat 21g (Saturated Fat 8g; Trans Fat 2.5g); Cholesterol 35mg; Sodium 230mg; Total Carbohydrate 60g (Dietary Fiber 1g); Protein 2g **Exchanges:** 1 Starch, 3 Other Carbohydrate, 4 Fat **Carbohydrate Choices:** 4

sweet success tip
To make these cupcakes for a wedding, double the recipe as many times as needed to serve your guests. More than doubling the recipe will create problems with the filling and bake time.

use a cake mix

Substitute 1 box milk chocolate cake mix for the Chocolate Cupcakes. Make cake mix as directed on box for cupcakes **except**—add 2 tablespoons unsweetened baking cocoa and 1 teaspoon vanilla. Bake 17 to 20 minutes. Fill, frost and garnish as directed in recipe.

chocolate ganache **mini cakes**

60 mini cakes   **PREP TIME: 1 Hour 10 Minutes** START TO FINISH: **2 Hours 20 Minutes**

MINI CAKES

- 1 box devil's food cake mix with pudding

  Water, vegetable oil and eggs called for on cake mix box

FILLING

- 2/3 cup raspberry jam

GLAZE

- 6 oz dark baking chocolate, chopped
- 2/3 cup whipping cream
- 1 tablespoon raspberry-flavored liqueur, if desired

GARNISH

- 60 Fresh raspberries, if desired

1 Heat oven to 350°F. Place mini paper baking cup in each of 60 mini muffin cups. Make cake mix as directed on box, using water, oil and eggs. Fill muffin cups 3/4 full.

2 Bake 10 to 15 minutes or until toothpick inserted in center of mini cake comes out clean. Cool 5 minutes. Remove mini cakes from pans; place on cooling racks to cool.

3 With end of round handle of wooden spoon, make deep, 1/2-inch-wide indentation in center of top of each mini cake, not quite to bottom (wiggle end of spoon in mini cake to make opening large enough).

4 Spoon jam into small resealable food-storage plastic bag; seal bag. Cut 3/8-inch tip off one bottom corner of bag. Insert tip of bag into opening in each mini cake; squeeze bag to fill opening.

5 Place chocolate in medium bowl. In 1-quart saucepan, heat whipping cream just to boiling; pour over chocolate. Let stand 3 to 5 minutes or until chocolate is melted and smooth when stirred. Stir in liqueur. Let stand 15 minutes, stirring occasionally, until mixture coats a spoon.

6 Spoon about 1 teaspoon chocolate glaze onto each mini cake. Garnish each with raspberry.

1 Mini Cake: Calories 120; Total Fat 8g (Saturated Fat 2.5g; Trans Fat 0g); Cholesterol 15mg; Sodium 80mg; Total Carbohydrate 10g (Dietary Fiber 0g); Protein 1g **Exchanges:** 1/2 Starch, 1 1/2 Fat **Carbohydrate Choices:** 1/2

sweet success tip

If you refrigerate these little desserts, let them stand at room temperature at least 20 minutes before serving.

chai latte **cupcakes**

24 cupcakes   PREP TIME: **50 Minutes** START TO FINISH: **2 Hours 25 Minutes**

CUPCAKES

- 1 box French vanilla cake mix with pudding
- 1 1/2 cups water
- 1/3 cup vegetable oil
- 3 eggs
- 1 package (1.1 oz) instant chai tea latte mix (or 3 tablespoons from larger container)

FROSTING AND GARNISH

- 4 oz white chocolate baking bars (from 6-oz package), chopped
- 1/3 cup butter or margarine, softened
- 4 cups powdered sugar
- 1/4 cup milk
- 1/2 teaspoon vanilla
- Ground cinnamon, if desired

1 Heat oven to 350°F. Place paper baking cup in each of 24 regular-size muffin cups.

2 In large bowl, beat cupcake ingredients with electric mixer on low speed 30 seconds. Beat on medium speed 2 minutes, scraping bowl occasionally. Divide batter evenly among muffin cups, filling each about 2/3 full.

3 Bake 18 to 23 minutes or until toothpick inserted in center of cupcake comes out clean. Cool 10 minutes. Remove cupcakes from pans; place on cooling racks to cool.

4 In medium microwavable bowl, microwave baking bars on High 30 seconds. Stir until melted; if necessary, microwave 15 seconds longer or until melted and smooth. Stir in butter until smooth. Add powdered sugar, milk and vanilla; stir until well blended.

5 Frost cupcakes. Sprinkle with cinnamon.

1 Cupcake: Calories 250; Total Fat 9g (Saturated Fat 3.5g; Trans Fat 0g); Cholesterol 35mg; Sodium 180mg; Total Carbohydrate 41g (Dietary Fiber 0g); Protein 1g **Exchanges:** 1 Starch, 1 1/2 Other Carbohydrate, 1 1/2 Fat **Carbohydrate Choices:** 3

sweet success tip

Chai is the Hindi word for a tea made with milk and a variety of spices such as cardamom, cinnamon, cloves, ginger, nutmeg and pepper.

espresso **cupcakes**

24 cupcakes   PREP TIME: **1 Hour 15 Minutes** START TO FINISH: **2 Hours**

CUPCAKES

   Chocolate Cupcakes (page 15)

1 tablespoon instant espresso coffee powder or granules

FILLING

1 container (8 oz) mascarpone cheese

2 teaspoons milk

2 teaspoons instant espresso coffee powder or granules

1 cup powdered sugar

FROSTING

4 oz semisweet baking chocolate, finely chopped

6 tablespoons butter or margarine, softened

3 tablespoons milk

1 teaspoon instant espresso coffee powder or granules

1/2 teaspoon vanilla

   Dash salt

3 cups powdered sugar

1 Make Chocolate Cupcakes as directed in recipe except—stir in 1 tablespoon instant espresso coffee powder or granules with the flour. Bake and cool as directed in recipe.

2 In medium bowl, beat filling ingredients with electric mixer on medium speed until smooth. Spoon mixture into decorating bag fitted with 1/4-inch (#9) writing tip.

3 To fill each cupcake, insert tip of bag into center of cooled cupcake; gently squeeze bag until cupcake expands slightly but does not burst (each cupcake should be filled with about 1 tablespoon filling).

4 In small microwavable bowl, microwave chocolate uncovered on High 45 seconds. Stir; continue microwaving and stirring in 15-second increments until melted. Cool slightly, about 5 minutes.

5 In another medium bowl, beat butter, 3 tablespoons milk, 1 teaspoon espresso powder, the vanilla and salt with electric mixer on low speed until well blended. Beat in 3 cups powdered sugar, 1 cup at a time, until smooth. Stir in melted chocolate until blended. Spoon mixture into decorating bag fitted with 3/4-inch (#824) star tip. Pipe frosting over tops of cupcakes. Store covered in refrigerator.

1 Cupcake: Calories 320; Total Fat 15g (Saturated Fat 6g; Trans Fat 1g); Cholesterol 30mg; Sodium 210mg; Total Carbohydrate 44g (Dietary Fiber 2g); Protein 3g **Exchanges:** 1 Starch, 2 Other Carbohydrate, 3 Fat **Carbohydrate Choices:** 3

sweet success tip

You can sprinkle the cupcakes with grated chocolate, mini chocolate chips or chocolate covered espresso beans.

use a cake mix

Substitute 1 box chocolate fudge cake mix for the Chocolate Cupcakes. Make cake as directed on box for cupcakes **except**—add 1 tablespoon instant espresso coffee powder or granules. Bake and cool as directed. Fill, frost and garnish as directed in recipe.

triple-chocolate **mini cups**

72 mini cups   **PREP TIME: 35 Minutes** START TO FINISH: **2 Hours 15 Minutes**

³/₄	cup butter or margarine
4	oz unsweetened baking chocolate
2	cups sugar
1¹/₂	cups all-purpose flour
¹/₂	cup unsweetened baking cocoa
2	teaspoons baking powder
¹/₂	teaspoon salt
4	eggs
1¹/₂	cups semisweet chocolate chips
6	dozen whole candied cherries, Hershey®'s Kisses® milk chocolates, unwrapped or pecan halves

1 Heat oven to 350°F. Place mini paper baking cups in mini muffin pan cups, or use mini foil muffin cups if you don't have mini muffin pans.

2 In 2-quart saucepan, melt butter and chocolate over low heat 6 to 10 minutes, stirring occasionally, until smooth. Cool 20 minutes. In large bowl, beat melted chocolate mixture, sugar, 1 cup of the flour, the cocoa, baking powder, salt and eggs with electric mixer on medium speed about 2 minutes, scraping bowl occasionally, until well blended. Stir in remaining ¹/₂ cup flour and the chocolate chips. Drop dough by rounded teaspoons into mini cups.

3 Bake 15 to 17 minutes or until edges are slightly firm (center will be slightly soft). Immediately top each with cherry, pecan half or chocolate, pressing slightly. Cool in pans about 10 minutes. Remove from pans; place on cooling racks to cool.

1 Mini Cups: Calories 100; Total Fat 4g (Saturated Fat 2.5g; Trans Fat 0g); Cholesterol 15mg; Sodium 55mg; Total Carbohydrate 15g (Dietary Fiber 0g); Protein 1g **Exchanges:** 1 Other Carbohydrate, 1 Fat **Carbohydrate Choices:** 1

HERSHEY'S and KISSES trademarks and trade dress are registered trademarks used under license.

sweet success tip
Top these little gems with an assortment of toppings so you have a variety to give or enjoy.

Special-Occasion Cupcakes   263

hot chocolate **cupcakes**

24 cupcakes   PREP TIME: **50 Minutes** START TO FINISH: **1 Hour 50 Minutes**

CUPCAKES
Chocolate Cupcakes (page 15)

FROSTING
Vanilla Buttercream Frosting
(page 20)
1 cup marshmallow creme

DECORATIONS
1/2 teaspoon unsweetened baking cocoa

12 miniature pretzel twists, broken in half

1 Make, bake and cool Chocolate Cupcakes as directed in recipe.

2 Make Vanilla Buttercream Frosting as directed in recipe. Measure 2 cups frosting into small bowl; stir in marshmallow creme. Spoon into resealable food-storage plastic bag; seal bag. Cut tiny hole in one bottom corner of bag. (Reserve remaining frosting for another use.)

3 Pipe 3 small dollops of frosting mixture on top of each cupcake to resemble melted marshmallows. Sprinkle with cocoa. Press pretzel half into side of each cupcake for cup handle.

1 Cupcake: Calories 350; Total Fat 13g (Saturated Fat 5g; Trans Fat 1.5g); Cholesterol 30mg; Sodium 220mg; Total Carbohydrate 56g (Dietary Fiber 1g); Protein 2g **Exchanges:** 1 Starch, 2 1/2 Other Carbohydrate, 2 1/2 Fat **Carbohydrate Choices:** 4

sweet success tip
Leftover frosting? Use it for ice cream topping. Just microwave uncovered on High for about 30 seconds or until hot.

use a cake mix

Substitute 1 box devil's food cake mix for the Chocolate Cupcakes. Make cake mix as directed on box for cupcakes. For the frosting, substitute 2 cups vanilla whipped ready-to-spread frosting (from 2 containers); stir in 1 cup marshmallow creme. Frost and decorate as directed in recipe.

mocha-caramel **cappuccino cupcakes**

6 jumbo cupcakes   **PREP TIME: 40 Minutes** START TO FINISH: **1 Hour 40 Minutes**

Chocolate Cupcakes (page 15)
4 3/4 teaspoons instant espresso granules
1/2 pint (1 cup) heavy whipping cream
2 tablespoons powdered sugar
2 tablespoons miniature semisweet chocolate chips
2 tablespoons caramel topping

1 Heat oven to 350°F. Place jumbo paper baking cups in each of 6 jumbo muffin cups or grease and flour 6 jumbo muffin cups, or spray with baking spray with flour.

2 Make Chocolate Cupcakes as directed in recipe except—stir in 4 teaspoons of the espresso granules with hot water and cocoa until dissolved. Divide batter evenly among muffin cups, filling each about 2/3 full.

3 Bake 20 to 25 minutes or until toothpick inserted in center of cupcake comes out clean. Cool 5 minutes; remove from pan to cooling rack to cool.

4 In small deep bowl, beat whipping cream, powdered sugar and remaining 3/4 teaspoon espresso granules with electric mixer on high speed until stiff peaks form.

5 To serve, place each cupcake in a coffee cup, if desired. Top each with about 3 tablespoons whipped cream, sprinkle with 1 teaspoon chocolate chips, and drizzle with 1 teaspoon caramel topping.

1 Cupcake: Calories 840; Total Fat 45g (Saturated Fat 18g; Trans Fat 5g); Cholesterol 125mg; Sodium 740mg; Total Carbohydrate 99g (Dietary Fiber 5g); Protein 9g **Exchanges:** 3 1/2 Starch, 3 Other Carbohydrate, 8 1/2 Fat **Carbohydrate Choices:** 6 1/2

sweet success tip

For a quick-and-easy topping, use refrigerated whipped cream topping from an aerosol can.

use a cake mix

Substitute 1 box devil's food cake mix for the Chocolate Cupcakes. Place jumbo paper baking cup in each of 8 jumbo muffin cups. Mix 1 1/4 cups warm water and 4 teaspoons espresso granules until granules are dissolved. Make cake mix as directed on box for cupcakes **except**—use espresso mixture, 1/2 cup vegetable oil and 3 eggs. Bake 21 to 29 minutes. Cool as directed on box. Frost and garnish as directed in recipe, using 1 1/4 cups whipping (heavy) cream, 2 tablespoons powdered sugar, 3 tablespoons each miniature chocolate chips and caramel topping. 8 jumbo cupcakes

peanut butter high hats

{ Bree Hester Carmichael, California Baked Bree www.bakedbree.com }

28 cupcakes   PREP TIME: **1 Hour 15 Minutes** START TO FINISH: **2 Hours 10 Minutes**

CUPCAKES

3	cups cake flour
1	tablespoon baking powder
1/2	teaspoon salt
1	cup butter, softened
2	cups granulated sugar
4	eggs
2	teaspoons vanilla
3/4	cup milk

FROSTING

1 1/2	cups butter, softened
1 1/2	cups creamy peanut butter
1	jar (7 oz) marshmallow creme
3	cups powdered sugar
2	teaspoons vanilla

CHOCOLATE COATING

3	cups milk chocolate chips (18 oz)
6	tablespoons vegetable or canola oil

1 Heat oven to 350°F. Place paper baking cup in each of 28 regular-size muffin cups. In medium bowl, stir together flour, baking powder and salt; set aside.

2 In large bowl, beat 1 cup butter and the granulated sugar with electric mixer on medium speed about 5 minutes or until light and fluffy. Add eggs, one at a time, beating well after each addition. Beat in 2 teaspoons vanilla. On low speed, alternately add flour mixture, about 1/3 of mixture at a time, and milk, about 1/2 at a time, beating just until blended. Divide batter evenly among muffin cups.

3 Bake 20 to 24 minutes or until toothpick inserted in center of cupcake comes out clean. Cool 5 minutes. Remove cupcakes from pans; place on cooling racks to cool.

4 In large bowl, beat 1 1/2 cups butter and the peanut butter with electric mixer on medium speed until smooth. Beat in marshmallow creme. On low speed, gradually add powdered sugar until blended. Add 2 teaspoons vanilla; beat 3 minutes longer.

5 Spoon frosting into decorating bag fitted with large round tip #1. On top of each cupcake, pipe frosting in circles making cone shape with peak in center. Refrigerate cupcakes at least 45 minutes to harden frosting before dipping in chocolate coating.

6 In 1 1/2-quart saucepan, heat chocolate chips and oil over low heat, stirring occasionally, until smooth. Dip cone-shaped frosting on each cupcake into chocolate coating to coat frosting completely, letting excess chocolate drip off. Refrigerate to set coating, about 5 minutes.

1 Cupcake: Calories 560; Total Fat 33g (Saturated Fat 16g; Trans Fat 0.5g); Cholesterol 80mg; Sodium 310mg; Total Carbohydrate 58g (Dietary Fiber 1g); Protein 7g **Exchanges:** 1 Starch, 3 Other Carbohydrate, 1/2 High-Fat Meat, 5 1/2 Fat **Carbohydrate Choices:** 4

sweet success tip

For the chocolate coating, you can use dark or semi-sweet chocolate chips.

use a cake mix

Substitute 1 box yellow cake mix for the cupcakes above. Make cake mix as directed on box for cupcakes **except**—make 28 cupcakes. Bake 16 to 18 minutes. Cool as directed on box. Prepare Frosting and Chocolate Coating as directed in recipe. Frost and decorate as directed in recipe.

pink lemonade **angel's wings cupcakes**

24 cupcakes   PREP TIME: **1 Hour** START TO FINISH: **1 Hour 50 Minutes**

CUPCAKES

2 3/4 cups all-purpose flour

3   teaspoons baking powder

1/2   teaspoon salt

3/4   cup shortening

1 1/2 cups granulated sugar

5   egg whites

2 1/2 teaspoons vanilla

3/4   cup milk

1/2   cup thawed pink lemonade concentrate (from 12-oz can)

PINK LEMONADE BUTTERCREAM FROSTING

6   cups powdered sugar

2/3   cup butter or margarine, softened

6   to 8 tablespoons thawed pink lemonade concentrate (from 12-oz can)

DECORATIONS

24   fudge-striped cookies, cut in half

Fine sparkling sugar (not coarse)

1   Heat the oven to 350°F. Place paper baking cup in each of 24 regular-size muffin cups; or grease and flour muffin cups, or spray with baking spray with flour. In medium bowl, stir together flour, baking powder and salt; set aside.

2   In large bowl, beat shortening with electric mixer on medium speed 30 seconds. Gradually add granulated sugar, about 1/3 cup at a time, beating after each addition. Beat 2 minutes longer. Add egg whites, one at a time, beating well after each addition. Beat in vanilla. On low speed, alternately add flour mixture, about 1/3 of mixture at a time, with milk and lemonade concentrate, beating just until blended.

3   Divide batter evenly among muffin cups, filling each about 2/3 full.

4   Bake 18 to 20 minutes or until toothpick inserted in center of cupcake comes out clean. Cool 5 minutes. Remove cupcakes to cooling racks to cool.

5   In large bowl, mix powdered sugar and butter with spoon or electric mixer on low speed. Stir in 6 tablespoons of the lemonade concentrate. Gradually beat in just enough remaining lemonade concentrate to make frosting smooth and spreadable. Spoon 1/2 cup frosting into small resealable food-storage plastic bag; set aside. Frost cupcakes with remaining frosting.

6   Cut 1/8-inch hole in one bottom corner of plastic bag. Pipe squiggly lines onto chocolate sides of cookie halves. Sprinkle with sparkling sugar. Press 2 cookie halves into cupcake to resemble wings.

1 Cupcake: Calories 360; Total Fat 12g (Saturated Fat 5g; Trans Fat 1.5g); Cholesterol 15mg; Sodium 160mg; Total Carbohydrate 60g (Dietary Fiber 0g); Protein 2g **Exchanges:** 1/2 Starch, 3 1/2 Other Carbohydrate, 2 1/2 Fat **Carbohydrate Choices:** 4

sweet success tip

You can use your favorite color or a variety of pastel-colored decorator sugars for the cupcakes if sparkling sugar is unavailable.

use a cake mix

Substitute 1 box white cake mix for the cupcakes above. Make cake mix as directed on box for cupcakes **except**—use 3/4 cup water, 1/2 cup thawed pink lemonade concentrate (from 12-oz can), 1/3 cup vegetable oil and 3 egg whites. Add a few drops red food color to batter, if desired. Bake and cool as directed on box. Frost and decorate as directed in recipe.

lemon meringue **cupcakes**

24 cupcakes   PREP TIME: 1 Hour START TO FINISH: 2 Hour 15 Minutes

CUPCAKES

   Lemon Cupcakes (page 17)
 1 jar (10 to 12 oz) lemon curd

MERINGUE

 4 egg whites
 1/4 teaspoon cream of tartar
 1 1/2 teaspoons vanilla
 2/3 cup sugar

1 Heat oven to 350°F. Place paper baking cup in each of 24 regular-size muffin cups; spray paper cups with baking spray with flour.

2 Make, bake and cool Lemon Cupcakes as directed in recipe.

3 With end of round handle of wooden spoon, make deep, 3/4-inch-wide indentation in center of top of each cooled cupcake, not quite to bottom. (Wiggle end of spoon in cupcake to make opening large enough.)

4 Spoon lemon curd into small resealable food-storage plastic bag; seal bag. Cut 3/8-inch tip off one bottom corner of bag. Insert tip of bag into opening in each cupcake; squeeze bag to fill opening.

5 Increase oven temperature to 450°F. In medium bowl, beat egg whites, cream of tartar and vanilla with electric mixer on high speed until soft peaks form. Gradually add sugar, 1 tablespoon at a time, beating continuously until stiff peaks form and mixture is glossy. Frost cupcakes with meringue; place on cookie sheet. Bake 2 to 3 minutes or until lightly browned.

1 Cupcake: Calories 230; Total Fat 9g (Saturated Fat 6g; Trans Fat 0g); Cholesterol 60mg; Sodium 210mg; Total Carbohydrate 34g (Dietary Fiber 0g); Protein 3g **Exchanges:** 1 Starch, 1 1/2 Other Carbohydrate, 1 1/2 Fat **Carbohydrate Choices:** 2

sweet success tip
Bake these gems in sparkling gold or silver cups and swirl on this fabulous meringue!

use a cake mix

Substitute 1 box lemon cake mix for the Lemon Cupcakes. Make cake mix as directed on box for cupcakes. Fill with lemon curd and make Meringue as directed in recipe.

pink champagne **cupcakes**

28 cupcakes   PREP TIME: **45 Minutes** START TO FINISH: **2 Hours**

CUPCAKES

White Cupcakes (page 16)

1 1/4   cups champagne

4   or 5 drops red food color

CHAMPAGNE FROSTING

1/2   cup butter or
margarine, softened

4   cups powdered sugar

1/4   cup champagne

1   teaspoon vanilla

4   to 5 drops red food color

GARNISH

Pink decorator sugar crystals

Edible pink pearls

1 Heat oven to 350°F. Place paper baking cup in each of 28 regular-size muffin cups. Make White Cupcakes as directed in recipe except—substitute 1 1/4 cups champagne for the milk and add 4 or 5 drops red food color. Divide batter evenly among muffin cups. Bake and cool as directed in recipe.

2 In medium bowl, beat frosting ingredients with electric mixer on medium speed until smooth. Frost cupcakes. Sprinkle with pink sugar and pearls.

1 Cupcake: Calories 280; Total Fat 10g (Saturated Fat 4g; Trans Fat 1g); Cholesterol 10mg; Sodium 150mg; Total Carbohydrate 43g (Dietary Fiber 0g); Protein 2g **Exchanges:** 1 Starch, 2 Other Carbohydrate, 2 Fat **Carbohydrate Choices:** 3

sweet success tip

There are many expensive champagnes available, but this is one time you might choose less expensive champagne. Have the champagne at room temperature when preparing the cake.

use a cake mix

Substitute 1 box white cake mix for the White Cupcakes. Make cake mix as directed on box for cupcakes **except**—use 1 1/4 cups champagne, 1/3 cup vegetable oil, 3 egg whites, and add 4 or 5 drops red food color. Bake and cool as directed on box. Frost and garnish as directed in recipe. 24 cupcakes

mini crumb cakes

6 mini cakes   **PREP TIME: 10 Minutes** START TO FINISH: **45 Minutes**

1¼ cups all-purpose flour
½ cup packed brown sugar
½ cup butter or margarine, melted
1 egg, beaten
¼ cup milk
1 teaspoon baking powder
½ teaspoon ground cinnamon
2 tablespoons powdered sugar

1 Heat oven to 350°F. Place paper baking cup in each of 6 regular-size muffin cups, or grease cups with shortening or spray with cooking spray. In large bowl, stir together flour, brown sugar and butter with spoon until crumbly. Reserve ⅓ cup mixture for topping.

2 Stir egg, milk, baking powder and cinnamon into remaining crumbly mixture until well mixed. Divide batter evenly among muffin cups. Sprinkle reserved crumbly mixture over batter.

3 Bake 20 to 30 minutes or until toothpick inserted in center of cake comes out clean. Cool 5 minutes. Remove cakes from pan; place on cooling rack. Before serving, sprinkle warm cakes with powdered sugar. Serve warm or cooled.

1 Mini Cake: Calories 330; Total Fat 17g (Saturated Fat 10g; Trans Fat 0.5g); Cholesterol 75mg; Sodium 210mg; Total Carbohydrate 41g (Dietary Fiber 1g); Protein 4g **Exchanges:** 1 Starch, 1 ½ Other Carbohydrate, 3 ½ Fat **Carbohydrate Choices:** 3

sweet success tip

Serve these sweet little coffee cakes for brunch. Place them on a pedestal serving platter.

butterfly cupcake petits fours

72 cupcake petits fours   PREP TIME: 2 Hours 30 Minutes START TO FINISH: 3 Hours 20 Minutes

CUPCAKES

White Cupcakes (page 16)

GLAZE

8   cups powdered sugar
1/2 cup water
1/2 cup light corn syrup
2   teaspoons almond extract

DECORATIONS

288 Pastel-colored chocolate
     covered candy pieces
     (from 12.6-oz bag)
144 Yogurt or white fudge-covered
     small pretzel twists
     Black string licorice, cut into
     144 (1/2-inch) pieces

1 Make, bake and cool mini version of White Cupcakes as directed in recipe variation. When cupcakes are cool, remove paper baking cups; turn cupcakes upside-down.

2 Meanwhile, in 2 1/2 quart saucepan, beat glaze ingredients until smooth. Heat over low heat just until lukewarm. Remove from heat. If necessary, add hot water, a few drops at a time, until glaze is pourable.

3 Place cupcakes, one at a time, on wire rack over large bowl. Pour enough glaze over top to cover top and sides. (Glaze can be reheated and used again.)

4 Place 4 candy pieces in a row in center of each cupcake. Press 2 pretzels, one on each side of row of candy pieces, to resemble wings. Use licorice pieces for antennae.

1 Frosted Cupcake Petit Four (Undecorated): Calories 120; Total Fat 2.5g (Saturated Fat 0.5g; Trans Fat 0g); Cholesterol 0mg; Sodium 45mg; Total Carbohydrate 24g (Dietary Fiber 0g); Protein 1g **Exchanges:** 1/2 Starch, 1 Other Carbohydrate, 1/2 Fat **Carbohydrate Choices:** 1 1/2

sweet success tip

For sparkly butterfly wings, brush pretzels with a little of the glaze, then sprinkle with colored sugar.

use a cake mix

Substitute 1 box white cake mix for the White Cupcakes. Make cake mix as directed on box for cupcakes. Divide batter evenly into mini muffin cups. Bake 14 to 18 minutes or until toothpick inserted in center of cupcake comes out clean. To make the glaze, use 6 cups powdered sugar, 1/4 cup plus 2 tablespoons water, 1/4 cup plus 2 teaspoons light corn syrup and 1 1/2 teaspoons almond extract. Glaze cupcakes and decorate with 144 mint candy drops, 96 mini pretzel twists and 48 pastel candy pieces as directed in recipe. 48 cupcake petits fours

pastel angel food cupcakes

26 cupcakes   PREP TIME: **50 Minutes** START TO FINISH: **1 Hour 45 Minutes**

CUPCAKES

1 1/2   cups powdered sugar
1   cup cake flour or
    all-purpose flour
1 1/2   cups egg whites (about 12 large)
1 1/2   teaspoons cream of tartar
1   cup granulated sugar
1 1/2   teaspoons vanilla
1/2   teaspoon almond extract
1/4   teaspoon salt
    Yellow, red and green liquid
    food color

PINK FLUFFY FROSTING

Fluffy White Frosting (page 21)
4 drops red food color

1 Move oven rack to lowest position. Heat oven to 375°F. Place paper baking cup in each of 26 regular-size muffin cups.

2 In medium bowl, mix powdered sugar and flour; set aside. In large bowl, beat egg whites and cream of tartar with electric mixer on medium speed until foamy. Beat in granulated sugar, 2 tablespoons at a time, on high speed, adding vanilla, almond extract and salt with the last addition of sugar. Continue beating until stiff and glossy. Do not underbeat.

3 Sprinkle powdered sugar-flour mixture, 1/4 cup at a time, over egg white mixture, folding in with rubber spatula just until sugar-flour mixture disappears.

4 Divide batter among 3 bowls. Carefully fold a few drops yellow food color into 1 bowl until desired shade. Repeat with red and green food color and remaining batter. In each muffin cup, spoon 2 tablespoons of each color batter next to each other; using knife, make "S" motion through batters to swirl.

5 Bake 15 to 20 minutes or until cracks in cupcakes feel dry and tops spring back when touched lightly. Remove from pan to cooling racks to cool.

6 Meanwhile, make Fluffy White Frosting as directed in recipe except—stir in 4 drops red food color with the corn syrup. Frost cupcakes.

1 Cupcake: Calories 110; Total Fat 0g (Saturated Fat 0g; Trans Fat 0g); Cholesterol 0mg; Sodium 55mg; Total Carbohydrate 25g (Dietary Fiber 0g); Protein 2g **Exchanges:** 1/2 Starch, 1 Other Carbohydrate **Carbohydrate Choices:** 1 1/2

sweet success tip

Egg whites will have better volume when beaten at room temperature in a bowl that is clean and dry. Don't let the egg whites stand at room temperature longer than 30 minutes.

use a cake mix

Substitute 1 box white angel food cake mix for the cupcakes above. Make cake mix as directed on box **except**—divide and color batters as directed in recipe. Divide and color batters as directed in step 4. Bake 13 to 21 minutes. Remove from pan to cooling rack. Cool completely, about 30 minutes. For frosting, use 1 container whipped fluffy white ready-to-spread frosting mixed with 4 drops red food color.

simply elegant **cupcakes**

For that special celebration to charm the bride or just to dazzle your guests, you can make these fanciful cupcakes to adorn your platters. Make one of your favorite cupcakes from the basics chapter, and prepare Vanilla Buttercream Frosting on page 20. Then start creating these stunning treats!

Spiky-Topped

Make 2 recipes of frosting. Tint frosting with blue paste food color. Frost cupcakes with thin layer of frosting. Pipe remaining frosting onto cupcakes using #9 round tip. Starting on outside edge, pipe first layer of spikes out over edge of cupcakes. Continue piping spikes in circular pattern ending with spikes standing up on top. Sprinkle with edible pearls.

Fancy Flower

Make 2 recipes of frosting; tint with pink paste food color. Pipe frosting onto cupcakes using #6 tip in a spiral pattern, starting at outside edge. Tint remaining frosting darker pink. Using pastry bag fitted with a #104 rose tip, form layered rose petals and add to cupcakes.

Petals and Lace

Pipe frosting onto cupcakes using #6 round tip. Sprinkle with decorator sugar. Melt 14-oz. bag of white confectionary coating wafers as directed on package; place in resealable food-storage plastic bag with one small corner cut off. Pipe 144 (1¾-inch) elongated petal shapes onto waxed paper. When set, top cupcakes with petal shapes. Tie with bow.

Strawberry Delight

Tint frosting with green paste food color. Pipe frosting onto cupcakes using #6 tip in a spiral pattern, starting at outside edge and ending with peak in center. Cut small gumdrops in half lengthwise for strawberries. Pipe purchased green frosting using small round tip to resemble strawberry tops.

mini cupcake **mortarboards**

72 cupcake mortarboards PREP TIME: **1 Hour 15 Minutes** START TO FINISH: **1 Hour 45 Minutes**

CUPCAKES

Yellow Cupcakes (page 14)

DECORATIONS AND FROSTING

1 box (4.5 oz) chewy fruit snack rolls (any flavor) or shoestring licorice

Vanilla Buttercream Frosting (page 20)

Food color

72 square shortbread cookies (from two 10-oz packages)

72 candy-coated chocolate candies or fruit-flavored candies

1 Make mini version of Yellow Cupcakes as directed in recipe variation. Bake and cool as directed. (Leave paper baking cups on cupcakes so mortarboards are quicker and easier to make and more portable to serve.)

2 To make tassels, cut 72 (2 1/2-inch) lengths from fruit snack rolls. Cut each into several strips up to 1/2-inch from 1 end. Roll uncut end between fingertips to make tassels. Or, cut several pieces of shoestring licorice into 2 1/2-inch lengths.

3 Make Vanilla Buttercream Frosting as directed in recipe. Tint frosting with food color to match paper baking cups.

4 Frost bottoms of cookies. Place 1 candy on center of each. For each mortarboard, place small dollop of frosting on bottom of cupcake; top with cookie, unfrosted side down. Press uncut end of fruit snack or 3 or 4 pieces of licorice into frosted cookie next to candy.

1 Cupcake Mortarboard: Calories 100; Total Fat 5g (Saturated Fat 3.5g; Trans Fat 0g); Cholesterol 15mg; Sodium 95mg; Total Carbohydrate 14g (Dietary Fiber 0g); Protein 1g **Exchanges:** 1 Other Carbohydrate, 1 Fat **Carbohydrate Choices:** 1

sweet success tip

Use paper baking cups for the cupcakes that match school colors to serve guests at a grad party.

 *use a* **cake mix**

Place mini paper baking cup in each of 60 mini muffin cups. Substitute 1 box yellow cake mix for the Yellow Cupcakes. Make cake mix as directed on box for cupcakes. Divide batter evenly among muffin cups, filling each about 2/3 full. (If using one pan, refrigerate batter while baking other cakes.) Bake 14 to 16 minutes or until toothpick inserted in center of cupcake comes out clean. (Leave paper baking cups on cupcakes so mortarboards are quicker and easier to make and more portable to serve.) Make 60 tassels. For the frosting, substitute 1 container vanilla creamy ready-to-spread frosting, stirring in food color to match paper baking cups. Continue as directed in recipe, using 60 cookies and 60 candies. 60 cupcake mortarboards

flower cupcakes

24 cupcakes   **PREP TIME: 1 Hour 10 Minutes** START TO FINISH: **2 Hours 25 Minutes**

CUPCAKES
White Cupcakes (page 16)

FROSTING
Vanilla Buttercream Frosting
(page 20)

DECORATIONS
30   large marshmallows
Colored sugar
Birthday candles, if desired

1 Make, bake and cool White Cupcakes as directed in recipe.

2 Make Vanilla Buttercream Frosting as directed in recipe. Frost cupcakes.

3 Using kitchen scissors, cut each marshmallow crosswise into 4 slices. Sprinkle slices with colored sugar. Arrange 5 slices on each cupcakes in flower shape. Place candle in center of each flower.

1 Frosted Cupcake (Undecorated): Calories 340; Total Fat 12g (Saturated Fat 5g; Trans Fat 1.5g); Cholesterol 15mg; Sodium 160mg; Total Carbohydrate 56g (Dietary Fiber 0g); Protein 2g **Exchanges:** ¹/₂ Starch, 3 Other Carbohydrate, 2 ¹/₂ Fat **Carbohydrate Choices:** 4

sweet success tip
Spray the blades of the scissors with cooking spray to prevent the marshmallows from sticking.

use a cake mix

Substitute 1 box white cake mix for the White Cupcakes. Make cake mix as directed on box for cupcakes. For the frosting, substitute 1 container vanilla or creamy white creamy ready-to-spread frosting. Frost and decorate as directed in recipe.

wedding **cupcakes**

26 cupcakes **PREP TIME: 1 Hour 15 Minutes** START TO FINISH: **4 Hours 5 Minutes**

FILLING

1	egg plus 3 egg yolks
1/2	cup granulated sugar
1 1/2	teaspoon finely grated lemon peel
1/3	cup fresh lemon juice (2 medium)
1/8	teaspoon salt
1/4	cup cold butter or margarine, cut up

CUPCAKES

White Cupcakes (page 16)

FROSTING

1 1/2	cup butter or margarine, softened
1	teaspoon kosher (coarse) salt
2	tablespoons milk
2	tablespoons fresh lemon juice
4	teaspoons grated lemon peel
3	teaspoons vanilla
5	cups powdered sugar

GARNISH

Edible pearls or decorator sugar, if desired

1 bag (16 oz) white candy melts or coating wafers

1 In 2-quart saucepan, mix all filling ingredients except butter with whisk. Heat to a simmer over medium heat, stirring constantly; simmer 4 to 5 minutes or until mixture thickens and coats back of wooden spoon. Into small bowl, strain sauce through strainer. Beat in butter with whisk. Press plastic wrap directly onto surface of lemon curd filling; refrigerate at least 3 hours or up to 1 week.

2 Heat oven to 350°F. Place baking cups in each of 26 regular-size muffin cups. Make, bake and cool White Cupcakes as directed in recipe.

3 Spoon filling into decorating bag fitted with round tip #6. Insert tip into center of cupcake, about halfway down. Gently squeeze decorating bag, pulling upwards until cupcake swells slightly and filling comes to the top.

4 In large bowl, beat all frosting ingredients with electric mixer on high speed about 3 minutes or until smooth and well blended, adding more lemon juice, 1 teaspoon at a time, if needed to get smooth but stiff consistency.

5 Spoon frosting into decorating bag fitted with star tip #7 . Generously pipe frosting in circular motion, leaving 1/4-inch border around cupcake. Sprinkle with edible pearls.

6 Melt candy melts as directed on package. Place melted candy in small resealable food-storage plastic bag; seal bag. Cut off tiny corner of bag. Squeeze bag to pipe 52 heart shapes onto waxed paper. Refrigerate 10 minutes to set. Garnish each cupcake with 2 hearts. Store in refrigerator.

1 Cupcake: Calories 390; Total Fat 19g (Saturated Fat 10g; Trans Fat 1.5g); Cholesterol 65mg; Sodium 260mg; Total Carbohydrate 51g (Dietary Fiber 0g); Protein 3g **Exchanges:** 1 Starch, 2 1/2 Other Carbohydrate, 3 1/2 Fat **Carbohydrate Choices:** 3 1/2

sweet success tip

If you need a bigger batch of cupcakes, you can double the recipe. More than doubling is not recommended for best results.

use a cake mix

Make filling as directed in recipe. Place baking cups in each of 24 regular-size muffin cups. Substitute 1 box white cake mix for the White Cupcakes. Make cake mix as directed on box for cupcakes **except**—add 1 teaspoon vanilla. Bake and cool as directed on box. Frost and garnish as directed in recipe. 24 cupcakes

vanilla bean calla lily cupcakes

18 regular and 18 mini cupcakes   PREP TIME: **1 Hour 10 Minutes** START TO FINISH: **6 Hours 20 Minutes**

2 oz vanilla-flavored candy coating (almond bark)

1 tablespoon light corn syrup

6 small yellow gumdrops
   White Cupcakes (page 16)

4 vanilla beans, cut in half, seeds scraped

1/2 teaspoon vanilla
   Vanilla Buttercream Frosting (page 20)
   Green decorating icing (from 6.4-oz can)

1 In small microwavable bowl, microwave candy coating uncovered on High 30 seconds; stir. Microwave about 30 seconds longer or until coating can be stirred smooth. Stir in corn syrup; cool 20 minutes. Wrap in plastic wrap; let stand at room temperature at least 4 hours or overnight.

2 Form calla lilies following directions on opposite page.

3 Make White Cupcakes as directed in recipe except—place paper baking cup in each of 18 regular-size muffin cups and mini paper baking cup in each of 18 mini muffin cups. Before adding sugar to shortening, place in medium bowl and stir in seeds of 2 of the vanilla beans and vanilla with whisk to evenly distribute.

4 Divide batter evenly among muffin cups, filling each about 2/3 full.

5 Bake regular cupcakes 18 to 20 minutes, mini cupcakes 12 to 16 minutes, or until toothpick inserted in center of cupcake comes out clean. Cool 5 minutes; remove from pans to cooling racks to cool.

6 Meanwhile, make Vanilla Buttercream Frosting as directed in recipe except—stir remaining vanilla bean seeds into powdered sugar with whisk to evenly distribute. Continue as directed. Frost each cupcake with about 2 generous tablespoons frosting. Place 1 calla lily decoration on each cupcake. Use green decorating icing to add stem and leaf on regular cupcakes.

1 Cupcake: Calories 370; Total Fat 13g (Saturated Fat 6g; Trans Fat 1.5g); Cholesterol 15mg; Sodium 170mg; Total Carbohydrate 59g (Dietary Fiber 0g); Protein 3g **Exchanges:** 1 Starch, 3 Other Carbohydrate, 2 1/2 Fat **Carbohydrate Choices:** 4

sweet success tip

After the calla lilies have chilled for an hour, you can shape the petal edges with a slightly rippled look. The flowers can be made up to 1 week in advance and stored in a sealed container.

to form calla lilies:

1. Knead candy coating mixture until smooth.

2. Using fingers, press ¼ teaspoon mixture into rounds, about ⅛ inch thick.

3. Fold sides of bottom halves of rounds together, overlapping slightly.

4. Cut each gumdrop lengthwise in half; cut each half into 3 pieces.

5. Insert gumdrop piece, sugar side up, into center as stamen.

white-on-white **cupcakes**

24 cupcakes   PREP TIME: **1 Hour 10 Minutes** START TO FINISH: **2 Hours 5 Minutes**

CUPCAKES
White Cupcakes (page 16)

FROSTING
Fluffy White Frosting (page 21)

GARNISH
1 package (4 oz) white chocolate baking bar

1 tablespoon powdered sugar

1 Make, bake and cool White Cupcakes as directed in recipe.

2 To make chocolate curls, pull a swivel-bladed vegetable peeler down the edge of white chocolate bar, using long, thin strokes.

3 Make Fluffy White Frosting as directed in recipe. Frost cupcakes. Using toothpick to lift curls, place about 2 teaspoons white chocolate curls on each cupcake. With small strainer, lightly sprinkle powdered sugar over cupcakes.

1 Cupcake: Calories 230; Total Fat 8g (Saturated Fat 2.5g; Trans Fat 1g); Cholesterol 0mg; Sodium 140mg; Total Carbohydrate 36g (Dietary Fiber 0g); Protein 3g **Exchanges:** 1 Starch, 1 1/2 Other Carbohydrate, 1 1/2 Fat **Carbohydrate Choices:** 2 1/2

sweet success tip

If you have only one 12-cup muffin pan, cover and refrigerate the rest of the batter while baking the first batch. Then bake the rest of the batter in the cooled muffin pan, adding 1 or 2 minutes to the bake time.

use a **cake mix**

Substitute 1 box white cake mix for the White Cupcakes. Make cake mix as directed on box for cupcakes. Make chocolate curls as directed in recipe. For the frosting, substitute 1 container fluffy white whipped ready-to-spread frosting. Garnish as directed in recipe.

monogrammed **cream-filled cupcakes**

24 cupcakes   **PREP TIME: 55 Minutes** START TO FINISH: **1 Hour 55 Minutes**

CUPCAKES

Chocolate Cupcakes (page 15)

FILLING

1 cup vanilla whipped ready-to-spread frosting (from 12-oz container)

$^{1}/_{2}$ cup marshmallow creme

FROSTING

1 cup chocolate whipped ready-to-spread frosting (from 12-oz container)

$^{1}/_{2}$ cup semisweet chocolate chips

2 teaspoons light corn syrup

DECORATION

3 tablespoons vanilla whipped ready-to-spread frosting (from 12-oz container)

1 Make, bake and cool Chocolate Cupcakes as directed in recipe.

2 With end of round handle of wooden spoon, make deep, $^{1}/_{2}$-inch-wide indentation in center of each cupcake, not quite to the bottom (wiggle end of spoon in cupcake to make opening large enough). In small bowl, mix 1 cup vanilla frosting and the marshmallow creme. Spoon into small resealable food-storage plastic bag. Cut $^{3}/_{8}$-inch tip off one bottom corner of bag. Insert tip of bag into each cupcake and squeeze bag to fill.

3 In small microwavable bowl, microwave chocolate frosting, chocolate chips and corn syrup uncovered on High 30 seconds; stir. Microwave 15 to 30 seconds longer; stir until smooth. Dip top of each cupcake in frosting. Let stand until frosting is set.

4 Spoon 3 tablespoons vanilla frosting into small resealable food-storage plastic bag. Cut tiny tip off one bottom corner of bag. Pipe initials or a squiggle shape on each cupcake.

1 Cupcake: Calories 260; Total Fat 12g (Saturated Fat 3.5g; Trans Fat 2g); Cholesterol 20mg; Sodium 210mg; Total Carbohydrate 37g (Dietary Fiber 1g); Protein 2g **Exchanges:** $^{1}/_{2}$ Starch, 2 Other Carbohydrate, 2 $^{1}/_{2}$ Fat **Carbohydrate Choices:** 2 $^{1}/_{2}$

sweet success tip

You can use a melon baller to take a small scoop out of the cupcakes for the filling.

use a **cake mix**

Substitute 1 box devil's food cake mix for the Chocolate Cupcakes. Make cake mix as directed on box for cupcakes. Frost and decorate as directed in recipe.

baby **rattle cupcakes**

24 cupcakes PREP TIME: **1 Hour 5 Minutes** START TO FINISH: **2 Hours 5 Minutes**

CUPCAKES

Yellow Cupcakes (page 14)

FROSTING

Vanilla Buttercream Frosting
(page 20)

DECORATIONS

Yellow and green decorating
icings (from 4.25-oz tubes)

Candy sprinkles and decors,
if desired

8 yards pastel satin or curling
ribbon ($^1/_4$ inch), cut into
12-inch pieces, if desired

24 paper lollipop sticks (4 $^1/_2$ inch)

24 small gumdrops
(from 10-oz package)

1 Make, bake and cool Yellow Cupcakes as directed in recipe.

2 Make Vanilla Buttercream Frosting as directed in recipe. Frost cupcakes. With yellow and green icings, pipe designs onto cupcakes. Decorate as desired with candy sprinkles.

3 With toothpick, poke hole in side of each cupcake. Tie ribbon bow in center of each lollipop stick. Add gumdrop to one end of each stick. Insert other ends of sticks into sides of cupcakes, just below frosting, to form rattles.

1 Frosted Cupcake (Undecorated): Calories 340; Total Fat 14g (Saturated Fat 8g; Trans Fat 0.5g); Cholesterol 60mg; Sodium 230mg; Total Carbohydrate 50g (Dietary Fiber 0g); Protein 2g **Exchanges:** 1 $^1/_2$ Starch, 2 Other Carbohydrate, 2 $^1/_2$ Fat **Carbohydrate Choices:** 3

sweet success tip

To make these cupcakes super easy, use lollipops or suckers instead of the lollipop sticks with gumdrops.

use a cake mix

Substitute 1 box yellow cake mix for the Yellow Cupcakes. Make cake mix as directed on box for cupcakes. For the frosting, substitute 1 container vanilla or creamy white creamy ready-to-spread frosting. Frost and decorate as directed in recipe.

baby's **booties**

16 booties (24 cupcakes)   **PREP TIME: 1 Hour 5 Minutes** START TO FINISH: **2 Hours 5 Minutes**

CUPCAKES
White Cupcakes (page 16)

FROSTING
Vanilla Buttercream Frosting
(page 20)

DECORATION
Sour candy straws
Candy decors

1 Make, bake and cool White Cupcakes as directed in recipe; color as desired.

2 Meanwhile, make Vanilla Buttercream Frosting as directed in recipe; color as desired.

3 Remove paper baking cups from cupcakes. Place 2 cupcakes upside down on separate plates. Cut small piece off side of a third cupcake to make a flat surface. Cut third cupcake horizontally in half. Place one half with cut side against cupcake on plate as shown in diagram. Place other half against second cupcake. Repeat with remaining cupcakes.

4 Frost cupcake booties, attaching toe piece to cupcake with frosting. Cut sour candy straws to form bows. Top with candy decors.

1 Frosted Bootie (Undecorated): Calories 520; Total Fat 18g (Saturated Fat 8g; Trans Fat 2g); Cholesterol 20mg; Sodium 250mg; Total Carbohydrate 84g (Dietary Fiber 0g); Protein 4g **Exchanges:** 1 ¹/₂ Starch, 4 Other Carbohydrate, 3 ¹/₂ Fat **Carbohydrate Choices:** 5 ¹/₂

sweet success tip
Wish you had pink or yellow booties? Add the color of your choice by stirring drops of food color into the frosting.

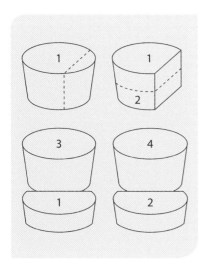

use a cake mix

Substitute 1 box white cake mix for the white cupcakes. Make cake mix as directed on box for cupcakes. For the frosting, substitute 2 containers vanilla creamy or whipped ready-to-spread frosting. Decorate as directed in recipe.

sunflower **cupcakes**

24 cupcakes   PREP TIME: **1 Hour 15 Minutes** START TO FINISH: **2 Hours 20 Minutes**

CUPCAKES

Yellow Cupcakes (page 14)

FILLING

1/3 cup lemon curd (from 11 1/4-oz jar)

1 package (3 oz) cream cheese, softened

FROSTING AND DECORATIONS

Fluffy White Frosting (page 21)

Yellow food color

4 to 5 tubes (4.25 oz each) yellow decorating icing

1/2 cup miniature semisweet chocolate chips

Sour candy straws, if desired

1 Make, bake and cool Yellow Cupcakes as directed in recipe.

2 By slowly moving end of round handle of wooden spoon back and forth, make deep, 3/4-inch-wide indentation in center of top of each cupcake, not quite to bottom (wiggle end of spoon in cupcake to make opening large enough).

3 In medium bowl, beat lemon curd and cream cheese with electric mixer on medium speed until blended. Spoon into small resealable food-storage plastic bag; seal bag. Cut 3/8-inch tip off one bottom corner of bag. Insert tip of bag into top of each cupcake; squeeze bag to fill cupcake.

4 Make Fluffy White Frosting as directed in recipe. Stir 4 drops food color into frosting until pale yellow. Frost cupcakes.

5 Place unopened icing tube in tall drinking glass filled with hot tap water for 15 minutes. Remove from water; wipe dry. Knead tube gently with hands to soften. Using leaf tip on icing tube, pipe 2 concentric circles of leaves, starting with outside edge of cupcake and working toward center; leave quarter-size area in center with just frosting. Carefully spoon 1 teaspoon chocolate chips onto center of each cupcake; press into frosting.

6 Using sour candy straws for stems and leaves, arrange cupcakes on serving tray. Refrigerate until ready to serve. Store in refrigerator.

1 Cupcake: Calories 350; Total Fat 15g (Saturated Fat 10g; Trans Fat 0g); Cholesterol 55mg; Sodium 210mg; Total Carbohydrate 50g (Dietary Fiber 0g); Protein 3g **Exchanges:** 1 Starch, 2 1/2 Other Carbohydrate, 3 Fat **Carbohydrate Choices:** 3

sweet success tip

You can find lemon curd in the baking aisle of the supermarket or with the jams and jellies. It's a sweet and tart sauce made with lemon juice, egg yolks, butter and sugar.

use a cake mix

Substitute 1 box yellow cake mix for the Yellow Cupcakes. Make cake mix as directed on box for cupcakes. For the frosting, substitute 1 container fluffy white whipped ready-to-spread frosting. Frost and decorate as directed in recipe.

cosmopolitan **cupcakes**

27 cupcakes **PREP TIME: 1 Hour 55 Minutes** START TO FINISH: **2 Hours 55 Minutes**

CUPCAKES

White Cupcakes (page 16)
1 cup milk
1 package (6 oz) fresh raspberries

RASPBERRY BUTTERCREAM FROSTING

Vanilla Buttercream Frosting (page 20)
3 to 5 tablespoons raspberry juice
Red food color
Pink decorating sugar

CHOCOLATE PURSE DECORATIONS

String licorice, cut into 27 pieces (1 1/2 inches)
White decorating icing (from 6.4-oz can)
27 smooth milk chocolate candies (from 9.5-oz bag), unwrapped
Assorted decors, if desired

1 Make White Cupcakes as directed in recipe except—place paper baking cup in each of 27 regular-size muffin cups, use 1 cup milk and lightly mash raspberries with fork; fold into batter just until incorporated.

2 Divide batter evenly among muffin cups, filling each about 2/3 full.

3 Bake 22 to 24 minutes or until toothpick inserted in center of cupcake comes out clean. Cool 5 minutes; remove from pans to cooling racks to cool.

4 Meanwhile, make Vanilla Buttercream Frosting as directed in recipe except—substitute raspberry juice for the vanilla and milk. Stir in 2 drops red food color. Frost each cupcake with about 2 tablespoons frosting. Sprinkle pink decorating sugar on small plate; roll edges of cupcakes in red sugar.

5 Bend 1 licorice piece and press into 1 cupcake for purse handle. Pipe decorating icing on front of 1 chocolate candy; press decors into icing. Place candy on cupcake, just overlapping ends of licorice, for purse. Repeat with remaining licorice, candies and cupcakes.

1 Cupcake: Calories 310; Total Fat 11g (Saturated Fat 4.5g; Trans Fat 1g); Cholesterol 15mg; Sodium 150mg; Total Carbohydrate 51g (Dietary Fiber 0g); Protein 2g **Exchanges:** 1 Starch, 2 1/2 Other Carbohydrate, 2 Fat **Carbohydrate Choices:** 3 1/2

sweet success tip

Serve these cupcakes without liners in martini glasses for a fun presentation.

use a cake mix

Substitute 1 box white cake mix for the White Cupcakes. Make cake mix as directed on box for cupcakes **except**—use 1 cup water, 1/3 cup vegetable oil and 3 egg whites. Lightly mash 1 package (6 oz) fresh raspberries with fork; fold into batter just until incorporated. Bake and cool as directed on box. Frost and decorate as directed in recipe.

key lime **cupcakes**

48 cupcakes **PREP TIME: 55 Minutes** START TO FINISH: **2 Hours**

TOPPING

1 box (4-serving size) vanilla instant pudding and pie filling mix

1 1/2 cups whipping cream

1/4 cup Key lime or regular lime juice

4 drops green food color

1 1/2 cups powdered sugar

CUPCAKES

1 box yellow cake mix with pudding

Water, vegetable oil and eggs called for on cake mix box

FROSTING

1 (12-oz container) fluffy white whipped ready-to-spread frosting

1 tablespoon Key lime or regular lime juice

1/2 teaspoon grated Key lime or regular lime peel

Small fresh lime wedges

1 In large bowl, beat pudding mix and whipping cream with whisk 2 minutes. Let stand 3 minutes. Beat in 1/4 cup Key lime juice and the food color; stir in powdered sugar until smooth. Cover and refrigerate.

2 Heat oven to 375°F. Place paper baking cup in each of 24 regular-size muffin cups. Make cake batter as directed on box, using water, oil and eggs. Using about 1/2 of the batter, spoon about 1 rounded tablespoon batter into each muffin cup. (Muffin cups will be about 1/3 full.) Refrigerate remaining batter.

3 Bake 12 to 16 minutes or until toothpick inserted in center of cupcake comes out clean. Remove cupcakes from pan; place on cooling racks to cool. Repeat with remaining baking cups and batter.

4 Remove paper baking cups from cupcakes. Swirl about 2 teaspoons topping on top of each cupcake.

5 Stir frosting in container 20 times. Gently stir in 1 tablespoon Key lime juice and the lime peel. Spoon frosting into 1-quart resealable food-storage plastic bag. Cut 1/2-inch opening from bottom corner of bag. Squeeze 1 rounded teaspoon frosting from bag onto topping. Garnish with lime wedge. Store in refrigerator.

1 Cupcake: Calories 140; Total Fat 6g (Saturated Fat 2.5g; Trans Fat 0.5g); Cholesterol 25mg; Sodium 115mg; Total Carbohydrate 19g (Dietary Fiber 0g); Protein 0g **Exchanges:** 1/2 Starch, 1 Other Carbohydrate, 1 Fat **Carbohydrate Choices:** 1

sweet success tip

Check your grocery store for seasonal fresh Key limes in bags to juice. You will need 5 Key limes to make about 1/3 cup juice.

cherry mini cakes

72 mini cakes   PREP TIME: **35 Minutes** START TO FINISH: **1 Hour 45 Minutes**

MINI CAKES

  Yellow Cupcakes (page 14)
1 package (0.14 oz) cherry-flavored unsweetened soft drink mix
1 teaspoon almond extract

GLAZE

1 bag (2 lb) powdered sugar (8 cups)
1/2 cup water
1/2 cup light corn syrup
2 teaspoons almond extract
2 to 3 teaspoons hot water

DECORATION

  Miniature red candy hearts or candy sprinkles

1 Make mini version of Yellow Cupcakes as directed in recipe variation except—stir in soft drink mix with the flour and add 1 teaspoon almond extract with the eggs. Bake and cool as directed.

2 Place cooling rack on cookie sheet or waxed paper to catch glaze drips. In 3-quart saucepan, mix all glaze ingredients except hot water. Heat over low heat, stirring frequently, until sugar is dissolved. Remove from heat. Stir in 2 teaspoons hot water. If necessary, stir in up to 1 teaspoon more hot water so glaze will just coat cakes.

3 Turn each cake so top side is down on cooling rack. Pour about 1 tablespoon glaze over each cake, letting glaze coat sides. Let stand until glaze is set, about 15 minutes. Top each cake with candy hearts.

1 Mini Cake: Calories 110; Total Fat 3g (Saturated Fat 1.5g; Trans Fat 0g); Cholesterol 15mg; Sodium 65mg; Total Carbohydrate 21g (Dietary Fiber 0g); Protein 0g **Exchanges:** 1/2 Starch, 1 Other Carbohydrate, 1/2 Fat **Carbohydrate Choices:** 1 1/2

sweet success tip

Perfect for a party! Bake the mini cakes up to 2 weeks ahead of time and freeze. Add the glaze when it's time for the party.

use a cake mix

Place mini paper baking cup in each of 60 mini muffin cups. Substitute 1 box yellow cake mix for the Yellow Cupcakes. Make cake mix as directed on box for cupcakes **except**— add 1 package (0.14 oz) cherry-flavored unsweetened soft drink mix and 1 teaspoon almond extract. Divide batter evenly among muffin cups, filling each about 1/2 full. (If using one pan, refrigerate batter while baking other cakes.) Bake 10 to 13 minutes or until toothpick inserted in center of cake comes out clean. Glaze and decorate as directed in recipe. 60 mini cakes

tres leches **cupcakes**

24 cupcakes   PREP TIME: **1 Hour 10 Minutes** START TO FINISH: **3 Hours 45 Minutes**

CUPCAKES

    White Cupcakes (page 16)
1   teaspoon rum extract
$3/4$ cup finely chopped pecans

SOAKING MIXTURE

$2/3$ cup canned sweetened
    condensed milk
    (not evaporated)
$1/4$ cup canned coconut milk (not
    cream of coconut)

RUM WHIPPED CREAM

1   pint (2 cups) heavy
    whipping cream
1   teaspoon rum extract

GARNISH

1   cup flaked coconut
$1/2$ cup chopped pecans

1 Make White Cupcakes as directed in recipe except—use 1 teaspoon rum extract for the 2 $1/2$ teaspoons vanilla and stir in $3/4$ cup pecans. Divide batter evenly among muffin cups, filling each about $2/3$ full.

2 Bake 18 to 20 minutes or until toothpick inserted in center of cupcake comes out clean. Cool 5 minutes; remove from pans to cooling racks. Cool 10 minutes longer.

3 Poke tops of cupcakes every $1/2$ inch with long-tined fork, wiping fork occasionally to reduce sticking. Place cupcakes in dessert cups. In small bowl, stir sweetened condensed milk and coconut milk with whisk until smooth. Slowly spoon 2 teaspoons milk mixture evenly over top of each cupcake, allowing mixture to soak into holes and drizzle down side. Cover; refrigerate at least 2 hours or overnight, until milk mixture on tops of cupcakes is absorbed.

4 In medium deep bowl, beat whipping cream and 1 teaspoon rum extract with electric mixer on high speed until stiff peaks form. Frost each cupcake with about 2 heaping tablespoons whipped cream; sprinkle with about 2 teaspoons coconut and 1 teaspoon pecans.

1 Cupcake: Calories 340; Total Fat 21g (Saturated Fat 9g; Trans Fat 1.5g); Cholesterol 30mg; Sodium 150mg; Total Carbohydrate 33g (Dietary Fiber 1g); Protein 4g **Exchanges:** 1 $1/2$ Starch, $1/2$ Other Carbohydrate, 4 Fat **Carbohydrate Choices:** 2

sweet success tip
For fun, serve these delicious cupcakes in elegant dessert dishes.

banana-turtle **torte cupcakes**

24 cupcakes   **PREP TIME: 55 Minutes** START TO FINISH: **2 Hours**

CUPCAKES

Chocolate Cupcakes (page 15)
3/4 cup chopped pecans
1 pint (2 cups) heavy whipping cream

CARAMEL SAUCE

1/4 cup butter
1/2 cup packed brown sugar
2 tablespoons light corn syrup
1 tablespoon milk

TOPPING

2 medium bananas
24 pecan halves

1 Make Chocolate Cupcakes as directed in recipe except—stir chopped pecans into batter. Bake and cool as directed.

2 In chilled large bowl, beat whipping cream with electric mixer on high speed until stiff peaks form; set aside. Cut cupcakes horizontally in half.

3 In 1-quart saucepan, melt butter over medium-high heat. Stir in brown sugar, corn syrup and milk. Cool 5 minutes.

4 Spread 1 heaping tablespoon whipped cream on each cupcake bottom. Thinly slice bananas; place 3 slices on top of whipped cream on each cupcake. Drizzle with 1 teaspoon caramel sauce; replace cupcake tops. Spread remaining whipped cream on cupcakes; drizzle with 1 teaspoon caramel sauce. Garnish each with pecan half.

1 Cupcake: Calories 320; Total Fat 20g (Saturated Fat 8g, Trans Fat 1.5g); Cholesterol 50mg; Sodium 200mg; Total Carbohydrate 31g (Dietary Fiber 2g); Protein 3g **Exchanges:** 1 Starch, 1 Other Carbohydrate, 4 Fat **Carbohydrate Choices:** 2

use a cake mix

Substitute 1 box devil's food cake mix for the Chocolate Cupcakes. Make cake mix as directed on box for cupcakes. Toss 3/4 cup finely chopped pecans with 1 1/2 tablespoons flour; stir into batter. Bake and cool as directed on box. Continue as directed in recipe.

banana-coffee caramel-filled cupcakes

{ **Anna Ginsberg Austin, Texas Cookie Madness www.cookiemadness.net** }

22 cupcakes   PREP TIME: 55 Minutes START TO FINISH: 2 Hours 35 Minutes

CUPCAKES

2	teaspoons instant coffee crystals
1	tablespoon boiling water
2	cups all-purpose flour
1	teaspoon baking soda
1/2	teaspoon salt
1/2	cup unsalted butter, softened
1 1/2	cups granulated sugar
3	medium bananas, mashed (1 1/2 cups)
1	teaspoon vanilla
2	eggs
1	cup sour cream

CARAMEL FILLING

1/2	cup granulated sugar
2	tablespoons water
1/4	cup unsalted butter, softened
1/4	cup whipping cream
1	teaspoon vanilla
1/8	teaspoon salt

COFFEE FROSTING

1/4	cup milk
2	tablespoons plus 1 teaspoon instant coffee crystals
1/2	cup unsalted butter, softened
3 3/4	cups powdered sugar

GARNISH

1	cup whipping cream, whipped
	Chocolate-covered coffee beans, if desired

1 Heat oven to 350°F. Place paper baking cup in each of 22 regular-size muffin cups. Dissolve 2 teaspoons coffee crystals in 1 tablespoon boiling water; set aside. In small bowl, stir together flour, baking soda and 1/2 teaspoon salt; set aside.

2 In large bowl, beat 1/2 cup butter and 1 1/2 cups granulated sugar with electric mixer on high speed about 2 minutes. Beat in bananas and 1 teaspoon vanilla. Add eggs; beat on high speed 1 minute, scraping bowl frequently. With spoon or on low speed, alternately add flour mixture and sour cream, stirring just until combined. Stir in coffee mixture. Divide batter evenly among muffin cups.

3 Bake 22 to 25 minutes or until toothpick inserted in center of cupcake comes out clean.

4 Meanwhile, in 1-quart heavy saucepan, heat 1/2 cup granulated sugar and 2 tablespoons water over medium heat, swirling saucepan until sugar is dissolved. Increase heat to high; cover and boil syrup 2 minutes. Uncover; continue boiling until sugar is dark amber in color. Remove saucepan from heat. Beat in 1/4 cup butter with whisk until smooth. Beat in 1/4 cup whipping cream. Beat in 1 teaspoon vanilla and 1/8 teaspoon salt with whisk. Cool completely.

5 Microwave milk on High 40 seconds or just until it begins to boil. Stir in 2 tablespoons plus 1 teaspoon coffee crystals until dissolved; set aside. In medium bowl, beat 1/2 cup butter and 1/2 cup of the powdered sugar with electric mixer on low speed until blended. Gradually beat in remaining powdered sugar. Add 1/2 of the milk mixture; beat on high speed. Add remaining milk mixture, beating until smooth.

6 Using melon baller, scoop out center of each cupcake, scooping almost to bottom of cupcake. Spoon 1 generous teaspoon caramel filling into each hole. Reserve remaining caramel filling.

7 Frost each cupcake and top with whipped cream; drizzle with reserved caramel filling. Garnish with coffee beans.

1 Cupcake: Calories 380; Total Fat 18g (Saturated Fat 11g, Trans Fat 0.5g); Cholesterol 70mg; Sodium 135mg; Total Carbohydrate 52g (Dietary Fiber 1g); Protein 2g **Exchanges:** 1/2 Starch, 3 Other Carbohydrate, 3 1/2 Fat **Carbohydrate Choices:** 3 1/2

use a cake mix

Substitute 1 box devil's food cake mix for the cupcakes above. Dissolve 2 teaspoons instant coffee crystals in 1 1/4 cups water. Make cake mix as directed on box for cupcakes **except**—use coffee mixture, 1/2 cup vegetable oil, 3 eggs and 1 cup mashed bananas (2 medium). Bake and cool as directed on box. Fill and frost 22 cupcakes as directed in recipe. Save 8 cupcakes for another use. 30 cupcakes

baked alaska **cupcakes**

24 cupcakes   PREP TIME: **50 Minutes** START TO FINISH: **3 Hours 45 Minutes**

CUPCAKES

White Cupcakes (page 16)
1 quart strawberry ice cream, softened

MERINGUE

4 egg whites
1/4 teaspoon cream of tartar
1 1/2 teaspoons vanilla
2/3 cup sugar

1 Make White Cupcakes as directed in recipe except—place paper baking cup in each of 48 regular-size muffin cups and spray with baking spray with flour. Fill cups only 1/3 full.

2 Bake 10 to 14 minutes or until toothpick inserted in center of cupcake comes out clean. Cool 5 minutes; remove from pans to cooling racks to cool.

3 Place 24 cupcakes in freezer plastic bag and freeze for another use. On top of each of the remaining 24 cupcakes, spoon and spread 2 heaping tablespoons ice cream. Cover; freeze at least 2 hours or overnight, until ice cream is hardened.

4 Heat oven to 450°F. In medium bowl, beat egg whites, cream of tartar and vanilla with electric mixer on high speed until soft peaks form. Gradually add sugar, 1 tablespoon at a time, beating until stiff peaks form and mixture is glossy. Spread over ice cream–topped cupcakes.

5 Bake 2 to 3 minutes or until lightly browned. Serve immediately.

1 Cupcake: Calories 250; Total Fat 9g (Saturated Fat 3.5g; Trans Fat 1g); Cholesterol 10mg; Sodium 150mg; Total Carbohydrate 36g (Dietary Fiber 0g); Protein 4g **Exchanges:** 1 1/2 Starch, 1 Other Carbohydrate, 1 1/2 Fat **Carbohydrate Choices:** 2 1/2

sweet success tip

Use the leftover cupcakes to make this recipe again for another get-together, or use them to make layered desserts with your favorite ice cream or whipped cream and toppings.

special serving and gift ideas

Serving Up Cupcakes

When you've made some really special cupcakes for a special occasion, you have to show them off! Here are some ways to display your scrumptious creations.

- Cupcake stands, pedestals and towers will show off your little cakes in style. You'll find them available at specialty shops or online. Or use tiered pedestals that hold several serving plates.

- Fill shallow baskets with cupcakes. Line the baskets with vintage print dish cloths or linen napkins. Or use shallow wooden boxes—a heart-shaped box would be perfect for a wedding, shower or Valentine's Day.

Dress Up Your Platters

Special cupcake wrappers, designed to hold already baked and decorated cupcakes, can add drama to your display. Paper leaves or doilies can also offer a "supporting role" under your cupcakes on the platter. Look for decorations at party stores or online.

Clever Ideas from Your Cupboards

Why not display your cupcakes in cups or glasses that coordinate with the flavor of the cupcakes? Serve Cosmopolitan Cupcakes (page 296) in martini glasses, or Margarita Cupcakes (page 52) in margarita glasses. Don't have a lot of specialty glasses? You can create a display by featuring a cupcake in a glass, in the center of a platter of cupcakes! Serve Mini Cupcake Banana Splits (page 148) in boat-shaped dishes or Mocha-Caramel Cappuccino Cupcakes (page 266) in coffee cups!

Gifting Cupcakes

The perfect gift for any occasion—cupcakes! Who wouldn't love some of these homemade, frosted goodies? The only trick is how to wrap them.

Gifting a Batch of Cupcakes

Use cookie tins. They're already festive and are easy to fill. For a special touch, fill the gaps between the cupcakes with candy. The candies are a bonus and will hold the cupcakes steady during transit.

Bakery boxes are made specifically for multiple cupcakes. Look for the kind that have cellophane on the cover—perfect for showing off your beautifully decorated creations!

Gifting a Single Cupcake

Place a cupcake in an individual cupcake box tied with a colorful ribbon. Use wire-edged ribbons for easy, elaborate-looking bows. Chinese take-out containers also make a great packaging choice, and they're available in import stores or online.

For a tea lover, why not place a single Chai Latte Cupcake (page 258) in a china teacup or coffee cup. Place the cup on a large piece of cellophane; gather up the edges and secure with tape. Don't forget the ribbon.

apple-fig bread pudding cupcakes with maple sauce

6 servings   PREP TIME: **30 Minutes** START TO FINISH: **1 Hour 10 Minutes**

CUPCAKES

- 7 cups cubed (1 inch) day-old French or Italian bread (from 1-lb loaf)
- 1 large cooking apple (Braeburn, Cortland or Granny Smith), peeled, chopped (1 1/2 cups)
- 1/2 cup chopped dried figs
- 1 cup packed brown sugar
- 1 cup milk
- 1/4 cup butter or margarine
- 1 teaspoon ground cinnamon
- 1/2 teaspoon vanilla
- 2 eggs, beaten

SAUCE

- 1/3 cup granulated sugar
- 1/3 cup packed brown sugar
- 1/3 cup heavy whipping cream
- 1/3 cup butter or margarine
- 1/2 teaspoon maple flavor

1 Heat oven to 350°F. Grease 6 jumbo muffin cups with shortening.

2 In large bowl, mix bread cubes, apple and figs. In small saucepan, cook 1 cup brown sugar, the milk and 1/4 cup butter over medium heat until butter is melted. Remove from heat; stir in cinnamon and vanilla. Pour over bread mixture in bowl. Add eggs; toss to coat.

3 Divide mixture evenly among muffin cups, filling to tops of cups. Bake 30 to 34 minutes or until center is set and apples are tender. Cool while making sauce.

4 In 1-quart saucepan, stir granulated sugar, 1/3 cup brown sugar, the whipping cream and 1/3 cup butter. Heat to boiling over medium heat, stirring occasionally. Remove from heat; stir in maple flavor.

5 Remove warm cupcakes from pan; place on serving plates. Spoon warm sauce over cupcakes.

1 Serving (1 cupcake and about 1/2 cup sauce each): Calories 660; Total Fat 26g (Saturated Fat 16g; Trans Fat 1g); Cholesterol 140mg; Sodium 450mg; Total Carbohydrate 98g (Dietary Fiber 3g); Protein 9g **Exchanges:** 2 1/2 Starch, 1/2 Fruit, 3 1/2 Other Carbohydrate, 5 Fat **Carbohydrate Choices:** 6 1/2

sweet success tip

For sweet indulgence, top with whipped cream and a toasted pecan.

sunnyside-up **bacon cupcakes**

24 cupcakes   PREP TIME: **50 Minutes** START TO FINISH: **1 Hour 50 Minutes**

CUPCAKES

2 1/3 cups all-purpose flour
2 1/2 teaspoons baking powder
 1/2   teaspoon salt
 1/2   teaspoon ground cinnamon
  1   cup butter or
       margarine, softened
  1   cup sugar
  3   eggs
  2   tablespoons maple-flavored
       syrup
  1   teaspoon vanilla
  1   cup milk
 3/4   cup crumbled crisply cooked
       maple-flavored bacon (9 slices)
       Vanilla Buttercream Frosting
       (page 20)
 24   butterscotch
       candies, unwrapped
       Black decorator sugar, if desired

1 Heat oven to 350°F. Place paper baking cup in each of 24 regular-size muffin cups.

2 In medium bowl, mix flour, baking powder, salt and cinnamon; set aside.

3 In large bowl, beat butter with electric mixer on medium speed 30 seconds. Gradually add sugar, about 1/4 cup at a time, beating well after each addition and scraping bowl occasionally. Beat 2 minutes longer. Add eggs, one at a time, beating well after each addition. Beat in maple syrup and vanilla. On low speed, alternately add flour mixture, about 1/3 of mixture at a time, and milk, about 1/2 at a time, beating just until blended. Stir bacon into batter.

4 Divide batter evenly among muffin cups, filling each about 2/3 full.

5 Bake 20 to 25 minutes or until golden brown and toothpick inserted in center comes out clean. Cool in pans 5 minutes. Remove cupcakes from pans; place on cooling racks to cool.

6 Meanwhile, make Vanilla Buttercream Frosting as directed in recipe. Frost cupcakes to look like the white of a sunnyside-up egg. For yolk, press 1 butterscotch candy in center of each cupcake. Sprinkle with black decorator sugar for pepper.

1 Cupcake: Calories 370; Total Fat 15g (Saturated Fat 9g; Trans Fat 0.5g); Cholesterol 65mg; Sodium 300mg; Total Carbohydrate 55g (Dietary Fiber 0g); Protein 3g **Exchanges:** 1 Starch, 2 1/2 Other Carbohydrate, 3 Fat **Carbohydrate Choices:** 3 1/2

sweet success tip

Short on time? Use a container of vanilla creamy ready-to-spread frosting instead of the Buttercream frosting.

use a cake mix

Substitute 1 box white cake mix for the cupcakes above. Make cake mix as directed on box for cupcakes **except**—use 1 cup water, 1/3 cup vegetable oil, 3 egg whites and 2 tablespoons maple-flavored syrup.
Stir in 3/4 cup crisply cooked and finely crumbled maple-flavored bacon (9 slices). Bake 15 to 22 minutes. Cool as directed on box. For the frosting, substitute 1 container vanilla creamy ready-to-spread frosting. Decorate as directed in recipe.

mango-jalapeño cupcake stacks

24 cupcakes   **PREP TIME: 15 Minutes** START TO FINISH: **1 Hour 15 Minutes**

CUPCAKES

2 3/4 cups all-purpose flour
   3   teaspoons baking powder
 1/2   teaspoon salt
 3/4   cup shortening
1 2/3 cups sugar
   5   egg whites
1 1/2 teaspoons vanilla
 3/4   cup mango nectar
 1/2   cup milk
   2   tablespoons grated lime peel
   1   tablespoon finely chopped jalapeño chile

CREAM CHEESE FROSTING

   1   package (8 oz) plus 1 package (3 oz) cream cheese, softened
 1/3   cup butter or margarine, softened
1 1/2 teaspoons vanilla
   3   to 5 teaspoons milk
   6   cups powdered sugar
   1   cup finely chopped peeled mango
   1   cup flaked coconut
       Grated lime peel, if desired

1 Heat oven to 350°F. Place paper baking cup in each of 24 regular-size muffin cups.

2 In medium bowl, mix flour, baking powder and salt; set aside.

3 In large bowl, beat shortening with electric mixer on medium speed 30 seconds. Gradually add sugar, about 1/3 cup at a time, beating well after each addition and scraping bowl occasionally. Beat 2 minutes longer. Add egg whites, one at a time, beating well after each addition. Beat in vanilla. On low speed, alternately add flour mixture, about 1/3 of mixture at a time, and mango nectar and milk, about 1/2 at a time, beating just until blended.

4 Divide batter evenly among muffin cups, filling each about 1/3 full.

5 Bake 18 to 20 minutes or until toothpick inserted in center comes out clean. Cool in pans 5 minutes. Remove cupcakes from pans; place on cooling racks to cool.

6 In large bowl, beat cream cheese, butter, vanilla and 3 teaspoons of the milk with electric mixer on low speed until smooth. Beat in powdered sugar, 1 cup at a time. Gradually beat in just enough remaining milk to make frosting smooth and spreadable.

7 Cut each cupcake horizontally in half. On each cupcake bottom, spread about 1 tablespoon frosting; top with 1 teaspoon mango and 1 teaspoon coconut. Cover with cupcake tops. Frost top of each cupcake with 1 heaping tablespoon frosting. Top each with about 1 teaspoon mango and 1 teaspoon coconut. Garnish with lime peel.

1 Cupcake: Calories 180; Total Fat 7g (Saturated Fat 2g, Trans Fat 1g); Cholesterol 0mg; Sodium 125mg; Total Carbohydrate 26g (Dietary Fiber 0g); Protein 2g **Exchanges:** 1/2 Starch, 1 Other Carbohydrate, 1 1/2 Fat **Carbohydrate Choices: 2**

sweet success tip

If fresh mango isn't available, use purchased refrigerated mango from a jar. You'll find it in the produce section.

use a cake mix

Substitute 1 box white cake mix for the cupcakes above. Make cake mix as directed on box for cupcakes **except**—use 3/4 cup mango nectar, 1/2 cup water, 1/3 cup vegetable oil, 3 egg whites, 2 tablespoons grated lime peel and 1 tablespoon finely chopped jalapeño chile. Bake and cool as directed on box. For the frosting, substitute 1 container cream cheese creamy ready-to-spread frosting. Layer with fruit and coconut as directed in recipe.

praline mini **bundt cakes**

12 mini cakes   PREP TIME: **25 Minutes** START TO FINISH: **2 Hours**

CAKES

Yellow Cupcakes (page 14)
1/2   cup chopped pecans
1/2   cup toffee bits

GLAZE

1/4   cup butter (do not use margarine)
1/2   cup packed brown sugar
2   tablespoons corn syrup
2   tablespoons milk
1   cup powdered sugar
1   teaspoon vanilla

GARNISH

1/4   cup toffee bits

1   Heat oven to 350°F. Spray 12 mini fluted tube cake pans with cooking spray with flour, or generously grease 12 jumbo muffin cups with shortening and lightly flour.

2   Make Yellow Cupcakes as directed in recipe except—stir in pecans and 1/2 cup toffee bits. Divide batter evenly among mini pans, filling each with about 1/2 cup batter.

3   Bake 20 to 25 minutes or until toothpick inserted in center of cake comes out clean. Cool 10 minutes. Remove cakes from pans; place on cooling racks to cool.

4   In 1-quart saucepan, melt butter over medium-high heat. Stir in brown sugar, corn syrup and milk. Heat to rolling boil over medium-high heat, stirring frequently. Remove from heat. Immediately beat in powdered sugar and vanilla with whisk until smooth. Immediately drizzle about 1 tablespoon warm glaze over each cake. Sprinkle each with 1 teaspoon toffee bits.

1 Mini Cake: Calories 570; Total Fat 29g (Saturated Fat 16g; Trans Fat 1g); Cholesterol 105mg; Sodium 420mg; Total Carbohydrate 72g (Dietary Fiber 1g); Protein 5g **Exchanges:** 1 1/2 Starch, 3 1/2 Other Carbohydrate, 5 1/2 Fat **Carbohydrate Choices:** 5

sweet success tip

Almond lovers can get a nut fix by substituting almonds for the pecans and almond extract for the vanilla.

use a cake mix

Spray 12 mini fluted tube cake pans with baking spray with flour, or generously grease 12 jumbo muffin cups with shortening and lightly flour. Substitute 1 box yellow cake mix for the Yellow Cupcakes. Make cake mix as directed on box **except**—add 1/2 cup chopped pecans and 1/2 cup toffee bits. Divide batter evenly among mini pans. Bake 18 to 23 minutes or until toothpick inserted in center of cake comes out clean. Glaze and garnish as directed in recipe.

molten caramel-apple cakes

6 cakes PREP TIME: **15 Minutes** START TO FINISH: **35 Minutes**

2 tablespoons cinnamon graham cracker crumbs (2 squares)

3 whole eggs

3 egg yolks

3/4 cup packed brown sugar

1 cup caramel topping

1/2 cup all-purpose flour

3/4 cup chopped peeled apple

Powdered sugar, if desired

1 Heat oven to 450°F. Spray bottoms and sides of 6 (6-oz) custard cups with baking spray with flour. Sprinkle 1 teaspoon cracker crumbs onto bottom and around side of each cup.

2 In large bowl, beat whole eggs and egg yolks with whisk until well blended. Beat in brown sugar. Beat in caramel topping and flour until well blended. Stir in apple. Divide batter evenly among custard cups. Place cups on cookie sheet with sides.

3 Bake about 15 minutes or until sides are set and centers are still soft but not liquid (tops will be slightly puffed). Watch carefully—cakes can overbake quickly. Remove from cookie sheet. Let stand 3 minutes.

4 Run small knife or metal spatula along sides of cakes to loosen. Immediately place heatproof dessert plate upside down over top of each cup; turn plate and cup over. Remove cup. Sprinkle cakes with powdered sugar. Serve warm.

1 Cake: Calories 380; Total Fat 5g (Saturated Fat 1.5g; Trans Fat 0g); Cholesterol 210mg; Sodium 250mg; Total Carbohydrate 75g (Dietary Fiber 1g); Protein 6g **Exchanges:** 1 1/2 Starch, 3 1/2 Other Carbohydrate, 1 Fat **Carbohydrate Choices:** 5

sweet success tip

To sprinkle the powdered sugar lightly onto the cakes, use a fine strainer.

molten butterscotch **cakes**

6 cakes PREP TIME: **15 Minutes** START TO FINISH: **35 Minutes**

6 teaspoons graham cracker crumbs
1 cup butterscotch chips (6 oz)
²/₃ cup butter or margarine
3 whole eggs
3 egg yolks
³/₄ cup packed brown sugar
¹/₂ cup all-purpose flour

1 Heat oven to 450°F. Spray bottoms and sides of 6 (6-oz) custard cups with baking spray with flour. Sprinkle 1 teaspoon cracker crumbs onto bottom and around side of each cup.

2 In 1-quart saucepan, melt butterscotch chips and butter over medium heat, stirring constantly. Remove from heat; cool slightly, about 5 minutes.

3 Meanwhile, in large bowl, beat whole eggs and egg yolks with whisk until well blended. Beat in brown sugar. Beat in butterscotch mixture and flour until well blended. Divide batter evenly among custard cups. Place cups on cookie sheet with sides.

4 Bake 12 to 14 minutes or until sides are set and centers are still soft (tops will be puffed and cracked).

5 Let cakes stand 3 minutes. Run small knife or metal spatula along sides of cakes to loosen. Immediately place dessert plate upside down over top of each cup; turn plate and cup over. Remove cup. Serve cakes warm.

1 Cake: Calories 550; Total Fat 34g (Saturated Fat 21g; Trans Fat 1g); Cholesterol 260mg; Sodium 220mg; Total Carbohydrate 56g (Dietary Fiber 0g); Protein 6g **Exchanges:** 2 Starch, 1 ¹/₂ Other Carbohydrate, 6 ¹/₂ Fat **Carbohydrate Choices:** 4

sweet success tip
When baking these delicious little cakes, watch the bake time for perfect molten filling.

molten chocolate **cakes**

6 cakes   **PREP TIME: 25 Minutes** START TO FINISH: **45 Minutes**

Unsweetened baking cocoa

6 oz semisweet baking chocolate, chopped

1/2 cup plus 2 tablespoons butter or margarine

3 whole eggs

3 egg yolks

1 1/2 cups powdered sugar

1/2 cup all-purpose flour

Additional powdered sugar, if desired

Sugared kumquats, if desired

1 Heat oven to 450°F. Grease bottoms and sides of 6 (6-oz) custard cups with shortening; dust with cocoa. In 2-quart saucepan, melt chocolate and butter over low heat, stirring frequently. Cool slightly.

2 In large bowl, beat whole eggs and egg yolks with whisk or egg beater until well blended. Beat in 1 1/2 cups powdered sugar. Beat in melted chocolate mixture and flour. Divide batter evenly among custard cups. Place cups on cookie sheet with sides.

3 Bake 12 to 14 minutes or until sides are set and centers are still soft (tops will be puffed and cracked).

4 Let cakes stand in cups 3 minutes. Run small knife or metal spatula along sides of cakes to loosen. Immediately place heatproof serving plate upside down over each cup; turn plate and cup over. Remove cup. Sprinkle with additional powdered sugar. Garnish with kumquats. Serve warm.

1 Cake: Calories 580; Total Fat 39g (Saturated Fat 23g; Trans Fat 1g); Cholesterol 260mg; Sodium 180mg; Total Carbohydrate 47g (Dietary Fiber 5g); Protein 9g **Exchanges:** 1 Starch, 2 Other Carbohydrate, 1 Medium-Fat Meat, 6 1/2 Fat **Carbohydrate Choices:** 3

sweet success tip

These warm, gooey cakes are delicious served with a small scoop of vanilla ice cream.

fire and ice **cupcakes**

{ Angie Dudley Suwanee, Georgia Bakerella www.bakerella.com }

36 cupcakes   PREP TIME: **1 Hour** START TO FINISH: **1 Hour 55 Minutes**

CHIPOTLE CHOCOLATE CUPCAKES

1 cup unsweetened baking cocoa
3/4 cup boiling water
2 1/2 cups all-purpose flour
3 teaspoons baking soda
1 teaspoon ground cinnamon
1/4 teaspoon salt
2 to 3 teaspoons ground chipotle chile pepper
1 cup butter, room temperature
2 cups granulated sugar
4 eggs
1 cup buttermilk
2 teaspoons vanilla
1 to 2 tablespoons chopped chipotle chilies in adobo sauce (from 7-oz can)

CHILE CHOCOLATE GANACHE

6 oz semisweet baking chocolate, coarsely chopped
3/4 cup heavy whipping cream
2 cups powdered sugar
1/2 teaspoon ground chipotle chile pepper

GARNISH

2 quarts cinnamon dulce de leche ice cream or cinnamon ice cream, softened slightly

Grated semisweet or dark chocolate, if desired

1 Heat oven to 350°F. Place paper baking cup in each of 36 regular-size muffin cups.

2 In small bowl, stir cocoa into boiling water; set aside. In medium bowl, mix flour, baking soda, cinnamon, salt and 2 to 3 teaspoons chile pepper; set aside.

3 In large bowl, beat butter and granulated sugar with electric mixer on medium speed 2 minutes or until light and fluffy. Add eggs, 1 at a time, beating well after each addition. Beat in buttermilk and vanilla (mixture will appear curdled). On low speed, alternately add flour mixture, about 1/3 at a time, and cocoa mixture, about 1/2 at a time, beating just until blended. Stir in chiles.

4 Divide batter evenly among muffin cups, filling each about 3/4 full.

5 Bake 16 to 20 minutes or until toothpick inserted in center of cupcake comes out clean. Cool 5 minutes; remove from pans to cooling racks to cool.

6 In small microwavable bowl, microwave chopped chocolate and whipping cream uncovered on High about 1 minute 30 seconds, stirring every 30 seconds, until melted and mixture can be stirred smooth. Gradually add powdered sugar and 1/2 teaspoon chile pepper, beating with whisk until smooth.

7 Remove paper liners from cupcakes. Cut each cupcake in half horizontally. Place top half of cupcake on serving plate top-side down. Place small scoop of ice cream on bottom half of cupcake; place remaining cupcake half cut-side down on top of ice cream. Top with another small scoop of ice cream. Drizzle each with about 1 tablespoon ganache; sprinkle with grated chocolate.

1 Cupcake: Calories 300; Total Fat 15g (Saturated Fat 9g; Trans Fat 0g); Cholesterol 60mg; Sodium 210mg; Total Carbohydrate 36g (Dietary Fiber 2g); Protein 4g **Exchanges:** 1 Starch, 1 1/2 Other Carbohydrate, 3 Fat **Carbohydrate Choices:** 2 1/2

sweet success tip

For a mildly spicy flavor, use less of chipotle chile pepper, but if you want true "fire" with super-spicy flavor, use more.

use a cake mix

Substitute 1 box devil's food cake mix for the Cupcakes above. Make cake mix as directed on box for cupcakes **except**—use 1 1/4 cups water, 1/2 cup vegetable oil, 3 eggs, 1 teaspoon ground cinnamon, 2 to 3 teaspoons ground chipotle chile pepper and 1 to 2 tablespoons chopped chipotle chiles in adobo sauce (from 7-oz can). Bake and cool as directed in recipe. Frost and garnish as directed in recipe.

Metric Conversion Guide

VOLUME

U.S. Units	Canadian Metric	Australian Metric
1/4 teaspoon	1 mL	1 ml
1/2 teaspoon	2 mL	2 ml
1 teaspoon	5 mL	5 ml
1 tablespoon	15 mL	20 ml
1/4 cup	50 mL	60 ml
1/3 cup	75 mL	80 ml
1/2 cup	125 mL	125 ml
2/3 cup	150 mL	170 ml
3/4 cup	175 mL	190 ml
1 cup	250 mL	250 ml
1 quart	1 liter	1 liter
1 1/2 quarts	1.5 liters	1.5 liters
2 quarts	2 liters	2 liters
2 1/2 quarts	2.5 liters	2.5 liters
3 quarts	3 liters	3 liters
4 quarts	4 liters	4 liters

WEIGHT

U.S. Units	Canadian Metric	Australian Metric
1 ounce	30 grams	30 grams
2 ounces	55 grams	60 grams
3 ounces	85 grams	90 grams
4 ounces (1/4 pound)	115 grams	125 grams
8 ounces (1/2 pound)	225 grams	225 grams
16 ounces (1 pound)	455 grams	500 grams
1 pound	455 grams	0.5 kilogram

MEASUREMENTS

Inches	Centimeters
1	2.5
2	5.0
3	7.5
4	10.0
5	12.5
6	15.0
7	17.5
8	20.5
9	23.0
10	25.5
11	28.0
12	30.5
13	33.0

TEMPERATURES

Fahrenheit	Celsius
32°	0°
212°	100°
250°	120°
275°	140°
300°	150°
325°	160°
350°	180°
375°	190°
400°	200°
425°	220°
450°	230°
475°	240°
500°	260°

NOTE: The recipes in this cookbook have not been developed or tested using metric measures. When converting recipes to metric, some variations in quality may be noted.

index

Page numbers in *italics* indicate illustrations

Recipe Testing and Calculating Nutrition Information

Recipe Testing:

- Large eggs and 2% milk were used unless otherwise indicated.

- Fat-free, low-fat, low-sodium or lite products were not used unless indicated.

- No nonstick cookware and bakeware were used unless otherwise indicated. No dark-colored, black or insulated bakeware was used.

- When a pan is specified, a metal pan was used; a baking dish or pie plate means ovenproof glass was used.

- An electric hand mixer was used for mixing only when mixer speeds are specified.

Calculating Nutrition:

- The first ingredient was used wherever a choice is given, such as 1/3 cup sour cream or plain yogurt.

- The first amount was used wherever a range is given, such as 3- to 3 1/2-pound whole chicken.

- The first serving number was used wherever a range is given, such as 4 to 6 servings.

- "If desired" ingredients were not included.

- Only the amount of a marinade or frying oil that is absorbed was included.

Y-Z